THE
BATTLE
OF
LEWISBURG

May 23, 1862

RICHARD L. ARMSTRONG

35th Star Publishing
Charleston, West Virginia
www.35thstar.com

ISBN-10: 0-9965764-2-8
ISBN-13: 978-0-9965764-2-0
Library of Congress Control Number: 2017951839

On the cover:
Lewisburg in the 1850s, from a painting by Edward Beyer
From the collection of Susan and Tom O'Hanlan, Liberty, South Carolina

Image of Colonel George Crook, National Archives
Image of General Henry Heth, Library of Congress

Design by: Studio 6 Sense, LLC • studio6sense.com

THE
BATTLE
OF
LEWISBURG

May 23, 1862

RICHARD L. ARMSTRONG

GENERAL HENRY HETH,
CONFEDERATE COMMANDER

"Victory was in my grasp, instead of which
I have to admit a most disgraceful retreat."

COLONEL GEORGE CROOK,
UNION COMMANDER

"…the neatest little
stand-up fight of the war"

DEDICATION

This book is dedicated to God, without Whose help, it would not have been written. It is further dedicated to the memory of Becky F. Armstrong, who read part of the manuscript before losing her battle with cancer. I also would like to dedicate this volume to the memory of the soldiers of both the North and South, who fought so valiantly for what they believed in.

ACKNOWLEDGEMENTS

Acker, G. Dudley, Jr., Flagstaff, Az. – Historian of 36th OVI for suggestions

Lowry, Terry – Charleston, West Virginia, for information

John Chapla – for information about 50th Va. Inf., losses, etc.

Charles Kellogg – for checking Monroe County, W. Va. items, and providing information

Tim McKinney – for information and proofreading

Staff of Clark County Heritage Center, Springfield, Ohio, for providing information

Nicholas LaCasse, Executive Director of the Greenbrier Historical Society

Robert M. Hicklin, Jr., Charleston Renaissance Gallery

Susan and Tom O'Hanlon, Liberty, South Carolina – a very special thanks for allowing the use of the Edward Beyer painting of Lewisburg in the 1850s.

Contents

INTRODUCTION

During the first year of the War Between the States, the Southern Government scampered to raise troops, arm them, and secure its borders. This was no easy task.

For the first time in history, railroads played an important and vital role. In Virginia, the Baltimore and Ohio Railroad, the Northwestern Virginia Railroad (a branch of the B. & O., joining that line at Grafton), the Virginia Central Railroad, and the Virginia and Tennessee Railroad were among the most important.

By early 1862, the B. & O. and the Northwestern Virginia lines were firmly under control of the United States forces. The Virginia Central Railroad, operating from Richmond to Jackson River Depot in Alleghany County, Virginia, was a vital life-line for the Confederate troops operating in Western Virginia. In the spring of 1862, the track of the V. C. R. R. ended at Jackson River Depot, however, grading and other work had been completed well past that point. The Virginia and Tennessee Railroad, running from Charlottesville, Virginia to Knoxville, Tennessee, was another vital link in the Southern rail system. Tons of supplies and countless troops poured into Virginia from Tennessee, and became a focus of the Federal Government.

While the larger (and better known) battles raged in Eastern and Northern Virginia, the Confederates in Western Virginia were often on the run, confronted by overwhelming forces and a supply line second to none. Many of the troops who had operated in Western Virginia during 1861, were moved to other points, leaving only small numbers to hold the broad frontier of Virginia.

Efforts were made to bolster the number of Southern soldiers in Western Virginia and elsewhere. The Confederate Government enacted what was called the Conscription Act (draft) in April 1862, making all healthy white men between the ages of 18 and 35 liable for a three-year term of service in the Confederate Army. This act also extended the terms of service of those already in service, who had enlisted for a one-year term.

The ranks of the militia regiments throughout the South were decimated by this act, and brought many new soldiers into the service. Confederate commanders scrambled to find weapons to arm their new recruits. Uniforms, provisions and other equipment was equally scarce. Training was of the "on-the-job" type.

Among the Confederate leadership in Western Virginia, such figures as General Robert E. Lee, General William Wing Loring, General Thomas J. "Stonewall" Jackson, General Edward Johnson, and General Henry Heth (among others), rose to prominence.

General Lee did not fare so well in Western Virginia during the 1861 campaign, and returned to Eastern Virginia in early 1862. General Loring rose to command the Army of Northwest Virginia following Lee's departure. He, too, was called away in late 1861 to assist Jackson in operations in Northern Virginia, leaving a small force under the command of General Edward Johnson to hold the Staunton and Parkersburg Turnpike. General Loring soon found himself being brought up on charges by Jackson, resulting in his being assigned to duty elsewhere, and his troops parceled out to other commands. Eventually, Loring would supersede Heth in command of the Southwestern Virginia Army.

General Henry Heth, formerly colonel of the 45th Virginia Infantry, found himself in command of a scattered force in Southwest Virginia. His force was spread out from Lewisburg to the Narrows of the New River, in Giles County, Virginia.

The Confederate forces were posted along the present-day border of Virginia and West Virginia, from Romney to Bristol, sometimes consisting of several brigades of troops, and other times, only a small force of several hundred men. These soldiers were so placed to protect the various in-roads leading to the Shenandoah Valley and the various railroads mentioned.

Equally scattered, but in greater numbers, better armed and equipped, were the Northern troops. These were variously commanded by such Generals as Nathaniel Banks, James Shields, William S. Rosecrans, Robert H. Milroy, George Crook, and Jacob D. Cox, to name a few. Many of these officers would later serve under the command of General John C. Fremont, who had won fame in the West, and became known as the "Pathfinder."

Generals Banks and Shields operated in the Northern Virginia area, confronting the Southern forces under General Thomas J. "Stonewall" Jackson, at Kernstown, near Winchester, Virginia in March 1862, forcing Jackson to retire to Harrisonburg.

General Milroy occupied the vicinity of Beverly, Randolph County, Virginia, on the Staunton and Parkersburg Turnpike, confronting Edward Johnson's troops at Alleghany Mountain and at Huntersville, in Pocahontas County, Virginia.

Further to the Southwest, were Generals Cox and Crook (and others), occupying a large portion of Western Virginia. The Kanawha and James River Turnpike, as well as Heth's position at the Narrows, were of particular interest to them.

General Rosecrans, the hero of Rich Mountain, commanded a large portion of Western Virginia. He was to be replaced by the Pathfinder, General John C. Fremont in March 1862.

The close proximity of these opposing forces often resulted in skirmishing, and an occasional battle. A few of the more notable battles fought along the line are Bartow (October 3, 1861), Camp Alleghany (December 13, 1861), Bath and Romney campaign (January 1862), Kernstown (March 23, 1862), Giles Court House (early May 1862), and Princeton (mid May 1862).

SETTING
THE STAGE

B y early March 1862, President Abraham Lincoln had conceived a plan to strike the Virginia and Tennessee Railroad at Knoxville, Tennessee. He believed that by sending a force along the Alleghany Mountain range (running to the southwest), he could take Knoxville.

To satisfy members of the Republican Party and to further his plan to cut the railroad at Knoxville, Lincoln created the Mountain Department on March 11, 1862. To command this new department, Lincoln chose the immensely popular Major General John Charles Fremont.[1]

Portions of the Department of Western Virginia and the Department of the Ohio were included in the newly formed Mountain Department. Lincoln's War Order defined the department in a different manner: "That the country west of the Department of the Potomac and east of the Department of the Mississippi be a military department ..."[2] To put it more

MAJOR GENERAL
JOHN C. FREMONT
National Archives

---

1   U. S. War Department. *The War of the Rebellion: A Compilation of the Official Records of the Union and Confederate Armies.* Washington, D. C., Government Publishing Office, 1880 – 1900, Series I, Volume 5, p. 54 (hereafter cited as OR).
2   Ibid.

precisely, the department consisted of Western Virginia, portions of Tennessee and Eastern Kentucky.[3]

The troops in Fremont's department were spread over a wide range of rugged terrain, most of it in present day West Virginia, and a portion of Virginia. On March 22, 1862, General William S. Rosecrans reported the strength and disposition of the troops of the Mountain Department to the Adjutant General.

Command	Commander	Total Strength
District of the Cumberland	Brig. Gen. R. C. Schenck	2,816
Cheat Mountain District	Brig. Gen. R. H. Milroy	6,084
Railroad District	Brig. Gen. B. F. Kelley	3,105
District of the Kanawha[4]	Brig. Gen. J. D. Cox	12,071
District of the Big Sandy River[5]	Col. J. A. Garfield	4,425
District of the Gap	Col. Carter	4,870
Total – Mountain Department		34,271

The troops were scattered across Western Virginia and Eastern Kentucky. General Rosecrans explained: "These troops, it will be perceived, guard a frontier 350 miles long, approached by roads more or less perpendicular to that line of frontier, with few cross-communications. They also guard the depots, bridges, and tunnels on 300 miles of railroad and 200 miles of water communication."[6]

General Fremont assumed command of the department on March 29, 1862, from Brigadier General Rosecrans, and established his headquarters at Wheeling, Va.

The President's plan to take Knoxville proved to be flawed and unrealistic. He completely underestimated the ruggedness of the Alleghany mountain range, and the obstacles Fremont's troops would face. On paper, Fremont commanded an army of more than thirty-four thousand men. In reality the number was far less. The exemption of the District of the Big Sandy River and the District of the Gap

---

3   Tom Chaffin. *Pathfinder: John Charles Fremont and the Course of American Empire.* New York, New York, Hill and Wang, 2002, p. 473 – 4. (hereafter cited as Chaffin).

4   Colonel George Crook's Third Provisional Brigade formed a part of this command.

5   Although the Big Sandy River (in Eastern Kentucky) and Gap (in Southwest Virginia) Districts officially belonged to Fremont's Mountain Department, they were exempted from his control by order of the Secretary of War. OR, Series I, Vol. 12, Part 1, p. 4.

6   OR, Series I, Vol. 12, part 3, p. 9-12

reduced Fremont's command by 9,125 men. Sickness, absentees, and detailed men further reduced the command by 6,269 men, leaving Fremont with fewer than 19,000 troops to accomplish his mission.[7] To further reduce their effectiveness, many of the troops were not properly trained and equipped.[8]

Lewisburg, the county seat of Greenbrier County, Virginia, lay inside the

GENERAL JACOB D. COX
National Archives

COLONEL GEORGE CROOK
Richard A. Wolfe Collection

bounds of the Mountain Department, and more specifically, within the area designated as the District of the Kanawha, commanded by Brigadier General Jacob D. Cox. A portion of Cox's troops were stationed at Summersville, in Nicholas County, Virginia, under the command of Colonel George Crook, of the 36th Ohio Infantry. Crook's men were well trained. An 1852 graduate of the United States Military Academy at West Point, New York, Crook was a stickler for discipline, and was determined that his men would be well drilled and trained. In December 1861, Crook had a shed built – 760 feet long, by 33 feet wide – so the men could drill regardless of the weather. The colonel personally drilled his men four to six hours a day, with Sunday's set aside as a day of rest.[9] These long hours of training paid off when the 36th Ohio fought its first battle at Lewisburg.

Private John T. Booth, Company G, 36th Ohio Infantry, recalled the shed: "During the early Winter [sic] months Col. Crook had an immense shed built in

---

7   OR, Series I, Vol. 12, part 1, p. 4

8   Chaffin, p. 473 – 4; OR, Series I, Vol. 12, part 3, p. 169

9   Martin F. Schmitt, Ed. General George Crook: His Autobiography. Norman, Ok., University of Oklahoma Press, 1946, p. 86 (hereafter cited as Schmitt); Ken Hechler. Soldier of the Union: Private George Hechler's Civil War Service. Charleston, W. Va., Pictorial Histories Publishing Company, 2011, p. 32 (hereafter cited as Hechler).

the valley just outside the village limits. Here in all kinds of weather during the Winter [sic], day after day, did the Colonel drill the regiment a portion of the day. Another portion was devoted to manual of arms and company drill, until at word of command the men moved with automatic precision."[10]

Scattered along the Alleghany range were a number of Confederate units. They too, were spread thin to cover multiple points. In the Shenandoah Valley, Major General Thomas J. "Stonewall" Jackson and Brigadier General Edward Johnson countered the movements of Brigadier General Robert H. Milroy, while the army of Major General Richard S. Ewell countered the movements of Major General Nathaniel Banks.

In Southwest Virginia, Brigadier General Henry Heth commanded the Army of New River, part of the Department of Southwest Virginia, which consisting of four brigades. The brigades were commanded by Brigadier Generals John S. Williams, Humphrey Marshall (District of Abington), Colonels Walter H. Jennifer and John McCausland.[11] These commands operated to counter movements along the Alleghany range by Cox's District of the Kanawha.[12]

On May 2, 1862, General Cox submitted a plan of operations to General Fremont. He wrote: "The Third Provisional Brigade, under Colonel George Crook, will consist of the Thirty-sixth Ohio, now at Summerville [Summersville]; the Forty-fourth Ohio, now at Gauley Bridge; the Forty-seventh Ohio, now at Gauley Mount (Tompkin's Farm), and the Eleventh Ohio, now at Winfield, but which will move forward as soon as the hurry of other transportation is a little over. With it will be a battery now forming out of infantry detachments from the regiments, and when it moves it will be accompanied by the First Battalion of Colonel William M. Bolles' Second (West) Virginia Cavalry."[13]

General Cox proposed to move the First and Second Brigades to Princeton or Pearisburg, to cut off the retreat of troops from Lewisburg, while Crook's Third Brigade moved forward by both the Wilderness Road and the turnpike to Lewisburg. Transportation, noted Cox, was the only cause of his delay.

The town of Lewisburg was officially created in 1782, named in honor of General Andrew Lewis. By 1860, it was a very modern town – having several hotels, a bank, a drug store, and served as a regular meeting point for the Virginia Supreme Court. One Union correspondent described the town in May 1862: "Lewisburg is a remarkably well built and appealing town, for it's [sic] size. It is situated … in a basin, completely surrounded by a ridge of hills. The houses are

---

10 *National Tribune*, Washington, D. C., June 24, 1886

11 Clement A. Evans, Ed. Confederate Military History. Atlanta, Ga., Confederate Publishing Company, Volume 2, Maryland and West Virginia, p. 58.

12 Jacob Dolson Cox. Reminiscences of the Civil War. New York, New York, Charles Scribner's Sons, 1900, p. 208

13 OR, Series I, Vol. 12, part 3, p. 128; Companies B, C, F H and I, 2nd (West) Virginia Cavalry

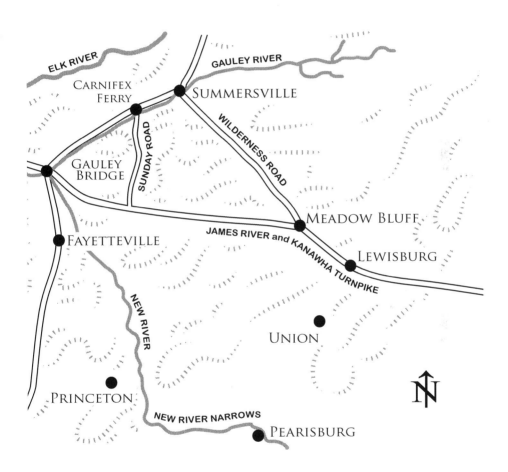

AREA OF OPERATIONS, MAY 1862

generally of brick, and two to three stories in height, and well built. ... It boasts of several churches, two school-houses, a bank, court-house and whipping post."[14]

As noted by the Union soldier, Lewisburg is situated between two ridges, in a small valley, earning it the nickname of "saucer village."[15] The town, which is the

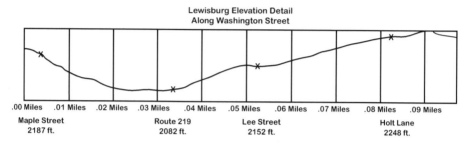

Lewisburg Elevation Detail
Along Washington Street

.00 Miles	.01 Miles	.02 Miles	.03 Miles	.04 Miles	.05 Miles	.06 Miles	.07 Miles	.08 Miles	.09 Miles

Maple Street 2187 ft.   Route 219 2082 ft.   Lee Street 2152 ft.   Holt Lane 2248 ft.

county seat of Greenbrier County, controlled the intersection of the James River and Kanawha Turnpike and the Huntersville Turnpike. Some 700 residents lived in the town in 1862.[16]

The James River and Kanawha Turnpike (present day Midland Trail, Route 60), runs roughly east and west through the town, while the Huntersville Turnpike (present day Route 219), runs roughly north and south. To the west, a ridge or plateau commands the town. This is where Colonel George Crook established his camp. A similar ridge lay on the eastern side of Lewisburg, about a mile distant from the western one. This ridge, soon to be occupied by Brigadier General Henry Heth's forces, somewhat commanded the western ridge and the town. Private John T. Booth, the historian of the 36th Ohio Infantry, noted that the eastern ridge was a strong position for troops facing west, while the western ridge was an equally poor one for troops facing east.[17]

The majority of the residents in Lewisburg, like most of Greenbrier County, were Southern sympathizers. One newspaper correspondent, signing himself "Alpha", reported on the voting in Lewisburg in May 1861: "Our election passed off more quietly than any one we have had for many a day. Indeed we had no cause to quarrel, for all were upon the same side of the question of the ratification of the ordinance of secession. Not one single vote was given against it."[18]

---

14   *Springfield Republic*, Springfield, Ohio, May 26, 1862

15   J. W. Benjamin. "Gray Forces Defeated in Battle of Lewisburg," *West Virginia History: A Quarterly Magazine*. Vol. XX, (October 1958), 25.

16   Captain Thomas T. Taylor, 47th Ohio Infantry, noted the figure at 1,500 inhabitants, but is believed to be too high (Taylor).

17   *National Tribune*, Washington, D. C., June 24, 1886

18   *Richmond Enquirer*, Richmond, Virginia, May 30, 1861.

An examination of the official results regarding the ordinance of secession shows that Greenbrier County cast 1,016 votes in favor and 110 votes against ratification of the ordinance.[19]

The vote was taken on May 23, 1861, amid much celebration as Southern troops left Lewisburg for the war. A year later, the scene presented in Lewisburg was a much different one as a battle raged in the streets of the town.

Lewisburg was militarily important, as it controlled the entrance into the Shenandoah Valley, and in the opposite direction, the Kanawha Valley, with its essential salt mines. Given the political feeling of the townspeople, Confederate soldiers and those termed "bushwhackers" could rely upon them for support.

In the early spring of 1862, Colonel Crook's scouts reported this activity to him. Crook proposed to occupy Lewisburg, take control of the turnpikes, and break up the support for the bushwhackers. His commanding officer, General Cox, agreed.

A small force of Confederates occupied Lewisburg in early May 1862, consisting of the Greenbrier Cavalry (Captain Benjamin F. Eakle), and Company E, Edgar's (26th) Battalion (Captain William H. Heffner).[20] A portion of Eakle's cavalry were sent out on picket near Bunger's Mills, about four miles west of town.

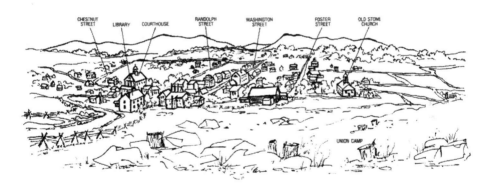

ARTIST'S CONCEPTION OF HOW LEWISBURG APPEARED IN MAY 1862, LOOKING EAST[21]

19 Jeffery C. Weaver. New River Notes. Available from www.newrivernotes.com/va/vasecesh.htm, last visited Nov. 2012.

20 Virgil A. Lewis. *History of West Virginia*. Philadelphia, Hubbard Brothers, Publishers, 1889, p. 410 (hereafter cited as Lewis); Tim McKinney. *The Civil War in Greenbrier County, West Virginia*. Charleston, W. Va., Quarrier Press, 2004, p. 170. (hereafter cited as McKinney).

21 The Battle of Lewisburg, Brochure, Greenbrier County Convention & Visitors Bureau, drawing based upon Edward Beyer's unpublished painting of Lewisburg in the 1850's.

THE

LEWISBURG RACES

May 12, 1862

Soon after Brigadier General Jacob D. Cox announced his plan to move against Heth's command, Colonel George Crook prepared to move on Lewisburg. The advance detachments of his brigade assembled on Little Sewell Mountain, about 20 miles west of Lewisburg. This advance detachment consisted of portions of three companies (D, F, and I) of the 47th Ohio, commanded by Captain John Wallace.[22]

Captain Wallace was joined on the morning of May 11th by another detachment from the 47th Ohio (companies B and E), along with three companies of the 2nd (West) Virginia Cavalry (Companies B, F, and H), and fifty men from the 44th Ohio. The men from the latter regiment were picked for their marching and fighting ability, five from each company. First Lieutenant James W. Shaw, Company G, commanded the detail, while Lieutenant Colonel Lyman S. Elliott (47th Ohio) commanded the entire force, numbering about 400 men.

Captain Thomas T. Taylor, of the 47th Ohio, had a few days earlier scouted much of the country about Lewisburg. He reported his findings to Colonel Elliott, who determined to make an advance on the town. The Union raiding party left Little Sewell Mountain about 6 p.m. on May 11th, and proceeded to Meadow Bluff.

---

22 About twenty men of Wallace's Company (D), and thirty men from Captain H. D. Pugh's Company (I), along with Captain Thomas T. Taylor's Company (F), composed the first part of Crook's advance force.

At Meadow Bluff, Elliott divided his command in two. Major John J. Hoffman, with about 162 cavalrymen from the 2nd (West) Virginia Cavalry, was sent to Blue Sulphur Springs, then to follow a road running from that point to its intersection with the main turnpike, just west of Lewisburg. Elliott hoped that the cavalrymen would successfully get into the rear of the Confederate Cavalry camped in the vicinity of Bunger's Mill, thereby cutting off their retreat. Meanwhile, Elliott with about 200 infantrymen would follow the turnpike in the direction of Lewisburg. The two planned to meet about 4 a.m. on the morning of May 12th.[23]

Proceeding on the turnpike road toward Lewisburg, Elliott and his men halted to rest in the Sinking Creek Valley.[24] In addition to allowing the men time to rest, it would give Major Hoffman's cavalry time to pass Blue Sulphur Springs and reach the turnpike road in rear of the enemy position. Many of the men wrapped themselves in their rubber blankets and were soon fast asleep.

Lieutenant James W. Shaw, Company G, 44th Ohio Infantry, noted a different reason for the halt in the Sinking Creek Valley. He wrote: "…we laid in ambush on the side of the road to catch a patrol that they [Confederates] always sent out to the Bluffs. The boys were very sleepy and cold, and wrapping their rubber blankets around them they laid down and were soon asleep."[25]

After about an hour, five men were sighted coming along the road – Rebel infantry, it was supposed. When the men discovered they were not alone on the turnpike, they tried to run. Lieutenant Shaw recounted the incident for the readers of the *Darke County Democrat*, from the point of view of the men they caught:

"One of them described the scenes and his feelings better than I can. He said that '"Cuffee,"' naming one of his party, '"said somebody's coming behind us. I run to de fence to git in de woods, when someting berry brack raised up, and I saw it was a man. Golly how dis nigra was scared. I jes pushed dem other niggas out of de road and didn't I go!"' The fact was he jumped a fence ten rails high and never touched it. The other four rolled over and through the fence somehow or other, and were breaking through the field, when hearing the click of the hammers of our rifles, they began to yell '"free blacks!"' '"free blacks!"' and stopped at our challenge."[26]

The five men stayed with the Northern forces, employed as cooks. Two remained with Company G, 44th Ohio and three remained with the 47th Ohio, the latter until 1865.[27]

23 McKinney, p. 170; Lewis, p. 210 – 11; OR, Series I, Vol. 12, part 3, p. 182; Joseph A. Saunier, Ed. A History of the Forty-Seventh Regiment Ohio Veteran Volunteer Infantry, Second Brigade, Second Division, Fifteenth Army Corps, Army of the Tennessee. The Lyle Printing Company, Hillsboro, Ohio, c. 1903, p. 75 (hereafter cited as Saunier).

24 Saunier, p. 75.

25 *Darke County Democrat*, Greenville, Ohio, June 11, 1862.

26 Ibid.

27 Ibid; Saunier, p. 75.

The men now aroused from their sleep, Elliott resumed the march toward Lewisburg and the junction with Hoffman's cavalry. He marched over Brushy Ridge to Helm's Chapel, and into Muddy Valley. While crossing Muddy Valley, the sound of a slight skirmish reached their ears, and they supposed it to come from Bunger's Mill. Colonel Elliott ordered his men to double-quick to the mill.[28]

Lieutenant Shaw recorded: "We were terribly foot sore and fatigued ... About five miles further on, we stumbled on the Rebel pickets and shot one and captured two, the remaining two escaping to Lewisburg. We then made quick time to the mill, and found the enemy had removed to the town on the morning before, just four hours after our scouts had last seen them."[29]

The Union infantry pushed on to the point where they were supposed to meet Major Hoffman's cavalry, and halted to wait for daylight. Lieutenant Shaw noted: "Here we dropped down in the road[,] in fence corners, or wherever we found a place, and fell asleep."[30]

Meanwhile, Major Hoffman's column cleared the Confederate pickets from the Blue Sulphur Springs road, and joined Elliott on the main turnpike. The exact time of their arrival is unclear. According to one account, they arrived at 2 a.m., while another gives the time as 4 a.m. It is more than likely that it was the latter.[31]

Resuming his march, Elliott moved his men forward at daybreak, and soon discovered the Confederates drawn up in line of battle on the heights, three-quarters of a mile west of Lewisburg. It was now about 5 a.m. on the morning of May 12th.

Having received word of the approach of Elliott's men, the Confederate force at Lewisburg, prepared to meet them, establishing a line of battle west of the town. The cavalry, about 90 strong, formed on the road, in the center of the line. The infantry formed their line of battle on either side of the cavalry, taking shelter behind the fences. The two forces appeared to be about equal in numbers.[32]

Lieutenant Shaw recalled: "At break of day we were aroused and found we were so stiff and lame from our severe marching and sudden cooling off, that we could hardly move. We hobbled along like we all had the rheumatism or gout for about 300 or 400 yards, when the Adjutant of the 47th rode back and told us the enemy were drawn up on the hill awaiting us. It was strange to see the boys straighten up, and I did not hear "'sore feet'" once afterward. From the disposition

---

28 Saunier, p. 75.

29 *Darke County Democrat*, Greenville, Ohio, June 11, 1862; Colonel Elliott noted in his report of expedition to Lewisburg that "We succeeded in capturing one and running two into the woods. One got away and started for the mill [or] for this place [Lewisburg]. Our cavalry had got across onto the same road and took this picket and two others." OR, Series I, Vol. 12, part 3, p. 182.

30 *Darke County Democrat*, Greenville, Ohio, June 11, 1862.

31 Record of Events Cards, Companies B and F, 2nd (West) Virginia Cavalry, Compiled Military Service Records, National Archives, Washington, D. C. (hereafter cited as RE).

32 Saunier, p. 76.

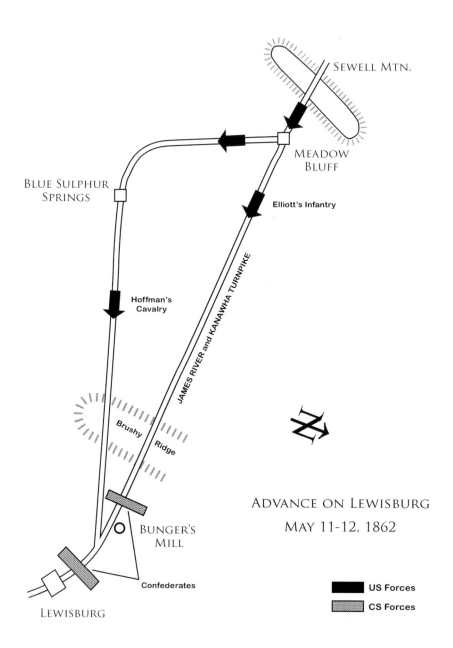

SEWELL MTN.

MEADOW
BLUFF

BLUE SULPHUR
SPRINGS

Elliott's Infantry

JAMES RIVER and KANAWHA TURNPIKE

Hoffman's
Cavalry

Brushy Ridge

ADVANCE ON LEWISBURG
MAY 11-12, 1862

BUNGER'S
MILL

Confederates

US Forces

CS Forces

LEWISBURG

of their forces, we thought that the three pieces of artillery, which we knew they had here some six days before, were posted at the brow of the hill to rake us."[33]

Elliott deployed his forces to meet the enemy. He placed his cavalry on the road in the center too meet those of the Southerners, and placed the companies of the 47th regiment on either side of the road to protect the flanks. Lieutenant Shaw described his orders: "Two detachments of the 47th were deployed as skirmishers on the flanks, and I was ordered to charge the battery if one should open on us"[34]

Once in position, Elliott ordered his men forward at a run. After firing several volleys into the Confederate ranks, the enemy "broke for Dixie."[35] Colonel Elliott succeeded in turning the Rebels' right flank, and at the same time, Major Hoffman made a charge on the enemy's center, overwhelming the Southerners. The Confederates broke and fled in the "wildest disorder."[36]

Lieutenant Shaw noted: "…to our surprise, after the first five or six shots of our skirmishers, the enemy broke and ran in the most cowardly manner. We immediately '"let slip"' our cavalry upon them, and then commenced the most exciting race I ever beheld. Away they went – pell mell – until they got to the town."[37]

Captain Thomas T. Taylor recorded the events of that morning: "Within a half mile from town the enemy were drawn up in battle array on a hill, when up went a shout from our boys. Capt. Wallace skirmished on the enemy's left and Capt. Pugh on the right. I and my boys formed the center – we advanced on double quick delivered a volley & charged. I then gave to the right & and away dashed our cavalry like hounds in the chase, boys whooping & yelling – balls whizzing, sabres clattering and dirt flying. It was a most exciting race & though we had not slept any and marched twenty miles we were apparently fresh. When Pugh's boys gave out I was ordered to deploy my company and did so. One volley and the Rebel infantry broke and fled."[38]

Another soldier described the incident for the *Springfield Republic*: "Lt. Col. Elliott ordered two companies to deploy as skirmishers, the others to advance up the road. When within 600 yards, the skirmishers opened fire. The first volley wounded the Rebel captain[39] in the shoulder. That was enough for the cowardly dogs. Without further resistance they ran. Company B, of the 22d [2nd] Virginia cavalry, after them; also, our infantry followed on the double quick. They went

---

33 *Darke County Democrat*, Greenville, Ohio, June 11, 1862.

34 Ibid.

35 McKinney, p. 170; OR, Series I, Vol. 12, part 3, p. 182

36 Saunier, p. 76.

37 *Darke County Democrat*, Greenville, Ohio, June 11, 1862

38 Letter dated May 12, 1862, Thomas Thomson Taylor Papers, Stuart A. Rose Manuscript, Archives and Rare Book Library, Emory University (hereafter cited as Taylor).

39 Identity unknown; not supported by official records.

helter-skelter, rapidly spluttering through Lewisburg, yelling like fiends, the Rebels firing as they run, but too cowardly to face about. When they fired, they would stick their guns behind and blaze away without aim."[40]

An account of the encounter published in the *Cincinnati Gazette* related: "Major Hoffman's cavalry fired upon them at a very long range, and pitched into them in a manner that gave them to understand that fighting or flying was the only alternative presented. The Rebels chose the latter alternative, and made track on the double quick, their infantry scattering in every direction. When our infantry heard the report of guns, and expecting that Rebels, of course, would defend vigorously the important place, though so tired that they could scarcely get one foot before the other, fired up, and, according to the statement of Lieut. Shaw of Co. G, 44th regiment, fresh men never rushed with more speed and determination after a flying enemy – Maj. Hoffman's cavalry chasing the Rebel cavalry pell mell through the main street of this beautiful country town, popping away at them every moment, and the infantry in hot pursuit in every direction, pursuing the Infantry of Jeff. Davis & Co., firing at them every chance they could get, even at fifteen hundred or two thousand yards off."[41]

Captain Taylor recalled the fighting in town and the cavalry chase: "... then we struck the town, volley after volley was fired by the Rebel cavalry, but they only increased the ardor of our men & it was worth a life time to see the race neck and neck up hill and to see the sabres rise and fall. About six o'clock we had complete possession of the town and our cavalry were in full puruit. Now a panic seemed to strike the Rebels and they threw saddle bags, muskets, carbines and shot guns, boots and everything else to the ground, in some instances they even dropped their saddles."[42]

Captain William Powell and the cavalry started chasing the Confederates and drove them through the town of Lewisburg, and to within a mile of White Sulphur Springs. At that point Powell halted and took charge of the spoils of war. Zouave, a newspaper correspondent, noted that "the speed of their horses saved them."[43]

While the cavalry pursued the fleeing Confederates, Elliott and his infantrymen took possession of Lewisburg, and took care of the few casualties they sustained in the attack. Captain Taylor noted that only two or three of the Union men were wounded, mostly by falling down in the chase.[44] The historian of the 47th Ohio wrote: "... our forces took possession of the city, capturing several pris-

---

40 *Springfield Republic*, Springfield, Ohio, May 26, 1862
41 *Morning Leader*, Cleveland, Ohio, May 27, 1862
42 Taylor, letter dated May 12, 1862
43 McKinney, p. 170-1
44 Taylor, letter dated May 12, 1862

oners, horses with equipments complete, and all the Camp and garrison equipage, hospital stores, etc., belonging to the enemy. … About six o'clock A. M. the struggle, so far as it could be participated in by the Infantry being over, the officers went to the best hotel in the city and ate the breakfast prepared for the Rebel officers …"[45]

Private J. C. Winans related an incident for the readers of the *Troy Times*: "One of the citizens of this place told me yesterday that the Captain of the Rebel force told them as he went flying through town, '"I can do nothing for you; there are three thousand d___d Yankees after me!"'"[46]

Private M. McMillin, a member of the 2nd (West) Virginia Cavalry, recalled his encounter with the Greenbrier Cavalry at Lewisburg that morning. "At my first coming to Lewisburg … we had the pleasure of meeting, just outside of your town, a company known to us as the "Greenbrier Cavalry." They gave us a very cordial greeting, that is of the kind in vogue at that time. After their formal greeting they treated us very kindly as they just passed on thro town which gave us full possession. I will say right here that immediately after their greeting I lost all the effection [sic] I ever had for a double-barrel shot gun. One volley from those guns made every hair on my head stand on end and become as rigid as icicles. It was a beautiful May morning, but somehow, my teeth rattled and chattered worse than if the thermometer had ben below zero."[47]

Not having further orders, Major Hoffman and the cavalry left Lewisburg at 2 p.m., intending to return to their old camp on Loup Creek.[48] They halted at Meadow Bluff for the night, resuming their march on the morning of the 13th. On the way, they met another column of troops advancing toward Lewisburg, and joined them.

Colonel Elliott and his small band of infantry remained in control of Lewisburg. The Union troops settled down to a regular routine, described by the regimental historian of the 47th Ohio: "The troops were in comfortable quarters in the Louisburg [sic] fair grounds, where they remained during the day. Colonel Elliott assumed command of the city, and for two days we were marched out of the city at dusk and back again to make the Rebel citizens believe we were receiving re-enforcements. We camped each night west of the city on a High Ridge, for fear of an attack on our small force, and the next morning march back to the city fair grounds."[49]

---

45 Saunier, p. 76
46 *Troy Times*, Troy, Ohio, May 29, 1862.
47 War Reminiscences, *Greenbrier Independent*, Lewisburg, W. Va., June 9, 1904
48 RE, Company B, 2nd (West) Virginia Cavalry.
49 Saunier, p. 76

Another account tells of the interaction with the residents of Lewisburg. "The inhabitants were frightened to death, expecting their houses to be burned, and every other calamity to befall them that war has inflicted. It astonished them beyond measure, that we, after a forced march of two days, and having just driven the Rebels from their houses, should encamp on a hill side in a drenching rain. They admit there is more quiet peace since our advent then there was before. Every store in the place is closed up. ... The inhabitants have a suit of clothes apiece, and don't know where the next is to come from. Silver and gold are curiosities, but every one is rich in confederate script. There is a Northern Methodist Church which the Rebels threatened to burn, on account of the Unionism of the members. The Irish have been singing glory to God ever since we have been here."[50]

The after-action report filed by Elliott noted that one Confederate was killed, six taken prisoner, and three baggage wagons captured.[51] The Record of Events column for Company B, 2nd (West) Virginia Cavalry records that they wounded 3, took 6 prisoners, captured 4 wagons, and 20 horses, in addition to a number of tents and other camp equipage.[52]

Private John A. McKee, a member of the 44th Ohio Infantry, recorded a slightly different statement regarding the wounded Rebels. He wrote: "We wounded one and captured five of their cavalry. The one that was wounded is in our hands and it is thought his wounds will prove fatal."[53]

Captain Stough, Company F, 44th Ohio, stated on June 16th: "We ... captured eight or ten of them & four teams and fifty or sixty guns, principally shot and rifle."[54]

Only one of the Federal cavalrymen was injured in the chase, he broke his collar-bone when he fell from his horse.[55]

Those soldiers and civilians taken prisoner on May 12th are:[56]

---

50   *Springfield Republic*, Springfield, Ohio, May 26, 1862

51   The identity of the man killed is not known. Lieut. Shaw, in his account, states that they wounded 12, took two prisoners and killed 2 or 3; OR, Series I, Vol. 12, part 3, p. 182; Theodore F. Lang. Loyal West Virginia From 1861 to 1865. Baltimore, Md., The Deutsch Publishing Co., 1895, p. 182 (hereafter cited as Lang); *Darke County Democrat*, Greenville, Ohio, June 11, 1862.

52   RE, Company B, 2nd (West) Virginia Cavalry.

53   James R. James. To See the Elephant: The Civil War Letters of John A. McKee (1861 – 1865). Leathers Publishing, Leawood, Ks., 1998, p 32 (hereafter cited as McKee). The identity of the wounded Confederate cannot be determined.

54   Letter of Captain Israel Stough to G. W. Tuttle, June 16, 1862, Greenbrier County Historical Society, Lewisburg, W. Va. (hereafter cited as Stough)

55   Letters and Diaries of Junius Marion Jones (Ms90-48), West Virginia Department of Archives and History, Charleston, W. Va. (hereafter cited as Jones). The identity of this trooper has not been determined.

56   Descriptive List of Rebel Prisoners Captured by the 2d Va. Cavalry at and near Lewisburg, Va. on the 11th [12th] day of May 1862. Entry 199 (Station Rolls), RG-109, National Archives. The date of capture for J. W. Williams also appears as May 8 and May 5, 1862.

Name	Age	Remarks
B. F. Harlow	27	Greenbrier Cavalry
J. W. Williams	17	Co. B, 22nd Virginia Infantry
Mathew Johnson	20	Greenbrier Cavalry
W. H. H. Hume	21	Greenbrier Cavalry
Ballard Smith	40	Citizen
Pere B. Wethered	70	Citizen

The two citizens were arrested by members of Company F, 2nd (West) Virginia Cavalry. The evidence against Ballard Smith, Jr., charged with treason, alleged that he was taken with a rifle and ammunition in his possession. James F. Byers stated that on May 12, 1862, he captured Smith "in arms against the government of the United States, as he was passing along a fence with rifle in hand and an abundant supply of ammunition on his person ..."[57]

A second affidavit in the case states that James Nichols "was present and assisted in the capture of one Ballard Smith ... that said Smith had a rifle in his hand and ammunition on his person and was in active resistance to the government of the United States, that said Smith had fired his gun once and reloaded the same to use it again against the federal troops."[58]

The evidence against Pere B. Wethered, also charged with treason, is much the same as that against Smith. James F. Byers stated that on May 12, 1862, he captured Wethered "a citizen in arms against the government of the United States, that said Weatherhead [sic] had arms in hands and ammunition on his person and when taken was in active resistance to the Federal government endeavoring to repel federal troops in their attack on Lewisburg."[59]

A second affidavit against Wethered states that James Nichols "... was present at and assisted in the capture of Pere Weatherhead [sic], that said Weatherhead [sic] had arms and ammunition on his person and when taken was in active resistance to the United States government..."[60]

Both men were placed in the jail at Lewisburg, and following the May 23rd battle, were sent with the other prisoners to Camp Chase Prison, in Ohio.

---

57 Ballard Smith File, Union Provost Marshal Records, M-0345, National Archives (hereafter cited as Provost Marshal).

58 Ballard Smith File, Provost Marshal

59 Pere B. Wethered File, Provost Marshal

60 Pere B. Wethered File, Provost Marshal

ADVANCE TO LEWISBURG

The 44ᵗʰ Ohio Infantry Advances

The 44ᵗʰ Ohio Infantry broke camp at Gauley Bridge about 4 p.m. on Sunday, May 11ᵗʰ, and marched to Gauley Mount (Tompkin's Farm), where they joined the main body of the 47ᵗʰ Ohio Infantry, and four mountain howitzers. Soon afterward, the combined force marched for Little Sewell Mountain. Along the way, Colonel William M. Bolles and two companies (C & I) of the First Battalion, 2ⁿᵈ (West) Virginia Cavalry, joined them.[61] The column halted for the night about 10 p.m.

The Ohio soldiers arose about 4 a.m. on the morning of May 12ᵗʰ, and started on their way an hour later, with the 44ᵗʰ Ohio in the advance. A halt was called about noon, allowing the men to take a quick meal and rest for a while. They resumed their march at 3:30 p.m., and camped for the night on the top of Big Sewell Mountain.

Arising again at an early hour, 3:30 a.m., on the 13ᵗʰ, the march continued across Little Sewell Mountain, to the banks of Meadow River. On the way, they met Major Hoffman's detachment of cavalry, returning from Lewisburg, which brought the welcome news that Lewisburg was taken. The column continued on to Meadow Bluff, reaching that point in the afternoon and halted. Major Hoffman and his three companies of cavalry returned with this force.

---

61 Although mustered into service as a loyal Virginia regiment, most of the men in the 2ⁿᵈ (West) Virginia Cavalry were from Ohio.

Late in the evening, a panicked report reached the camp, claiming the Rebels were ready to attack Elliott's small detachment at Lewisburg. The 44th Ohio was quickly ordered to fall in, and marched to Elliott's aid about 7 p.m. After marching until midnight, the weary soldiers camped for the night within six miles of Lewisburg. Lieutenant Colonel H. Blair Wilson and Adjutant John G. Telford continued on to Lewisburg, to inform Elliott that help was on the way.

Up at daybreak on the 14th, the 44th Ohio ate a quick breakfast, and started for Lewisburg, in the midst of a thunderstorm. One soldier noted: "The roads being mainly a reddish clay, soon became almost impassable, and of all the miles, the last six were the hardest."[62] The regiment arrived at Lewisburg at about 10:30 a.m., and went into camp on the western heights overlooking town. The threatened attack proved to be only a rumor.

The 36th Ohio Infantry Advances

The 36th Ohio Infantry had spent the winter at Summersville, in Nicholas County, and welcomed the exciting news that they were about to leave that place. The order to prepare to march by daylight on the morning of May 12th was announced to the regiment at dress parade on Sunday evening. Most believed they would move to Meadow Bluff. The men of Company B, however, felt only disappointment, as they would remain behind to guard the post at Summersville.

The company and supply wagons, along with the ambulances, would also leave Summersville for Lewisburg on the following morning, traveling along the Wilderness Road to Meadow Bluff, and then follow the turnpike road to Lewisburg.

About 5:30 a.m. on the morning of May 12th, the 36th Ohio marched out of town, guided by Dr. William P. Rucker. Wading across the Gauley River at Brock's Ferry, the Ohioans marched about 8 miles, then turned to the right and climbed to the summit of a dry ridge, on what was called the Cold Knob route. They followed this ridge for about 8 miles, without any water. The trail, or rather path that they followed, was a bridle path through the mountains, and they were forced to march single file.

About 3 p.m. the weary men halted on the banks of Big Grassy Creek and ate their dinner. After resting a couple of hours, they resumed their march about 5 p.m., and continued on until it got dark. They went into camp for the night in a deep hollow, on the waters of Big Brushy Creek, having marched twenty-four "Va. miles" that day.[63]

---

62   *Springfield Republic*, Springfield, Ohio, May 26, 1862

63   Lester L. Kempfer. The Salem Light Guard: Company G, 36th Regiment Ohio Volunteer Infantry, Marietta, Ohio 1861-5. Adams Press, Chicago, Ill. 1973. p. _(hereafter cited as Salem Light Guard).

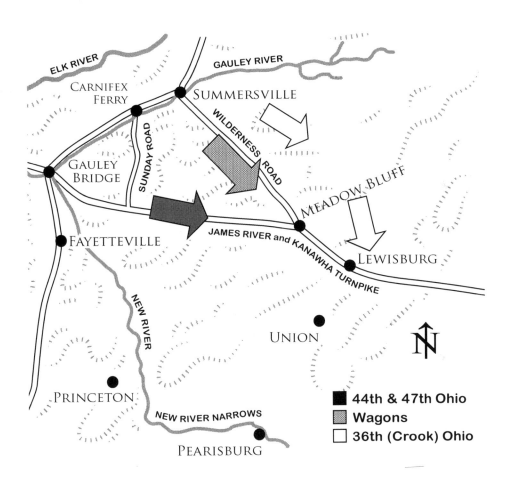

The men arose at 3 a.m. on the morning of May 13[64], ate their breakfast and started on through the mountains at 4 a.m. Halting at 7 a.m. in a field of ramps[64], the men helped themselves to the onion-like root. By 1 p.m., the column had passed the summit of Cold Knob, and from the southeast slope of the mountain, admired the panoramic view before them. Once again, they went into camp in the wilderness, halting just before dark on Brown's Creek.

Crook and his men resumed the march about 3:30 a.m. on the morning of May 14th, after breakfasting on dry crackers. About 5 a.m. it began to rain and continued throughout the day. The column reached the village of Frankford about 8 a.m. and sought shelter in the many abandoned houses, where they remained until the morning of the 15th. While at Frankford, Crook learned of Colonel Elliott's success in occupying Lewisburg.

One of the Ohio men described the village, which he called Frankfort, stating that it "is a pretty place, with commodious dwellings, two neat churches and a large seminary."[65]

On the morning of May 15th, the Ohio soldiers resumed their march (6:30 a.m.), and entered Lewisburg about 11 a.m. They entered the town from the east (Huntersville Turnpike), marched down the main street, and turned right at the intersection of the James River and Kanawha turnpike. They followed this road to the heights on the west side of town, where they set up camp, joining the 44th Ohio and a detachment of the 47th Ohio, already in camp.

Earlier that morning, Colonel Bolles and his battalion of cavalry arrived. About 12 p.m., the wagon trains loaded with supplies and sick soldiers, along with the band of the 44th Ohio reached Lewisburg. It is likely that the battery of mountain howitzers also arrived at Lewisburg on the 15th, although no mention is made of their arrival. According to the regimental history of the 47th Ohio, the battery commanded by 1st Lieutenant John G. Durbeck, left the camp at Meadow Bluff for Lewisburg on the 16th. This is highly unlikely as Colonel Crook marched for Jackson River Depot early on the morning of the 16th, and he mentioned the battery of mountain howitzers as taking part in the expedition.

During the day (15th), members of the 44th Ohio visited Lewisburg. Several noted that the townspeople were afraid of the Northern soldiers.[66] Another soldier noted that "Lewisburg is a pretty good looking one horse town." [67] Private Asa

---

64 A variety of wild leeks, found in the wilds of the Appalachian Mountains.

65 *The Home News*, Marietta, Ohio, June 6, 1862

66 Joseph Pearson Diaries, West Virginia Collection, West Virginia University, Morgantown, W. Va. (hereafter cited as Pearson Diary)

67 The Salem Light Guards, p. 59

Sackman, of Company G, 44[68] Ohio, agreed that it was a "tolerable nice town but the streets is vary [sic] narrow."[68]

One of the 44th Ohio band members, Private Charles Ramsey, commented on the court house and the temperament of the citizens: "The court house is far ahead of Springfield. In the public square is a whipping block or post for whipping slaves. It excited considerable curiosity. The most of the regiment were like myself, had never seen anything of the kind. The citizens are all secesh but are very kind and agreeable."[69]

Private Ramsey continued, commenting on how the demeanor of the citizens has changed in the first few days the Union troops were in Lewisburg: "The citizens are beginning to find out that the Yankees are gentlemen and are beginning to make their appearance. The first day or so we were here there was scarcely a lady to be seen but yesterday I met quite a number on the street. There is no doubt but that they were badly scared."[70]

Another Union soldier, Private J. C. Winans, had this to say about the residents of Lewisburg: "The people here call us Yankees – I think we will soon yank the secesh out of them."[71]

For a number of the men of Company K, 36th Ohio Infantry, their arrival at Lewisburg was a sort of homecoming. Years earlier, settlers from Greenbrier County moved westward into the Jackson County area of Ohio. The descendants of these settlers now returned to their ancestral homes as part of an army of occupation.[72]

The Union force occupying Lewisburg (3rd Provisional Brigade, Kanawha Division) consisted of the following units, all under the command of Colonel George Crook:

> 36th Ohio Infantry (9 Companies) – Lieutenant Col. Melvin Clarke
>
> 44th Ohio Infantry – Colonel Samuel A. Gilbert
>
> 47th Ohio Infantry (detachment) – Lieutenant Colonel Lyman S. Elliott
>
> 2nd (West) Virginia Cavalry (battalion) – Lieutenant Colonel William M. Bolles
>
> Four brass 12-pound howitzers – 1st Lieutenant John G. Durbeck, 47th Ohio

---

68 Asa Sackman Diaries, 1861 – 1862 (MS-0404), San Diego State University, San Diego, California (hereafter cited as Sackman Diary).

69 Letters of Charles Ramsey, 44th Ohio Volunteer Infantry Band, May 15, 1862 (transcript in author's collection; hereafter cited as Ramsey Letter)

70 Ramsey Letter, May 18, 1862

71 *Troy Times*, Troy, Ohio, May 29, 1862

72 Eugene B. Willard, Ed. A Standard History of The Hanging Rock Iron Region of Ohio, Volume I, The Lewis Publishing Company, n.p., 1916, p. 467 (hereafter cited as Hanging Rock Iron Region)

About sundown on the evening of May 15th, Colonel Crook ordered his command to prepare rations for five days. An inspection of arms was held, and the men who could not withstand a march of thirty miles a day for five days were ordered to fall out. One 44th Ohio solder noted that "a few stepped out very reluctantly."[73] Another noted in his diary that the command drew rations and cooked all night in preparation for the march.[74]

Colonel Crook also reported his arrival at Lewisburg to Captain G. M. Bascom, Assistant Adjutant General for General Cox. The colonel complained that the camp did not have a good source of water, and that the only source for good water was at the Greenbrier River Bridge, about 3 miles east of Lewisburg. He also informed Cox that he would leave Lewisburg on the morning of May 16th, on a raid to Jackson River Depot on the Virginia Central Railroad. He planned to take all of his available force; the 36th Ohio, 44th Ohio, 2nd (West) Va. Cavalry, and 4 mountain howitzers. In his absence, Lieutenant Colonel Elliott, would be in command of the post at Lewisburg, with 98 men of the 47th Ohio, along with 150 men from each of the other two regiments.[75]

Crook informed Cox of his intention to continue his march from Jackson River Depot in the direction of Buchanan, having learned of some Rebel provisions stored there, as well as several squads of the enemy.[76]

E. J. Allen, a secret service operative on Fremont's staff, reported Crook's purpose: "Having received reliable information that General Heth had carried all of his stores to Buchanan by way of Covington and boat down [the] James River and was taking them from thence to Bonsack's Station by wagons. That there was a force of about 500 North Carolina troops at Buchanan and about 600 men at Bonsack's – some of the stores were being forwarded to Dublin Depot – it seemed to be the impression among Heth's men that it was his intention to push on a quantity of the stores to Dublin Depot; keep the line of the Tennessee road open in case he desired to fall back toward Lynchburg. [Crook marched] with the intention of capturing these stores, transportation and troops ..."[77]

---

73   Diary entry dated May 15, 1862, John E. Harrison Diaries, Stuart A. Rose Manuscript, Archives, and Rare Book Library, Emory University (hereafter cited as Harrison Diary)

74   Pearson Diary

75   Crook to Bascom, May 15, 1862, Vol. II, E-961, Records of the United States Army Continental Command, 1821 – 1920, RG-393, National Archives, Washington, D. C. (hereafter cited as RG-393); *Troy Times*, Troy, Ohio, May 29, 1862.

76   Crook to Bascom, May 15, 1862, RG-393

77   OR, Series I, Vol. 12, part 3, page 204-05

CHAPTER FOUR

THE JACKSON
RIVER DEPOT
EXPEDITION

May 16 – 19, 1862

Friday, May 16th

The Union soldiers arose at their usual time, about 4 a.m., on the morning of May 16th in their camp on "Lewisburg Hights [sic]."[78] They quickly assembled for the days march, eating some crackers and cold beef for breakfast, but not taking time to make coffee.[79] Colonel Crook's command consisted of the 36th and 44th Ohio Regiments, the Second Battalion of the 2nd (West) Virginia Cavalry, and Durbeck's Battery of four mountain howitzer's; less than 1,500 men in all. Each man carried several days' rations in his haversack, a gum and woolen blanket, their muskets and ammunition. Their knapsacks were left behind, in charge of the men remaining at Lewisburg as guards.

Captain Lysander W. Tulleys noted in his journal that "Gen'l. Crook thought [the] war about to close, & feared this would be our only chance to distinguish ourselves!"[80]

By 6:00 a.m., the 44th Ohio led the column out of camp, followed by the 36th Ohio, the cavalry and artillery. Private John E. Harrison noted in his diary: "We

---

78   Salem Light Guard, p. 60

79   Harrison Diary

80   Lysander W. Tulleys Journal, Kent State University Libraries, Special Collections and Archives, Kent, Ohio (hereafter cited as Tulleys); this was obviously written after the war.

marched through Lewisburg, accompanied by our band, which played for us till we reached the eastern border of the town, where they halted."[81]

Private Junius M. Jones, 2nd (West) Virginia Cavalry, noted the appearance of the citizens in Lewisburg as the cavalry passed through: "All the citizens looked gloomy. The ladies – some had snotrags to their faces to catch the precious southern tears. The men consold [sic] themselves in southern style by smoking their pipes with cane stems about two feet long. Some of their under lips hung as if they had had a brick hanging to them, they would have hung no lower."[82]

Not long into the march, it began to rain and continued for about an hour, making the roads very slippery and muddy. Three miles from Lewisburg, Crook arrived at the Greenbrier River Bridge, a substantial covered bridge about 375 feet in length.

After crossing the river about 7 a.m., the column halted while the major of the 44th Ohio returned to Lewisburg for a fresh horse. This halt also allowed time for the cavalry to come up, costing them several hours of marching time.

On the move once again, the column halted about noon near White Sulphur Springs to rest and eat dinner. One soldier recalled that they halted at a covered bridge spanning a creek, with a house nearby. The house was occupied by several Negro women and children, who were most hospitable. They gave up all the milk they had, and then carried water for the thirsty men. Here the cavalry moved into the advance of the column.[83]

Resuming their march about 1 p.m., they reached White Sulphur Springs, but did not halt. The appearance of the hotel and town caused quite a stir among the soldiers. "The buildings," wrote Private John E. Harrison, "are splendid, several of them of brick being 4 stories high. The town is at least a mile long and all shaded with the most beautiful pine trees."[84] Another soldier commented: "As we passed through [the town], exclamations of surprise and approbation at the beauty of the place, were made throughout the command."[85]

The Northern soldiers now commenced foraging as they went along. Near White Sulphur they picked up three horses, several guns and a quantity of bacon. In addition, at least one Confederate soldier was arrested. The man was seriously ill, and after examination and much debate, it was decided to parole him rather than endanger his life by moving him. The parole of Lieutenant Milton

81   Harrison Diary
82   Jones Diary
83   Harrison Diary; Pearson Diary
84   Harrison Diary
85   *Springfield Republic*, Springfield, Ohio, May 30, 1862

Humphreys went totally unrecorded in the official records; however, Humphreys recounted the incident in his diary.[86]

At some point, Colonel Crook learned from his scouts that the Moccasin Rangers[87] had a rendezvous point about 8 miles beyond White Sulphur Springs. The scout reported about four hundred of the Rangers at that point.

Hoping to capture them and rid the region of these detestable bushwhackers, Crook divided his command. The cavalry was sent by the Old Sweet Springs route to Callaghan's, with the intention of driving the Rangers westward into an ambush. The infantry and artillery continued to move eastward along the turnpike, until a suitable place was found to set up an ambush. According to the plan, the two columns would reunite at Callaghan's Station.

As they approached the Alleghany Mountains east of White Sulphur Springs, the road passed through a deep hollow between two high ridges. Soon after entering the hollow, at least one company of the 44th was ordered to load and conceal themselves on the mountainside along the road.

According to an account of the march on Callaghan's Station, from Theodore Lang's *Loyal West Virginia*, the battalion of the 2nd (West) Virginia Cavalry had a "serious contest" with the Rangers and captured six Rebel captains. After this brush with the Rangers, Captain Powell charged the station and captured two more officers and twenty-five men. The prisoners were held at Callaghan's to await the arrival of Crook and the main column.[88]

Trooper Jones recalled their ride to Callaghan's: "We all had our gum coats on & the citizens thought that we were secesh; we came to a house where a captain of the western rangers was taking dinner. He came out to us & said that he belonged to the rangers & had been after Rosecrans all winter. The Col. told him that he was the man that he was after. He [the captain] started to run. They boys fired upon him & he came back. We got him and another."[89]

Secret Service agent E. J. Allen, in his report to General Fremont, noted that when the cavalry reached the rendezvous point at Callaghan's, most of the

---

86 Milton Humphreys Diary, Acc. No. 1578, Albert & Shirley Small Special Collections Library, University of Virginia, Charlottesville, Va.; Diary of Asa Sackman mentions the capture of a Rebel lieutenant near the springs (Asa Sackman Diaries, Special Collections and University Archives, Library and Information Access, San Diego State University, San Diego, Ca. – hereafter cited as Sackman Diary).

87 E. J. Allen, Fremont's intelligence officer, called them Mountain Rangers rather than Moccasin Rangers. (OR, Series I, Vol. 12, part 3, p. 204-5

88 Lang, p. 183; Sutton, in his history of the 2nd West Virginia Cavalry, says only five captains and twenty-five men were taken at Callaghan's (J. J. Sutton, History of the Second West Virginia Cavalry Volunteers, During the War of the Rebellion. Portsmouth, Ohio, 1892, p. 53 [hereafter cited as Sutton]); according to available prisoner of war records, only two men were taken prisoner on this date – Captain John S. Sprigg and Private Andrew Jackson "Jack" Chewning. No large number of the Rangers are recorded as being captured here, unless they were all paroled and released. No mention, however, of this happening has been found, and besides, it is rather unlikely that Crook would allow the hated bushwhackers a chance at freedom.

89 Jones Diary

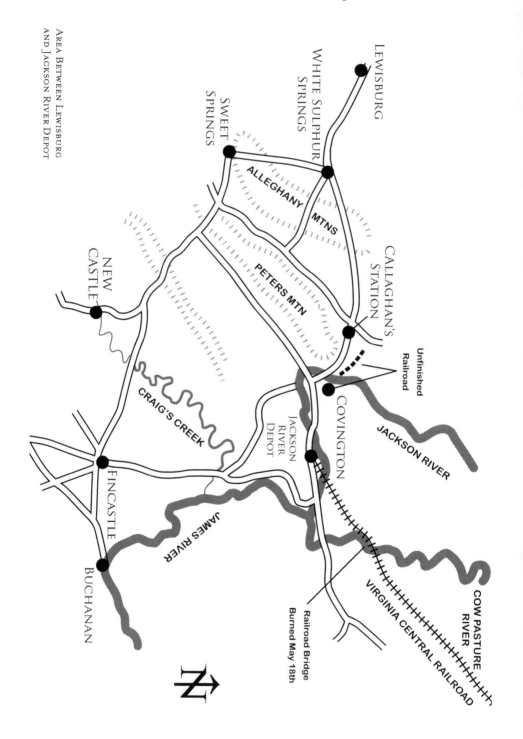

AREA BETWEEN LEWISBURG
AND JACKSON RIVER DEPOT

LEWISBURG

WHITE SULPHUR SPRINGS

SWEET SPRINGS

ALLEGHANY MTNS

CALLAGHAN'S STATION

PETERS MTN

NEW CASTLE

Unfinished Railroad

COVINGTON

JACKSON RIVER

JACKSON RIVER DEPOT

CRAIG'S CREEK

FINCASTLE

JAMES RIVER

COW PASTURE RIVER

BUCHANAN

VIRGINIA CENTRAL RAILROAD

Railroad Bridge Burned May 18th

N

Rangers had gone. Only Captain John S. Sprigg and a few other bushwhackers were found.[90]

Meanwhile, Crook and his infantry waited in a drizzling rain for the Rangers to appear. About 6 p.m., some of the cavalry returned and reported the capture of eight prisoners to the colonel. The prisoners, according to their report, included a captain and a surgeon. They reported that several ineffective shots had been fired at the Rebels, who had immediately surrendered.[91]

Reforming his men, Crook continued his eastward march through Alleghany Pass, into Alleghany County, Virginia. It was after dark when he arrived at Callaghan's, where they went into camp for the night in a field along the road. The Ohio soldiers were tired, having marched 22 miles that day. One soldier noted that they "laid down with very tired legs & feet to rest, after making us some coffee and eating some raw bacon & crackers (the most healthy victuals a man can live on) …"[92] Another soldier wrote: "We built some fires and made some coffee in our tin cups, ate a scanty supper and lay down on the wet ground to sleep. Just before we lay down it commenced raining, so that we were all wet before we got covered up."[93] Private Joseph Pearson, of the 44th Ohio, referred to the camp as "Camp Misery."[94]

Saturday, May 17th

The soldiers arose at 3 a.m. to get ready for the days march, which commenced at daybreak. Marching conditions were miserable recalled one soldier, noting that the roads were nearly shoe mouth deep in thin mud. In addition, rain showers fell off and on for several hours.[95]

After sloshing through eight miles of mud, the column reached Covington about 7 a.m. Trooper Jones noted in his diary that they expected a fight when they got to Covington, but no Rebels showed their faces. Jones recorded that one Rebel resident "told someone that he would shute [shoot] the guide. We took him in."[96]

Trooper Jones continued: "After we crossed the bridge in the first brick house a little boy about 2 or 3 years of age waved his hat out of the second story window & hallooed for the Union; it does my sole [sic] good to hear [it]. It was our guides

---

90 OR, Series I, Vol. 12, part 3, p. 204-5

91 Harrison Diary; the captain taken was undoubtedly John S. Sprigg. The identity of the surgeon and other prisoners taken remains unknown. See a later comment about a surgeon being paroled on May 21.

92 Salem Light Guard, p. 60

93 Harrison Diary

94 Pearson Diary

95 Harrison Diary

96 Jones Diary

family – he had been driven from home when the war broke out; his family were overjoyed to see him."[97]

Private John E. Harrison wrote about the town and their halt there: "This is the county seat of Alleghany county and is a very nice little town – houses mostly brick. We were halted, just at the bridge over Jackson River, the town being just on the other side."[98] The infantry rested about an hour along the river, in a meadow. The cavalry remained in Covington for two or three hours, allowing the infantry time to get ahead of them. While waiting, the cavalrymen helped themselves to as much Rebel corn as they could find. Those foraging succeeded in collecting a large quantity of forage (oats and corn), and about one thousand pounds of meat.[99] Undoubtedly, the foragers were directed by their guide, Dr. William P. Rucker, a former resident of Covington.

Resuming his march at 9 a.m., Crook passed over the covered bridge across the Jackson River (about 300 feet in length), then turned to the right and passed through the town.

In their march to Jackson River Depot, the column passed under the railroad bed several times. The passages were walled and arched completely with a blue looking stone, but no rails were laid. "This railroad has been in our sight the greater part of the time since we left Lewisburg."[100]

So far, the only Union casualty was one of the cavalrymen (of Company H) who accidently shot himself through the heel.[101]

Shortly before noon, and some four miles from Covington, the sound of gunfire brought the column to a halt. Several shots were fired from the mountainside into the advance of Crook's column as they passed through a rocky place near a bridge across the river.

Companies A, G, and D of the 36th Ohio Infantry, and the 2nd (West) Virginia Cavalry were deployed to meet the resistance. After about an hour, some of the cavalry returned to the head of the column with "an old Jay hawk which they said had fired on them and they at him, but no one was hurt. He was a hard looking old customer."[102]

Private Samuel J. Harrison, 44th Ohio, commented on the occasion in a letter home: "… we caught a few of the rascals along the road. One very old man (about 65 or 70 years of age) who was up on the side of the mountain and he had an old

---

97   Jones Diary; the guide was Dr. William P. Rucker.

98   Harrison Diary

99   *Springfield Republic*, Springfield, Ohio, May 30, 1862; Harrison Diary

100 Harrison Diary. The graded railroad bed was prepared much quicker than laying of the rails.

101 Pearson Diary; Jones Diary. The identity of the trooper remains unknown.

102 Harrison Diary; Salem Light Guard, p. 60-61

United States musket. He had shot once, & was in the act of loading when the advance guards caught him. I think it will go pretty hard with him."[103]

At least a portion of the cavalry must have accompanied Colonel Crook's infantry (based on the above statements). Diaries of the cavalrymen indicate that the cavalry remained behind in Covington for several hours. Those who remained behind caught up with the advance of Crook's command while they were searching for the bushwhackers. Trooper Jones noted in his diary that "they caught one & shot another – the rest got away. They had a jug of whiskey & were having a frolick [sic]."[104]

Colonel Crook and his men continued on toward Jackson River Depot, fully expecting to have a fight with a Rebel force there. Upon reaching the depot about 1 p.m., they found it all but deserted; the Rebels having fled days before. Zouave, the newspaper correspondent, noted that the telegraph operator and railroad agent fled over the neighboring hills as our advance arrived at the depot.[105]

Other accounts claim that the telegraph operator was captured while trying to make his escape with his instruments.[106] If the telegrapher was indeed taken prisoner, his name has not been recorded in any surviving record, and was likely paroled.

Another soldier noted that a small squad of men was seen running from a bridge across the Jackson River. "One man was caught. He was too drunk to run."[107]

A depot employee identified only as a Mr. Cupter[108] was detained at the depot by the Northern soldiers. He was released when Crook marched back toward Lewisburg the following day.[109]

In an account of the march by Private J. M. Parks, 36th Ohio, the correspondent noted the capture of a "major surgeon" and a lieutenant at Jackson River Depot. According to Parks, the surgeon's parents lived in Lewisburg, and were present when he was marched through the streets to the guard house.[110] The identity

---

103 Samuel J. Harrison Records, Letter from Samuel J. Harrison to Mother, 21 May, 1862. Ohio History Connection, Columbus, Ohio (hereafter cited as S. Harrison Letters). This was most likely John Allen, a citizen and resident of Alleghany County.

104 Jones Diary

105 *Springfield Republic*, Springfield, Ohio, May 30, 1862

106 OR, Series I, Vol. 12, part 1, p. 811

107 Ken Hechler. Soldier of the Union: Private George Hechler's Civil War Service. Pictorial Histories Publishing Company, Charleston, W. Va., 2011, p. 56 (hereafter cited as Hechler). Captain Marshall Triplett, John Allen, William M. Brown and Henry G. Hall were taken prisoner on this date. Private Joseph Pearson noted in his diary that a captain, lieutenant and a bushwhacker were taken that day. (Pearson Diary)

108 Probably John Cooper – the records show a John Cooper was employed at Jackson River Depot during the war; no one by the name of Cupter lived in Alleghany County in 1860.

109 *Lynchburg Daily Republican*, Lynchburg, Va., May 26, 1862

110 *Jackson Standard*, Jackson, Ohio, June 12, 1862

of the two prisoners mentioned in Parks account cannot be determined, however, it is believed that the surgeon referred to was either Samuel M. McPherson, or his brother, John H. McPherson, sons of Greenbrier County Clerk of Court, Joel McPherson. Private Asa Sackman, 44th Ohio, noted in his diary that a surgeon was tried, and given a parole of honor.[111] Unfortunately, none of the accounts give the surgeon's name.

Ohioan John T. Booth noted that "We captured one Captain; one Surgeon; one Quarter Master; one telegraph Operator and twelve men. Also quite a lot of flour, bacon, wheat, wagons, mules and horses, and other army stores to a very considerable amount." Booth, in an 1886 article, claimed the battle of Lewisburg was fought in retaliation for the raid on Jackson River Depot.[112]

The Union soldiers caused quite a stir among the residents of Alleghany County, and it appears that many were moving about – whether to catch a glimpse of the "Yankees", or trying to escape their clutches. Trooper Jones recorded the following in his diary: "We went up to the Jackson R. depot capt[ured]. a wagon load of nigers [sic] & another full of white ladies & one or two men. The telegraph operator just left before we got there. He destroyed the battery."[113]

Jackson River Depot served as the western terminus of the Virginia Central Railroad, running from Richmond to that point. This road, after the war, became part of the Chesapeake and Ohio (C&O) Railroad. Besides the railroad depot, there was a telegraph office, a store, a hotel, along with several other buildings.[114]

The telegraph office was found to be intact, with recent messages strewn about the room. By reading these messages, it was learned that Alleghany County Provost Marshal William Skeen had telegraphed Major General Thomas J. "Stonewall" Jackson at Staunton, asking for assistance. In addition, the telegram noted that the militia of Greenbrier and Monroe counties had been called out. Among the papers was Jackson's response, stating that a force would be sent from Staunton, and that General Floyd would send two regiments by way of Sweet Springs.[115]

While Colonel Crook and his subordinates debated the contents of these telegrams, the men of the command spread out and searched the surrounding buildings. Several barrels of salt were discovered, along with several barrels of whiskey. The officers quickly took charge of the whiskey, and to the dismay of

111 Sackman Diary

112 Marie Mollohan. Another Day in Lincoln's Army: The Civil War Journals of Sgt. John T. Booth. iUniverse, Inc., Lincoln, NE, 2007, p. 227 (hereafter cited as Another Day); Mss 180, John T. Booth Papers, Diary:,Ohio History Connection, Columbus, Ohio (hereafter cited as Booth); National Tribune, Washington, D. C., June 24, 1886

113 Jones Diary

114 Harrison Diary

115 OR, Series I, Vol. 12, part 3, p. 204-5

those present dumped the contents on the ground. Among other articles picked up were twenty-two barrels of flour, a considerable amount of tobacco, some molasses and vinegar.[116]

Foraging parties spread out across the countryside to gather supplies. About two miles downriver, the raiders came upon a mill, where they confiscated 150 bushels of wheat and 10 barrels of flour. Other parties picked up a large amount of hams and bacon, and a quantity of sweet or ginger cakes. Having such a quantity of supplies to remove, the soldiers began collecting horses, mules and wagons to carry it all away. The Union men took six or eight wagons and teams to remove the supplies.[117] Private John F. Harrison noted in his diary that in addition to the quantity of supplies, "Our officers got several contrabands here and on the road…"[118]

While Colonel Crook and his officers debated what to do next, a messenger arrived with orders to return to Lewisburg and reinforce General Cox.[119] That settled the matter; they would return to Lewisburg the next morning.

A strong guard was posted about the depot, with cavalry videttes[120] thrown out on the roads leading into and from the depot. The remainder of Crook's force went into camp in a grove of trees near the depot on the bank of the Jackson River.[121] The men had marched at least 17 miles that day; some more than that in their quest for Rebel forage and supplies.[122]

The weather cleared up nicely late in the evening, and remained so all night. Colonel Crook directed his men to sleep on their arms as he expected to be attacked that night or early the next morning.

The threat posed by a Confederate force from the direction of Staunton getting in their rear, demanded attention. A detachment of cavalry was sent to burn the railroad bridge across the Cowpasture River, some ten miles to the east of Jackson River Depot. Dr. Rucker, Crook's guide, now took the lead in destroying the bridge.[123] This action and his serving as a guide to Crook's invading force, later led a Alleghany County Grand Jury to return a total of sixteen indictments against Rucker.

A rough mountain path, said to be impassable by horsemen, led to the bridge. Dr. Rucker, with his knowledge of the area, was called upon by Colonel Crook to

116 Salem Light Guard, p. 61; Harrison Diary

117 Salem Light Guard, p. 61; Harrison Diary; S. Harrison Letters

118 Harrison Diary

119 *Springfield Republic*, Springfield, Ohio, May 30, 1862

120 Videttes – refers to a mounted sentinel stationed in advance of pickets.

121 Salem Light Guard, p. 61

122 Harrison Diary

123 Letters and Memoirs of James Abraham, 1st & 2nd West Virginia Cavalry, U. S. Army Military History Institute, Carlisle Barracks, Pa.; *Springfield Republic*, Springfield, Ohio, May 30, 1862; OR, Series I, Vol. 12, part 3, 204-5

lead the cavalry along this path and destroy the bridge. Crook wanted Rucker to take three hundred of the cavalry, but Rucker told Crook that he would take fifty picked men and complete the task. Crook would not hear of it, and insisted that he take more men. A compromise was finally reached and Rucker agreed to take seventy-five men (Company C, 2nd (West) Virginia Cavalry) with him to carry out his orders regarding the bridge from General Fremont.[124]

Dr. Rucker set out in the pouring rain. The Jackson River was rising rapidly, and was already past fording four miles below the depot, where they must cross. Determined to carry out his orders, Rucker pressed on, swimming the river.

When within a mile of the railroad bridge, the raiders met a Union man who lived on the path. From him they learned that a considerable force of Confederate cavalry guarded the bridge, commanded by a Captain Jones. With such a sizable guard, it would be impossible for them to burn the bridge, the man warned. Determined, Rucker continued.

When the doctor and his raiding party reached a point within a quarter of a mile of the bridge, they charged full speed upon the bridge, making all the noise possible. Hopefully, the Confederates would think Crook's entire force was upon them. The ruse worked perfectly. Not a shot was fired by the scattering and panic stricken Rebels. By ten o'clock on the morning of May 18, 1862, the Cowpasture Bridge was in flames.[125]

Sunday, May 18th

The men of the invading force arose at their accustomed hour, prepared breakfast, and were ready to meet the expected attack at daybreak. The nervous soldiers anxiously peered through the swirling fog, but the attack never materialized. The fog burned off by about 8 o'clock, and it proved to be a rather nice day.

That morning, Lieutenant Thomas F. Garlough, Company F, 44th Ohio Infantry, and a squad of men scoured the countryside for horses to press into service. He returned about noon with a nice herd.

Private Samuel J. Harrison wrote: "Well, mother I had an old fashioned dinner in part last Sunday 39 miles from here at Jackson's River Station on the Jackson River. I'll tell you what it was, it was green onion blades. We took them in a secesh garden, we just stripped the patch. About the only inhabitants there

---

124 General Fremont had employed Rucker as part of the secret service, and assigned him to duty with Crook. Rucker and Crook developed a friendship that lasted throughout the war. RE, Company C, 2nd West Virginia Cavalry.

125 There are several dates given for the burning of the bridge. According to the OR, the date was May 20, 1862. In other wartime accounts, the dates range between May 17th and May 19th, with the most accurate date being May 18th.

is left as far as we've been is the Irish and negroes, and the Irish say they will die before they will fight against the Yankees."[126]

At some point on the morning of May 18th, Fountain Morrison was discovered by some of Colonel Bolles' cavalry along the road with a gun in his hands. Suspecting he was up to no good, they arrested the 62 year-old resident of Alleghany County.

As Morrison desired to visit his nearby home to get some clothing, a detail of men accompanied him to the farm. Upon their arrival, they discovered the Quartermaster of the 36th Ohio already at the farm, loading up Morrison's stock of bacon. Lieutenant Levi Barber wrote: "Among the prisoners was one man who has a large family of grown up children, some daughters that are young ladies, and one that is married. We took him away from home but allowed him to go to his house under guard for some clothes. When they came to the house, I was there with a company of men getting his bacon and what grain we wanted for our teams. We took his four horses and wagon, loaded it with bacon and grain. When the guards brought the old man down to the house, such a sight I never saw, nor never wish to again. Such crying, hollering you never heard. He is wealth[y] and has a large and very fine home, some 30 or 40 slaves, some of them the finest looking women I have ever seen amongst slaves. They begged to have us take them along. One fine looking Negro woman dressed very nice with a babe in her arms, said she would lay her babe down on the ground and leave it if I would only take her along. But with the white daughters it was different. They took hold of me with both arms and would cry and say, '"Oh Mr. Officer, Take all we have got, but spare our Dear Pa. He is a passionate man. He has done wrong we know it. We have told him so. But do, do spare him. He won't do so any more.'"""[127]

Once the bridge burning party and the foraging parties returned to Jackson River Depot, the command started back to Lewisburg about 11:30 a.m. As the column passed through Covington, Dr. Rucker's wife, children and servants joined the march and accompanied her husband back to Lewisburg. Upon reaching that point, Rucker and his family continued on to Nicholas County, where he owned a large plantation.

E. J. Allen, Fremont's secret service agent, noted in his report that on the return, "Some prominent active secessionists of the county were arrested, and a notice posted on the court-house in Covington warning all secessionists against maltreatment of Union men under penalty of punishment. A number of Union men came out in our rear."[128]

---

126 S. Harrison Letters

127 Letters of Captain Levi Barber, Jr., Ancestors of Eugene Ashton Andrew
(http://www.geneal.net/138.htm), last visited April 19, 2016)

128 OR, Series I, Vol. 12, part 3, p. 204-5

About 3:00 p.m., it began to rain, continuing for the rest of the evening, making the road a muddy mire to march in.[129] The column halted at Callaghan's and went into camp just before dark. At that point, Crook intended to send a force of cavalry by way of Sweet Springs to Buchanan to accomplish the original mission. Being met at Callaghan's by another courier with an order from General Fremont to fall back to the Gauley River, the order was countermanded.[130]

Private John E. Harrison, 44th Ohio, recorded in his diary: "We were in a miserable plight, being wet, hungry and given out. My feet were so sore I could scarcely walk, as were all the rest as far as I could learn. Some of us made coffee in our tins and ate some crackers; others lay down in the rain without having a bite. Some sat up and kept a fire of rails nearly all night. We spread some of our blankets on the wet ground, and 2 or 3 of us lay down in a place, and covered with the balance of them. We lay with our accouterments on and our guns by our sides as usual on a march."[131]

Monday, May 19th

After a light breakfast, Crook's command continued at daylight toward Lewisburg. The weather was very cloudy and cool; the road a muddy mess. The rain had caused the streams to rise, and the men had to wade across them. Private Harrison recorded: "…we waded one [stream] some 8 or 9 times, knee deep each time, and two or three others once apiece about the same depth. We also waded about the same number of branches, from ankle to half knee deep."[132]

By 11:00 a.m., the Union troops reached a point in sight of White Sulphur Springs, where they halted to rest and eat. To their relief, the clouds had scattered and the warming light of the sun shown upon them. Hoping to raise the men's spirits a bit, Colonel Gilbert dipped into the store of ginger cakes taken at the depot, and gave each man two of the cakes.[133]

After an hour, the march resumed. At White Sulphur Springs each company was permitted to halt for a moment and get a drink of water. Private John E. Harrison wrote: "I observed one house more closely than I did before. It was a brick house 4 stories high, and I would judge at least 600 feet long. I supposed it to be some kind of institution of learning."[134] Harrison's brother, Samuel, wrote in

---

129 Harrison Diary
130 OR, Series I, Vol. 12, part 3, p. 204-5; Harrison Diary
131 Harrison Diary
132 Harrison Diary
133 Harrison Diary
134 Harrison Diary

a letter home, noting that a secession flag was captured at White Sulphur, which they dragged in the dust as they passed through the streets of Lewisburg.[135]

Private Asa Sackman, Company G, 44th Ohio, noted in his diary that after they had gone past White Sulphur Springs, that one of the cavalrymen rode up to the colonel and told him they had just passed a Rebel flag. The colonel immediately sent a Sergeant and four men back to retrieve it.[136]

After a 23 mile march, Crook arrived back at Lewisburg on the evening of the 19th, and went into camp. The men were weary and footsore, from having marched with wet shoes.[137] The band of the 44th Ohio met the column about two miles outside of Lewisburg, and escorted it back into the town, playing "Hail Columbia," "The Girl I Left Behind Me," and various other tunes.

Besides being followed by a number of Union men on the march from Covington, a number of Negroes also made their way to freedom. Zouave, the *Springfield Republic* correspondent, wrote: "A great crowd of contrabands followed in our back walk; nearly every commissioned officer [in] some of the companies have one working for them, for his bread, meat and clothes."[138]

Private Harrison recorded in his diary: "We got to town a little before sundown, and passed on to our camp ground just at the west side. We stacked arms and went back to the edge of town where our knapsacks were stored and took them out to camp. We then fixed up our little tents of gum blankets as we had them before. Our prisoners were lodged in the jail at the courthouse. We had marched a distance of 24 miles today, over a most extremely hard road, which I think is pretty good for "blue bellied yankees" to perform among the mountains of Virginia."[139]

Upon reaching his headquarters, Crook learned that the order to fall back to Gauley River had been countermanded. However, another order awaited him, directing him to move by the Palestine road to reinforce General Cox. He was to make this march on the morning of May 20th.[140] Evidently that order was also countermanded, as Crook remained in camp at Lewisburg.

Several days later, the department commander, Major-General John C. Fremont, issued the following congratulatory note to Crook:

---

135   S. Harrison Letters
136   Sackman Diary
137   Salem Light Guard, p.61; Harrison Diary; *Springfield Republic*, Springfield, Ohio, May 30, 1862
138   *Springfield Republic*, Springfield, Ohio, May 30, 1862
139   Harrison Diary
140   OR, Series I, Vol. 12, part 3, p. 204-5

HEADQUARTERS MOUNTAIN DEPARTMENT
MAY 22ND, 1862.

To Col. Geo. Crook,

Commanding Brigade, Lewisburg, Va.

The commanding general directs me to make you his thanks for your well conceived and handsomely executed dash up the Central Railroad.

ALBERT TRACEY,
COL. AND A. A. G.[141]

Southern newspaper accounts of Crook's raid on Jackson River Depot are filled with accusations against Dr. William P. Rucker. The *Lynchburg Republican* reported on May 26th: "It is true that Dr. Rucker, and one Allen,[142] who was once a Railroad conductor on the [Virginia] Central railroad, are with them, as officers; Rucker as Colonel. This man Rucker is a notorious scoundrel; once killed a man in Alleghany, and plead his own case, and was acquitted. He is having every man who was his personal enemy arrested, and carried off as prisoner, and his property destroyed. A number of negroes and several wagons and teams were carried off by the thieves."[143]

Another account, also from the *Lynchburg Republican*, went so far as to accuse Margaret Rucker of being a spy for the Confederates, while her husband was away from home. The report continued: "In the raid upon Jackson river [sic] the Yankees brought forty wagons with them, and carried off one hundred and ten, loaded with all imaginable kinds of property they had stolen. Rucker himself seized the carriage and horses of an aged widow lady in Covington to carry off his wife and children."[144]

According to Booth's account, sixteen prisoners were taken on the march to Jackson River Depot. This agrees with a notation in Joseph Pearson's diary. Corporal David Todd Gilliam, Company I, 2nd (West) Virginia Cavalry, told a different story, writing: "The fruit of this expedition were 20 prisoners, 20 horses & mules and a large quantity of stores. The Rebels had one killed and one wounded."[145]

Prisoner of War records, however, have been found for only eleven of those captured. Their names are as follows:

141 *The Yankee*, Lewisburg, Va., May 29, 1862

142 OR, Series I, Vol. 12, part 3, p. 204-5

143 *Lynchburg Daily Republican*, Lynchburg, Va., May 26, 1862

144 *Lynchburg Daily Republican*, Lynchburg, Va., May 30, 1862

145 David Todd Gilliam Autobiography, West Virginia Collection, West Virginia University, Morgantown, W. Va., (hereafter cited as Gilliam).

Date	Name	Unit	Remarks
May 16, 1862	Sprigg, John S.	Moccasin Rangers	Taken at Callaghan's
May 16, 1862	Chewning, A.J.	22nd Va. Infantry	Taken at Callaghan's
May 17, 1862	Allen, John	Citizen	Taken in Alleghany County, Va.
May 17, 1862	Brown, William M.	Citizen	Taken in Alleghany County, Va.
May 17, 1862	Hall, Henry G.	22nd Va. Infantry	Taken in Alleghany County, Va.
May 17, 1862	Triplett, Marshall	Rangers	Taken in Alleghany County, Va.
May 18, 1862	Morrison, Fountain	Citizen	Taken in Alleghany County, Va.
May 18, 1862	Sampson, Andrew J.	Citizen	Taken in Alleghany County, Va.
May 19, 1862	Sprowl, William B.	Citizen	Taken between Covington and White Sulphur Springs
May 19, 1862	Crawford, S. Owen	Citizen	Taken in Alleghany County, Va.
May 19, 1862	Crawford, William	Citizen	Taken in Alleghany County, Va.

These men, along with those taken on May 12th at Lewisburg, and a number of other men being held at Lewisburg, remained there until after the battle of Lewisburg, on May 23rd. After that time, the prisoners were sent to Wheeling, and subsequently to Camp Chase Prison, in Ohio. The prisoners whose names are not known may have been released on parole before being sent on to Camp Chase.

According to an article appearing in the *Covington Virginian* in the 1960s, a citizen of Alleghany County by the name of James N. Vowels (Vowles), reportedly was taken prisoner by Crook's forces, on order of Dr. William P. Rucker. A diligent search of the surviving records failed to support this report. It is likely Vowels was among those paroled by Crook's forces before the battle on May 23rd.

Captain Stough, Company F, 44th Ohio Infantry, reported that Crook's men were fired on by Rangers or Bushwhackers on their return, and had harsh words for them: "We were fired upon at two different times by these scoundrels without effect, however, & could I have had my way about it, every mother's son should have swung and danced on a rope's end until life would have been extinct for they are nothing but a cowardly set of cut throats and murderers and should not be entitled to the rights of prisoners of war."[146]

During the time between their return from Jackson River Depot and the battle on May 23rd, the Union soldiers rested and attended to various duties of camp life, including drill, scouting and picket duty. Private Asa Sackman, Company G, 44th Ohio, recorded in his diary for May 20th, that the colonel allowed them to lay in bed until they felt like getting up. Later that evening, an inspection of arms was held for the command.[147]

Colonel Crook ordered a military commission convened on May 21st, to hear evidence against many of the citizens arrested since May 12th. Affidavits were prepared in the cases, to be sent with the prisoners to Camp Chase prison, in Ohio. Sergeant Major Wallace Stanley, 36th Ohio Infantry, served as clerk for the commission.[148]

Among those appearing before the military commission was a Confederate Surgeon captured a few days earlier at Callaghan's. Private Sackman noted in his diary that the surgeon was released on his parole of honor.[149] There may have been others released in a similar way, but their names do not appear in the prisoner of war records.

While the commission was gathering evidence against the citizens, Company F, 2nd (West) Virginia Cavalry went out on a scout toward Union, in Monroe County. The scouts learned at Union that General Henry Heth's command was at nearby Salt Sulphur Springs. They returned to Lewisburg at once with that news. Along the way, one soldier from the 22nd Virginia Infantry was captured and placed in jail with the other prisoners at Lewisburg.[150]

Colonel Crook, expecting a flank or rear attack on his position at Lewisburg, established strong picket posts on all of the roads leading into the town. The pickets on the James River and Kanawha Turnpike took their position at the eastern end of the Greenbrier Bridge, three miles from Lewisburg. From the Union camp, the distance was a mile further. Second Lieutenant Josiah B. Martin, Company C, 36th Ohio Infantry commanded the pickets. A smaller detail of cavalry took up a position between the bridge and town, as a support for Lieutenant Martin. One account places their position on the hill east of Lewisburg, where General Heth would form his line of battle the next morning.

Private John E. Harrison noted in his diary: "It was rumored through the camp today, & yesterday also that there were 3000 Rebels advancing on us, but I

---

146 Stough

147 Sackman Diary

148 Another Day, p. 233

149 Sackman Diary; thought to be Samuel M. or John H. McPherson, both of whom were physicians and residents of Lewisburg.

150 RE, Company F, 2nd West Virginia Cavalry.

don't place any confidence in the report yet."[151] Sergeant Major Wallace Stanley, 36th Ohio, echoed Harrison's report, recording in his journal "Reports say the enemy is at hand, let him come."[152]

On May 21, 1862, Crook reported to Captain G. M. Bascom, A. A. G. to General Cox, that "My scouts returned from Union this evening with a prisoner from Gen. Heath [sic] command, whom they captured at Union, he says that some 3,000 men were at the Narrows on New River yesterday morning under Gen. Heth; that Gen. Marshall was near Princeton with a similar number of men. I think they intended attacking me, but my march to J. River Depot will probably divert them. I am on the watch for them. ... I want my company from Summersville very much as it is one of my biggest companies. My scout from Sweet Spring & Fincastle has not returned yet ... I have sent to Gauley for the remainder of my ordnance & to get some additional transportation. I hope Gen. Heth will march on me here. If you will advise me when you attack Marshall I will make a simultaneous attack on Heth."[153]

Sometime during the day, Colonel Crook ordered Lieutenant Colonel Elliott and the handful of companies belonging to the 47th Ohio Infantry to return to Meadow Bluff, and rejoin the main portion of their regiment.

Scouting parties were sent out as a matter of routine. One such group went out on May 22nd, under the command of Captain Arthur D. Eells, Company F, 2nd (West) Virginia Cavalry. "The day previous to the battle of Lewisburgh [sic] Captain Eells with a small detail of men was sent out by General Crook on a reconnoitring [sic] expedition. On this expedition he came very near being captured, having gone very nearly within the lines of the enemy's pickets. He and his men escaped by strategy, as he personally learned from prisoners captured in the Lewisburgh fight the next day. While at a farmer's house he learned facts that were of sufficient moment to put him on the alert, and in a very careless way gave orders to his men to fall back to the main force, indicating that there was quite a force close at hand. One of the men at the farm house was a Rebel soldier in citizen's dress, who at once reported these facts to the enemy, as one of the prisoners told Captain Eells the next day that they thought by letting him go that they would likely capture the main body of men, not supposing that he would ventur [sic] to come so near their lines with such a small squad of men. Captain Eells and his men after having got a reasonable distance from the enemy made good time in getting back to headquarters with his men, and reached camp at about nine o'clock in the evening of the twenty-second of May and made his report to General Crook, giving him valuable information."[154]

---

151 Harrison diary

152 Another Day, p. 234

153 Crook to Bascom, May 21, 1862, RG-393

154 H. C. Williams & Bro. History of Washington County, Ohio, with Illustrations and Biographical Sketches. H. Z. Williams & Bro., publishers, Cleveland, O., 1881, p. 249 (hereafter cited as History of Washington County, Ohio).

CONFEDERATE APPROACH

M a y   1 9 – 2 3 ,   1 8 6 2

W hile Colonel Crook and his men were busy at Jackson River Depot, Brigadier General Henry Heth was preparing to move against Lewisburg. During the day of May 19th, Heth ordered the 22nd and 45th Virginia Regiments to get ready to move. Similar orders were issued to Lieutenant Colonel William W. Finney's newly formed battalion, the 8th Virginia Cavalry, and to several companies of artillery. In total, Heth's force amounted to about 2,300 men.[155] Some accounts place Heth's strength at around 3,000 men, and others at no more than 2,000.[156]

General Heth's force consisted of (numbers approximate):

Infantry – just over 1,900 strong, composed of the 22nd Virginia Infantry (Colonel George S. Patton), 45th Virginia Infantry (Colonel William H. Brown), and two battalions commanded by Lieutenant Colonel William W. Finney and Major George M. Edgar. The entire force was known as Edgar's Battalion. Colonel Finney's battalion was formed of detachments of the 50th Virginia Infantry

---

155 Heth's official report of the battle states that his force consisted of 2000 infantry, 3 batteries of artillery, and about 100 cavalry. It is immediately evident that 2100 men composed the force. Adding the artillerymen and the possibility of additional cavalry, a total of 2,300 men is not too far off. Captain Edwin H. Harman, 45th Virginia Infantry, placed Heth's force at not more than 2,000 men. (Civil War Correspondence, A&M 1508, letter of E. H. Harman, May 25, 1862 [hereafter cited as Harman, WVU]).

156 Smith Family Letters, Ms1996-018, Virginia Polytechnic Institute & State University, Blacksburg, Va. (hereafter cited as Smith Letters): Hiram F. Devol says Heth had 2,500 men, one-third more than Crook (H. F. Devol, Biographical Sketch, Hudson-Kimberly Publishing Co., Kansas City, Mo., 1903, p. 28 [hereafter cited as Devol]); Harman, WVU.

(Companies F & I), and two companies of the 51st Virginia Infantry.

Major Edgar's battalion was composed of several militia regiments from Western Virginia, the remnants of the 59th Virginia Infantry, and very likely the men belonging to Captain Lewis A. Vawter's Western Artillery[157]. Many of the men in the battalion had joined the army a few days before going into battle.

Cavalry – about 200 strong, under the command of Colonel James M. Corns, 8th Virginia Cavalry. Captain John P. Sheffey mentions that Colonel Corns had command of the mounted men at Lewisburg, while an unknown number of dismounted men (without horses) fought with the infantry, under the command

GENERAL HENRY HETH
Library of Congress

COLONEL GEORGE S. PATTON
The Glenwood Estate, Charleston, West Virginia

of Lieutenant Colonel Alphonso F. Cook. Captain Benjamin F. Eakle's Greenbrier Cavalry was present, attached to the 8th Regiment at the time.

Artillery – about 200 strong, consisting of four different companies; Bryan's Battery (Captain Thomas A. Bryan), Lowry's Battery (Captain William M. Lowry), Otey's Battery (detachment, Captain George G. Otey), and a detachment of Chapman's Battery (Captain George B. Chapman).

Captain W. W. Woodward, Company C, 44th Ohio Infantry, in his account of the battle published in the *Dayton Weekly Journal*, reports Heth's force as more

---

157 Two days after the battle of Lewisburg, Captain Vawter submitted a requisition at Salt Sulphur Springs, signing it as Captain, Company F, Edgar's Battalion. This company later became Company C, 30th Battalion Virginia Sharpshooters (Compiled Service Record, Lewis A. Vawter, 30th Battalion Virginia Sharpshooters, RG-109, National Archives, Washington, D C.).

than 3,100 men. He cited captured morning reports and statements taken from the prisoners as the basis for this number.[158]

Lieutenant James W. Shaw, 44th Ohio Infantry, was a little more specific in his account appearing in the columns of the *Darke County Democrat*. "The whole force attacking numbered 3,000 infantry of the 22nd, 50th, and 51st Virginia, Edgar's battalion, 150 of Jenkins' cavalry, and five batteries of 100 men each and 8 guns in all; 1 twelve pound smooth bore, 4 ten pounders rifled, and three mountain howitzers."[159]

One of the most misunderstood aspects of Heth's command is the makeup of his artillery arm. In his official report, Heth mentioned that he brought "3 batteries" to Lewisburg. One must ask what constitutes a battery. The generally accepted definition is that a battery consists of four or six pieces of artillery. These are referred to as sections – two guns forming a section. Therefore, if Heth brought "3 batteries" to the field of Lewisburg, one can assume there were between twelve and eighteen pieces of artillery.

Most accounts of the battle of Lewisburg indicate Heth brought six pieces of artillery with him, and left four of them in the hands of the victorious Federals. A careful analysis of the available records and accounts reveals that Heth brought from eight to ten pieces of artillery to the battlefield at Lewisburg. Not all of them, however, were brought into action.

An account, credited to Captain G. Gaston Otey, published in the *Lynchburg Virginia*, placed Heth's force "at about 1,800 in number ... the 22d, 45th and 50th Virginia regiments, Edgar's battalion, one company of cavalry, two guns of the Otey battery, two guns of Lowry's battery, one gun of Chapman's battery and two guns of Bryan's battery,..."[160]

According to the foregoing statement, Heth had a total of seven pieces of artillery engaged at Lewisburg. Corporal Charles C. Baughman, a member of Otey's Battery, noted in a letter that "we had 11 pieces in the action and lost 4 of them, Bryant [sic] lost 3 and we lost one."[161]

Besides the four guns captured on the battlefield by Crook's men, an additional three or four guns were spiked and abandoned at or near the Greenbrier River Bridge at present day Caldwell. Heth's demoralized men salvaged only two guns – Captain George G. Otey saved one, and Captain George B. Chapman saved his 24 pounder.

---

158 *Dayton Weekly Journal*, Dayton, Ohio, June 10, 1862. Woodward wrote that Heth had 2,800 infantry, 300 cavalry, and one company of artillery.

159 *Darke County Democrat*, Greenville, Ohio, June 11, 1862. The lieutenant does not mention the 45th Virginia Infantry in his account.

160 *Lynchburg Daily Virginia*, Lynchburg, Va., May 27, 1862, copied in the June 5, 1862 issue of the *Wilmington Journal*.

161 Letters and Papers of Charles C. Baughman, Eleanor S. Brockenbrough Library, The Museum of the Confederacy, Richmond, Va. (hereafter cited as Baughman).

One of the few Confederate newspaper accounts of the battle named the units which left the Narrows of the New River after dark on May 19th. The writer, identified only as "Dane," noted that the 22nd and 45th Regiments, Finney's Battalion, and the 8th Virginia Cavalry, along with two guns of Otey's Battery, four of Bryan's Battery, and three from Lowry's Battery composed the column.[162] Dane, however, did not mention Chapman's gun or Vawter's Western Artillery in his account. By adding Chapman's 24-pounder, a total of ten pieces of artillery made the trip to Lewisburg.

Casualty records for the Battle of Lewisburg show several men from Captain Lewis A. Vawter's company as being killed or wounded in the fighting. It is very likely that the Western Artillery company had been disbanded when General Heth reorganized his command a short time before leaving camp at New River, and formed part of Edgar's Battalion of Infantry.

It is known that a total of five companies of artillery were assigned to Heth's command prior to the Lewisburg battle. A letter signed by four artillery captains, announced that First Lieutenant John Floyd King had been elected by them to command a battalion of artillery in Heth's command. The May 8, 1862 letter asked that King be commissioned as major, and was signed by Bryan, Lowry, Chapman and Vawter.[163] Although Captain George G. Otey's company was assigned to Heth, his name does not appear on the letter.

The following table gives a picture of Heth's artillery just before the Battle of Lewisburg:

---

162 *Richmond Daily Dispatch*, Richmond, Va., June 3, 1862

163 Compiled Service Records of General & Staff Officers & Non-Regimental Enlisted Men, M331, file of John Floyd King, National Archives, Washington, D. C. (hereafter cited as Staff File)

Company	Guns Assigned	Iron 6-pounder (smooth-bore)	6-pounder rifled	12-pounder (smooth-bore)	12-poundeer Howitzer	12-pounder Mtn. Howitzer	24-pounder	Unknown size	On Detached Service	Guns at Lewisburg	Saved	Captured	Spiked & Abandoned
Captain Lowry	2	1		1						2		2	
Captain Bryan	5	3	1	1					2	3		1	2
Captain Chapman	5	2			2		1		4	1	1		
Captain Otey	4		1	1				2	2	2	1	1	
Captain Vawter[164]	2					2				2			2
Total	18	6	2	3	2	2	1	2	8	10	2	4	4
Alternate Total	16	6	2	3	2	0	1	2	8	8	2	4	2

There are so many conflicting accounts regarding the number of artillery pieces brought into action and lost at Lewisburg, it is difficult to determine the truth of the matter. The figures presented in the above table are believed to be the most accurate numbers.

After dark on the evening of May 19th, Heth moved his command across the New River and went into camp on the northern bank, near the mouth of Wolf Creek. At dawn the following morning, Heth started for Lewisburg, about 47 miles away, marching ten or twelve miles that day, camping for the night on the farm of Captain Hugh S. Tiffany, in Monroe County, Virginia.

Major General William W. Loring, now in command of the Department of Southwest

MAJOR GENERAL WILLIAM
W. LORING

Museum of the Civil War

---

164 Captain Vawter's "Western Artillery" was most likely broken up by General Heth in the May 15, 1862 reorganization of his command. Should this be the case, the totals shown should be reduced by 2 guns (see Alternate Total line).

Virginia, and Heth's superior, learned that Crook had captured the telegraph office and its papers at Jackson River Depot, and that Crook had fallen back to Lewisburg. Loring cautioned Heth that Crook had been strongly reinforced, and that if Heth continued on to Lewisburg, he risked being overwhelmed by a force on his left flank.[165] Confident that his men could easily overwhelm the Union forces at Lewisburg, Heth pressed on.

CAPTAIN EDWIN H. HARMAN
History of Tazewell County and Southwest Virginia

Continuing the march on May 21st, Heth moved as far as Salt Sulphur Springs, near Union, going into camp about 3 p.m. There it was learned that a small force of the enemy were in possession of the town of Union[166] Colonel Finney's Battalion and two guns of Otey's Battery went forward to drive the enemy out and occupy the town. The Yankees retreated without contest.[167]

Two deserters from the 47th Ohio Infantry straggled into Heth's camp that evening.[168] It was learned from them that Crook's force consisted of two regiments of infantry and 500 cavalry, about 2,500 men in all. Captain Edwin H. Harman, 45th Virginia, noted: "We have a good many men here under Gen. Heth. I think enough for the work we have to do, and if they are not very particular, we will get at them where they are not expecting us."[169]

While in camp at Salt Sulphur Springs, Heth took the time to respond to several communications from General Loring. Heth reported that he was within 24 miles of Lewisburg. "I think I have pretty accurately ascertained that the force of the enemy does not exceed three regiments of infantry, 300 or 400 cavalry, with six or eight pieces of artillery."[170] Heth was a little strong on his estimate of

165 Loring, OR, Series I, Vol. 12, part I, p. 810.

166 Crook's scouting force from Company C, 2nd West Virginia Cavalry

167 *Richmond Whig*, Richmond, Va., May 28, 1862; there is no mention of this encounter in the Union records.

168 Confederate Prisoner of War records at the National Archives identify these two men as Corporal Jno. B. Davis, and Private Jacob Nutter, both of Company F, 47th Ohio Infantry. Both are listed as having been captured at Lewisburg, one on May 19 (Davis), and the other on May 23, 1862 (Nutter). Both were confined at Richmond on May 30, 1862, and released on June 24, 1862, by order of General Witcher.

169 Edwin Houston Harman Papers, 1856 – 1984, Ms1990-019, letter dated May 21, 1862, Special Collections, Virginia Polytechnic Institute and State Library, Blacksburg, Va. (hereafter cited as Haman VT)

170 OR, Series I, Vol. 12, part I, p. 811

Crook's strength. He faced only two regiments of infantry, a battalion of cavalry (five companies), and four mountain howitzers.

Late on May 23, 1862, following the battle of Lewisburg, Heth wrote his after-action report at Union, Monroe County, Virginia. In it, he now estimated Crook's strength as "about 1,500 men (infantry) – two regiments – two mountain howitzers, and about 150 cavalry."[171] He confidently added "My chance of success was good, provided I could surprise the enemy and get into position. This I succeeded in doing far beyond my expectation."[172]

About 5 a.m. on the morning of May 22nd, Heth left Salt Sulphur Springs and headed for Lewisburg. As the Confederates passed through the town of Union, some 30 or 40 men who were sick, injured, or otherwise unfit to fight, were left in the care of the townspeople. Late that evening, Heth arrived at a point within two miles of the Greenbrier River Bridge, where he halted and went into camp for the night. A strong picket guard from the 22nd Virginia Infantry was stationed between their camp and the bridge.

The men of Heth's command slept on their arms that night, without fires, tents, or food. First Lieutenant William F. Bahlmann (Company K, 22nd Virginia), in charge of the pickets, recalled that his men stayed near the bridge with only their overcoats to protect them from the cold. This close to the enemy, they could only "grin and bear it."[173]

Sergeant S. W. N. Feamster, of the Greenbrier Cavalry, recalled: "…the night before [the Battle of Lewisburg] our command came down to the Monroe Draft and lay there that night. Our Reg't. [8th Virginia Cavalry] had orders to charge the pickets at the Bridge (Greenbrier) at the signal to be given by the infantry firing from Caldwell's house a short distance from the Bridge. The signal was given about the peep of day and we were on our horses ready to make the charge and did charge the pickets. They had pickets

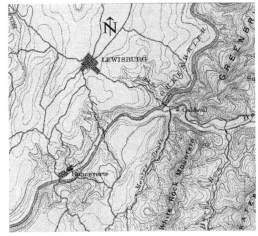

TOPOGRAPHICAL MAP OF LEWISBURG AREA 1887
US Geological Survey
https://ngmdb.usgs.gov/topoview/
viewer/#10/38.0600/-80.4302

171 OR, Series I, Vol. 12, part I, p. 812

172 OR, Series I, Vol. 12, part I, p. 812

173 "Down In The Ranks: Recollections of Captain William F. Bahlmann, Confederate Officer" *Journal of the Greenbrier Historical Society*, Volume II, No. 2 (October 1970), p. 41 – 93. (Hereafter cited as Bahlmann).

stationed every few hundred yards from there to Lewisburg. Our object was to capture the pickets before they could give word to Gen'l. Crooks [sic] at Lewisburg that we were coming."[174]

Heth started his advance on Lewisburg about 4:00 a.m. on the morning of May 23, 1862, a year to the day after the secession vote in Lewisburg. His advance cavalry and infantry quickly drove in the enemy pickets, taking some of them prisoner.

The advance infantry company got within 100 yards of the pickets before they fired upon the advancing Confederates. The Southern troops returned fire. Then the cavalry rushed across the bridge into the Union pickets, dispersing them, killing two and taking three prisoners.[175]

Captain John P. Sheffey, 8th Virginia Cavalry, wrote: "The pickets at the bridge were easily driven in, some were killed and some captured by the mounted companies of our cavalry under Col. Corns. Lt. George W. Holderby [Co. E] was wounded and Lt. Alexander H. Samuels [Co. E] had his horse killed."[176]

Private Joseph A. Brown, Company H, 22nd Virginia Infantry, recalled the events of the evening of May 22nd and the early morning of the 23rd. "The night was spent by the weary soldiers in a gorge of the mountain on the roadway... It was a night of anxiety to the soldier boys, who felt instinctively the anticipated activities of the next day. Everything was hushed and quiet, that the watchful enemy might not discover the army and the high hopes of the Confederate brigades. Just as the day was dawning, the splendid Greenbrier Cavalry was observed in waiting position. On the summit over-looking the Greenbrier bridge (a covered bridge) was easily seen a company of infantry ready and in order. At a signal the activities opened. Captain Echols [Eakle] charged through the bridge, and made a dash for the town of Lewisburg three miles distant and all the way up hill. Simultaneously the company over-looking the bridge descended in cooperation with the cavalry charge. At the same time these successful maneuvers were made, the entire column of Confederates joined in the movement for the capture of Lewisburg. No more buoyant hopes ever thrilled a soldier's heart than we Dixie boys felt in our confidence of victory."[177]

---

174 "A Civil War Event" *Journal of the Greenbrier Historical Society*, Volume VI, No. 3 (1995), p.19 – 37. (Hereafter cited as A Civil War Event).

175 Baughman; Smith Letters – Smith only reports two prisoners taken. Records of the Union forces do not list any men from the picket guard as being killed, only that six infantrymen were captured.

176 James I. Robertson, Jr. Soldier of Southwestern Virginia: The Civil War Letters of Capt. John Preston Sheffey. Louisiana State University Press, Baton Rouge, La., 2004. (hereafter cited as Sheffey). Lieutenant Samuels horse was not killed at the bridge, but on the way up the hill to Lewisburg; see recollections of Sergeant Feamster quoted below.

177 Joseph Alleine Brown. The Memoirs of a Confederate Soldier. Sam Austin Publishing, Forum Press, Abington, Va., 1940, p. 19 (hereafter cited as Brown).

Colonel James M. Corns
Diana Kinzer Heath

Captain Benjamin F. Eakle
Bill Turner, Clinton MD

An unidentified solder of the 36th Ohio Infantry, recorded some incidents of the attack on the picket post. He noted that John Hampton, one of those taken prisoner, "fought bravely till he was forced to surrender."[178]

Sergeant Anderson, of Wilson's Company, is reported as having "killed 4 of the enemy with a stick and then got away from them." Another of the pickets, according to this source, "out ran the Rebel cavalry and got away. He said they must get better horses if they wanted to take him."[179]

"…Lt. [Josiah B.] Martin of Co. C – in charge of the picket at Greenbrier bridge, who after firing into the enemy as they approached, retreated across it, formed, and as soon as a sufficient number had crowded on it, poured a volley into them which killed 3 and wounded some half dozen men. He then retreated into the woods up the river but not soon enough to prevent 5 of his men being taken prisoner."[180]

The number of prisoners taken was reported by Confederates newspapers as ten or twelve.[181] Lieutenant Colonel Edwin H. Harman, 45th Virginia Infantry, reported that the picket of twelve men was captured; other letters record the number at two or three. The official records show the loss in Federal prisoners as nine men, a mix of cavalry (3) and infantry (6).[182]

---

178 Another Day, p. 234

179 Another Day, p. 234

180 *Home News*, Marietta, Ohio, June 6, 1862; official records show six of the 36th Ohio taken prisoner.

181 *Richmond Daily Dispatch*, Richmond, Va., June 3, 1862; *Richmond Whig*, Richmond, Va., May 28, 1862

182 Harman VT; This number was determined from Muster Rolls, Compiled Service Records, Union Casualty reports, Confederate prisoner of war records, and newspaper accounts.

In his official report of the battle, General Heth noted that "Most of his pickets were captured, and I attained without firing a shot that position in front of Lewisburg which I would have selected."[183]

One Union diary noted that the Confederate advance was dressed in U. S. uniforms, and in this manner approached the pickets without alarming them.[184]

After crossing the bridge and securing the position, General Heth ordered Captain Bryan to post two pieces of artillery near the bridge as part of a rear guard. Captain Bryan chose two six-pounders to place on a hill near the bridge.[185] The captured Union pickets were undoubtedly left in charge of a squad of men at the bridge.

The bridge secure, Heth ordered his men forward, double quicking the three mile, up-hill march to Lewisburg. Lieutenant Colonel Finney, commanding the two battalions, led the advance, followed by the 22nd Virginia, 45th Virginia, the cavalry and artillery.[186] A small force of cavalry went in front of Finney, to ferret out any remaining pickets. Somewhere along the way, the Confederates dispersed at least one group of Federal cavalry pickets. Sergeant S. W. N. Feamster recalled: "As Captain [Alexander H.] Samuels and myself were coming up River Hill we came across two or three sets of pickets. We were riding at full speed and one set of pickets as we approached them jumped over the breast works into the brush and fired on us and shot Capt. Samuels horse… the rest of the regiment were coming on after us & we hurried on and never slackened our speed until we reached the top of Waggoners Hill & the pickets all broke and run, there we had to wait for the infantry to get up.[187]

Traveling at a double quick pace, it would have taken between forty-five minutes and an hour for the infantry to reach the ridge overlooking town. Heth's men were in high spirits, likely because Lewisburg was home to many of them. Captain Sheffey, 8th Virginia Cavalry, noted that "The men advanced with the utmost enthusiasm …"[188]

Private Joseph A. Brown, 22nd Virginia Infantry, recalled: "With elastic step we pursued the up grade of the mountain. Indulging ourselves in bombastic glee

183 OR, Series I, Vol. 12, part I, p. 812. This statement, however, is incorrect, as other accounts tell of shots being exchanged with the Union pickets.

184 Jones Diary

185 "Notes on Confederate Artillery Service," by Milton W. Humphreys. *Journal of the United States Artillery*, Volume IV (1895), p. 41 – 2; J. Gray McAllister. Family Records: Compiled for the Descendants of Abraham Addams McAllister and his wife Julia Ellen (Stratton) McAllister, of Covington, Virginia. Easton, Pa., Press of the Chemical Pub. Co., 1912, p. 29-30. (hereafter cited as McAllister)

186 Gleaves Family Letters, letter of E. H. Harman to Captain Robert H. Gleaves, June 3, 1862. www.gleavesfamily.com/home/letters/html, last visited January 2016. (hereafter cited as Gleaves)

187 A Civil War Event, p. 24; Samuels was not a captain, but a lieutenant, and belonged to the 8th Virginia Cavalry.

188 Sheffey, p. 107

that at last we were to have a decisive "set to" with the Yanks, whom we had for months tried to tempt to meet us in combat. Each Confederate soldier felt himself on the eve of a glorious success. John McMullen plucked a sprig of evergreen and pinned it on the lapel of his coat, quoting Scott's celebrated poems, *Charge, Chester, Charge* an *On, Stanley, On.* In exultation over our anticipated victory, snatches of songs and merry jokes now and then varied the monotony of the triumphant march. As we reached the outskirts of Lewisburg, a Lt.-Colonel shouted in a loud voice, "Come on boys, we've got them by the umbilicus, come on." [189]

189 Brown, p. 19

IN THE UNION CAMP

May 23, 1862: 4:00 – 5:30 a.m.

Drummer's Call[190] and Reveille sounded at 4:15 a.m. on the morning of May 23rd. As the camp started stirring and forming for roll call, the distant rattle of gunfire reached the camp. The sound carried well in the cool morning air. "...a shot or two was heard at Greenbrier Bridge. In a few moments after, a round of 12 or 20 shot[s] admonished us that our pick[ets] were being engaged. We were ordered to fall in with arms and accoutrements. The sharp firing going on informed us that the pickets were being driven in, and the enemy approaching in force."[191]

Within minutes of the sound of gunfire, two cavalrymen dashed into camp and reported to Colonel Crook, who was standing outside his quarters. After listening to what they had to say, Crook immediately went to Captain Jewett Palmer, Jr., commander of Company G, 36th Ohio Infantry, and ordered him to form his men at once. He directed Palmer to march to Greenbrier Bridge and support the picket guard.

Private George Hechler, one of Palmer's men, recalled: "We had just gotten up when our captain came around and told us to get into ranks with arms only, and then we knew there would be something to do."[192]

---

190 Drummer's Call – also known as first call; beaten by the lead drummer fifteen minutes prior to duty. It assembled the other musicians and warns the troops to get ready. All of the drummers then beat the second call for formation.

191 *Springfield Republic*, Springfield, Ohio, June 2, 1862

192 Hechler, p. 59

Captain William W. Woodward, Company C, 44th Ohio, noted that the outer pickets (at Greenbrier Bridge) were cut off by the Confederate cavalry, and could not send word to camp. Only when the inner pickets were attacked, was the alarm given.[193]

Captain John Beckley (Company C, 36th Ohio), recalled: "…had it not been for a Cavalry picket stationed who rode into camp and gave the alarm, we would have been completely surprised. As it was we had but about ten minutes to form our companies before the firing commenced."[194]

A letter written by Major John J. Hoffman, 2nd [West] Virginia Cavalry, following the battle, sheds a little more light on the events of that Friday morning: "Two mounted Pickets of Capt. Powell's Co. 2d Virginia Cavalry, were taken prisoner. They were stationed at the Bridge and came in and gave the alarm and were ordered to return to their guard, and while advancing at full speed ran directly into the front of the enemy's column and were taken."[195] Major Hoffman fails to explain the loss of a third member of the cavalry taken prisoner.

Corporal David Todd Gilliam, one of the cavalrymen, recalled things differently: "About daybreak orderlies passed from tent to tent with the exclamation – '"Up boys the enemy is upon us!"' Quickly and quietly the regiment was in arms and in the saddle. There was no bugle call, no roll of drums, no audible notes of preparation. Everything was conducted with the utmost secrecy."[196]

Sergeant James Haddow, Company F, 36th Ohio, told his wife that the enemy "had secretly gained their position by the cavalry swimming the river below and cutting off our pickets."[197] There is, however, no evidence to support Haddow's claim; besides, the river was running high and swift, making it unlikely it was forded.

Trooper J. M. Jones wrote that he was aroused about daylight by the bugler sounding "to horse."[198] George Jenvey, a bugler, from Marietta, Ohio, stated that he was awakened by the bugle sounding "Boots and Saddles."[199]

Company D, 44th Ohio Infantry, commanded by Captain Lysander W. Tulleys, was camped about 400 yards closer to the town than Palmer's men, and close to Crook's headquarters. Captain Tulleys overheard the cavalryman report

---

193 *Dayton Weekly Journal*, Dayton, Ohio, June 10, 1862

194 *The Athens Messenger*, Athens, Ohio, June 5, 1862

195 *Jackson Standard*, Jackson, Ohio, June 5, 1862.

196 Gilliam

197 "Sergeant Haddow Writes Home." *Journal of the Greenbrier Historical Society*, Volume VI, No. 6, (1998), p. 48 – 52.

198 Jones Diary; Trooper Todd Gilliam recorded that "about daybreak orderlies passed from tent to tent with the exclamation – "Up boys the enemy is upon us!". He added that there was no bugle calls and no drum rolls. (Gilliam)

199 *Home News*, Marietta, Ohio, June 6, 1862

that a Rebel force was approaching and that the pickets had been driven in. "Crook," noted Tulleys, "was incredulous."[200]

Captain Tulleys observation of Crook's reluctance to believe that the Confederates were actually attacking his camp raises some interesting questions. During the days prior to the battle, his scouts had learned of Heth's presence at Salt Sulphur Springs in Monroe County. Rumors of an impending attack spread through the Union camp for several days. Local Negroes were predicting an attack. Why, then, would Crook be surprised by the sudden appearance of an enemy force?

Captain William W. Woodward, Company C, 44th Ohio Infantry, reported that Crook knew of the enemy's intention to drive him out of Lewisburg, and of their approach. "By midnight," Woodward noted, "all were under

CAPTAIN LYSANDER W. TULLEYS
Kent State University

arms."[201] This statement is contradicted by numerous other accounts of the early morning events of May 23rd.

Captain Tulleys hurried to the tents of his company and ordered his men to fall in. By the time the long-roll sounded, Company D was already in line. "All was excitement in camp" noted Tulleys.[202]

Colonel Crook directed Tulleys to take the lead, and then added that it was "improbable that any considerable force of Rebels was threatening us; that a lot of bushwhackers had probably frightened the picket, and anticipated nothing serious."[203]

The colonel further directed Tulleys to take his company, along with Palmer's, and "go out to the bridge, ascertain the trouble and report. If he should meet any force of Rebels, he was to deploy his company as skirmishers, gradually fall back and report the situation."[204]

The colonel's instructions and comments caused Captain Tulleys to be less cautious than he should have been. The men of Company D, 44th Ohio also had

---

200 Tulleys; *National Tribune*, Washington, D. C., June 24, 1886

201 *Dayton Weekly Journal*, Dayton, Ohio, June 10, 1862

202 Tulleys; Long-roll – all of the drummers beat a continuous roll, signaling the troops to prepare as quickly as possible for some type of action.

203 Tulleys

204 Tulleys

their doubts about seeing any action, commenting when they were being sent out to skirmish with the enemy "should there be any."[205]

Captain Tulleys with 40 men of Company D, 44th Ohio started along the turnpike into Lewisburg at quick time. There was no hurry; the captain did not expect any trouble until they reached the Greenbrier River Bridge.[206]

About halfway through the town, Colonel Samuel Gilbert approached Captain Tulleys and asked if he had ordered his men to load their weapons. Tulleys had not, believing there was no immediate need to do so. The captain halted his men and ordered them to load their muskets.[207]

While halted, a matronly lady came from her nearby home, and, in trembling voice and tearful eye, inquired the reason for the early morning warlike activity. "Nothing serious, I think," replied Tulleys, and resumed his march.[208]

Cavalryman Gilliam related another encounter that morning as the skirmishers moved through the town: "In passing through town the inhabitants who were very jubilant and the women taunted our soldiers saying: - '"Our men are going to take breakfast with us this morning"', to which a soldier retorted: - '"I'm thinking ma'm that some of your men will breakfast in hell this morning."[209]

As the men from the 44th Ohio passed through town on the turnpike, Captain Palmer's company from the 36th Ohio came up about hundred yards in their rear. When about a hundred yards from the eastern ridge overlooking Lewisburg, the road passed through the bluff of the ridge. At this point, Tulleys' men formed into line of battle across the road. As this maneuver was taking place, Palmer's company advanced to within 30 yards of their position.

The morning was foggy, and it was easy to become confused. The two companies discovered a group in the road ahead of them, and thought they were the pickets retiring from Greenbrier Bridge. When within one hundred yards of the group, the Union men were met with a sharp volley. Private George Hechler noted: "Most of them were concealed behind a small house, surrounded by shade trees and shrubberies behind fences, and lying in the tall grass."[210]

An account of the battle written by a soldier named Shoemaker appeared in the *Gallipolis Journal*, in which he noted that the men under Captain's Tulleys and Palmer were "Deceived by the fog, they mistook a body of Rebels for our pickets,

---

205 William Wyles Collection, Oscar Hale Papers, Donald C. Davidson Library, University of California, Santa Barbara, California (hereafter cited as Hale).

206 Tulleys

207 Tulleys

208 Tulleys

209 Gilliam

210 Hechler, p. 59 - 60

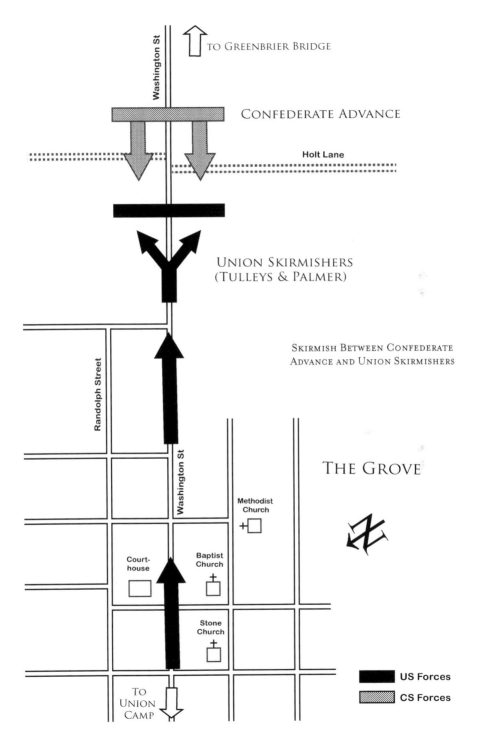

TO GREENBRIER BRIDGE

CONFEDERATE ADVANCE

Holt Lane

UNION SKIRMISHERS
(TULLEYS & PALMER)

SKIRMISH BETWEEN CONFEDERATE
ADVANCE AND UNION SKIRMISHERS

Washington St

Randolph Street

THE GROVE

Methodist
Church

Courthouse

Baptist
Church

Stone
Church

Washington St

TO
UNION
CAMP

US Forces

CS Forces

approached within close range, and it was not until they received a volley, that they discovered their mistake."[211]

Private Oscar Hale, Company D, 44th Ohio wrote: "Our Com[pany] being sent on to skirmish with the enemy should there be any. We had not advanced through town before we saw coming what we supposed to be the picket guard coming to camp & sent out two men to tell them to keep in our advance but when within a few rods they were ordered to surrender but refusing were fired on but without effect. They instead of being our pickets were the enemy."[212]

The two cavalrymen who had reported the advance of the Confederates were in Tulleys advance, per Crook's instructions. As they reached the top of the hill, Tulleys noticed they were met by other horsemen. Becoming suspicious, Tulleys slowed his march and sent a corporal and another soldier forward to see what was going on.[213]

When the two men drew near the horsemen on the hill, they were ordered to reverse their arms and surrender. The corporal refused and they hurried back to inform Tulleys what was happening. Several shots were fired at them, without doing any harm.[214]

Oscar Hale, a member of Tulleys company, noted that as soon as the two men were fired upon, the company formed in line of battle. Almost immediately, they were fired upon by what Hale reported to be a "whole regiment" of the enemy, killing one man, wounding 1st Lieutenant Samuel C. Howell and several privates. including Hale.[215]

The newspaper correspondent of the *Springfield Republic*, identified as Zouave, wrote a similar account: "As it [Company D] was raising [climbing] the ridge of hills opposite to the encampment, they saw a body of men standing in line, but it being foggy and smoky, they were unable to determine who they were, and supposed them to be our pickets. Two men beckoned to them to come on, crying come on boys, it's all right, come on. The two men advanced, and actually got within ten steps and commanded to reverse arms and surrender. They refused and gave the alarm. Captain Tulleys instantly charged from the march by flank to line, and ordered his men to deploy, when the whole Rebel battalion opened. One man was killed and several wounded; among them, Lieutenant Howell, who was shot through the leg, above the knee, but still continued with his men, urging

211 *Gallipolis Journal*, Gallipolis, Ohio, June 12, 1862

212 Hale

213 Tulleys; in his account, he identifies the corporal as Corporal Hamilton. A check of the roster of Company D does not show a corporal by that name in the company. There is, however, a sergeant by the name of Hamilton.

214 Tulleys

215 Hale

them on. The Company replied in earnest, and the volleyed thunder showed that we had a heavy force to contend with."[216]

Captain Tulleys noticed an open space on the right of his company, through which he saw a regiment of Rebels drawn up in line of battle, sheltered by a fence. Clearly visible in the billowing smoke, Tulleys could see that the enemy had bayonets fixed.[217]

"Right oblique. By company into line. Double Quick, March!"[218] Tulleys ordered rapidly, intending to deploy his men as skirmishers. Before the men could get into line, the Rebel force poured a volley into them.

Not waiting for further orders, the company fell to the ground, seeking what little shelter they could find. After the volley, those able to do so, sought shelter behind a rail fence on their right and among some nearby trees, where they returned fire. Captain Tulleys cautioned his men not to waste ammunition, to take careful aim and bring down a "Johnnie" with every shot.[219]

While the men of the 44th Ohio were taking fire, Captain Palmer's company from the 36th Ohio, were trying to get into a position to help their comrades. Still in column formation, Palmer ordered his men to scatter and lie down. They hastily obeyed; some taking shelter behind the fence, others dropping to the street. Musket balls struck all around the soldiers, throwing up dirt and debris; many of the balls passed uncomfortably close to the soldier's heads. Private John T. Booth noted: "I don't believe I ever tried to occupy less space in my life than upon that occasion."[220]

Private Hale continued: "We immediately deployed taking shelter behind a rail fence and maintained our ground against fearful odds for (20) twenty minutes when we were compelled to fall back to prevent being cut off from the main body."[221]

Because of their position, the men of Company G could not fire without endangering the men of the 44th. Booth, as he hugged the ground and wiped the dirt out of his eyes, glanced at his watch – it was 5:01 a.m.[222]

216 *Springfield Republic*, Springfield, Ohio, June 2, 1862
217 Tulleys
218 Tulleys
219 Tulleys; Hale
220 *National Tribune*, Washington, D. C., June 24, 1886
221 Hale
222 *National Tribune*, Washington, D. C., June 24, 1886; Virgil A. Lewis. History of West Virginia (In two parts). Philadelphia: Hubbard Brothers, Publishers, 1889, p. 211, says the battle began at 5:15 a.m., and lasted about an hour. (hereafter cited as Lewis)

THINGS BEGIN
TO HEAT UP

Confederates Take Position

May 23, 1862: 4:00 – 5:30 a.m.

The Confederate advance forces rapidly took possession of the hill overlooking Lewisburg and in sight of Crook's position on the opposite side of town. Sergeant S. W. N. Feamster recalled: "Gen'l. Crook had gotten warning the night before [and] he had sent out a double picket force & we knew by the beating of the drums that he knew of our approach – The dogs every where around were barking. Whilst we were there at Waggoner's the Federals were firing on us & we defended ourselves as best we could until the infantry & artillery reached us."[223]

It was just after daylight when the main force of the Confederates arrived on the ridge line. Captain Edwin H. Harman, 45th Virginia Infantry, noted that by the time they arrived on the ridge, Crook's men could be seen in position on the opposite ridge. Captains Tulleys' and Palmer's skirmishers were not yet visible to the Confederates, but soon would be.

Upon arriving at the top of the hill, General Heth commenced forming his line of battle. Colonel Finney, commanding the lead unit, was ordered to deploy

---

[223] A Civil War Event, p. 24

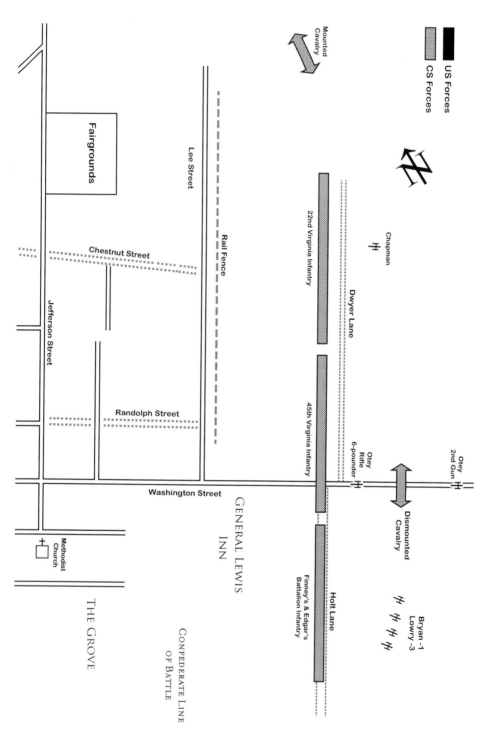

to the left of the road. The 22nd Virginia was sent to the right, and the 45th Virginia filled the center of the line, across the road.[224]

The Confederate line of battle occupied the area that is now Holt Lane and Dwyer Lane, covering a distance of about three-quarters of a mile.[225] The dismounted men of the 8th Virginia Cavalry, commanded by Lieutenant Colonel Cook was ordered to form about 300 yards in rear of the main line (probably in the center), as a reserve force. The mounted cavalrymen, commanded by Colonel James M. Corns, were spotted by a Federal soldier to the far right of the position occupied by the 22nd Virginia Infantry.[226]

One Union soldier observed the Confederates arrival, and noted that they "came up with great rapidity and boldness."[227]

Captain Harman later explained the purpose of placing the 45th Virginia in the center. It was thought that the enemy would concentrate their strength on that point, and not on the flanks. As it turned out, the opposite occurred. Had the 45th Virginia been on the left of the line in place of Finney's Battalion, the result would have been quite different, theorized Captain Harman after the battle.

Very few details concerning the placement of the artillery at Lewisburg is known. Only bits and pieces have survived, along with a great deal of conjecture. It is known, however, that the artillery was first positioned on the crest of the hill overlooking Lewisburg. A. S. Johnston, in his history of Chapman's Battery, notes that "Chapman's gun was posted on the right of the road entering Lewisburg from the south [east], while Bryan's was on the left;"[228] Other accounts place Lowry's two guns on the left with Bryan's gun. It is thought that these occupied the high ground near present Teaberry Road, on the Confederate left. Captain George G. Otey brought two guns to Lewisburg, and seems to be last to arrive on the field. His two pieces remained in the center of the line, on or near the main road, supporting the 45th Virginia.

A letter written by Edward Smith, Assistant Commissary & Subsistence officer in the 45th Virginia Infantry, notes that Bryan's and Lowry's companies were positioned on the hill in rear of Edgar's Battalion (Finney's), with Chapman in rear

224 Gleaves; A letter from Shannon Butt places the 45th Virginia to the left of the main road, with Edgar's Battalion on the extreme left (Shannon Butt Papers, Virginia Historical Society, Richmond, Va., hereafter cited as Butt).

225 Lt. Col. Finney's Battalion occupied the area on the left of the line near present day Holt Lane, from the turnpike road to what is now the road to Ronceverte. The 45th Virginia occupied a grove of trees at the crown of the hill above present day Lee Street, while the 22nd Virginia was on the right, in a wheat field near what was then the fairground (see map for location); Otis K. Rice. A History of Greenbrier County. McClain Printing Co., Parsons, W. Va., 1986.

226 National Tribune, Washington, D. C., November 4, 1886

227 Booth Papers

228 A. S. Johnston. Captain Beirne Chapman and Chapman's Battery: An Historical Sketch. Union, W. Va., n.p., 1903 (hereafter cited as Johnston)

of the 22nd Virginia. He recorded that one gun of Otey's Battery came up late in the action, while another advanced on the "street", passing the 45th Regiment.[229]

Further evidence as to the position and number of artillery pieces can be found in a letter written by Shannon Butt, a Monroe County physician: "A portion of the artilery [sic] on the street, and portions with the two Regiments."[230] An 1886 account of the battle, published in the *National Tribune,* stated that six guns were planted on the right of the turnpike, beyond the grove.[231]

General Heth, in his after-action report, stated: "While deploying and getting my batteries into position the enemy, evidently in order to cover the retreat of his wagons, threw forward his smallest regiment, sending one-half to the right and the other to the left of the main approach to the town. I advanced to meet him."[232]

Soon after 5:00 a.m., the Confederate line of battle appeared along the summit of the ridge, on either side of the road. Private John T. Booth observed: "It appeared to me as the sight met my gaze at that moment as though by magic they sprang out of the ground on which they stood."[233]

The order for the Federal skirmishers to lie down caused some confusion in the Rebel line. Private Hechler (36th Ohio) wrote: "Now they [Confederates] stopped, thinking they had us all killed, but what was their surprise when we all jumped up and commenced retreating and firing!"[234]

About five minutes later, the Confederates brought up two pieces of artillery to the summit of the turnpike, and began to unlimber them. Tulleys and Palmer's men were immediately ordered to fall back and use the houses and outbuildings of the town for cover. From their position on the right of the road (facing the enemy), they did their best to hold the Rebels in check.[235]

Private Hechler recalled: "They now commenced a furious cannonading, with one and then increased to eight pieces of artillery. They did some wild shooting. Before commencing to bombard us, they had raised a shout, calling: "'Lewisburg is ours!'""[236]

A Confederate account appearing in the *Richmond Whig,* noted that the battle commenced at 7 a.m. on the left of their line. "...Bryant's battery [was] throwing shell into the lower portion of the town and upon a hill covered with

229 William E. Duncan Letter Book, 1862, Letter of Edward Smith, David M. Rubensteiin Rare Book & Manuscript Library, Duke University, Durham, N. C. (hereafter cited as Duncan)

230 Butt

231 *National Tribune,* Washington, D. C., November 4, 1886. This is a Union recollection, and refers to the Confederate left.

232 OR, Series I, Vol. 12, part I, p. 812; the force spotted by Heth, and taken for two small regiments, was the skirmishers thrown out by Crook.

233 *National Tribune,* Washington, D. C., June 24, 1886

234 Hechler, p. 60

235 *National Tribune,* Washington, D. C., June 24, 1886

236 Hechler, p. 60

a thick undergrowth of trees, where the enemy were thought to be posted. This cannonading continued for some time without being returned by the enemy, when the order was given for the infantry to advance, which they did in good order, the 22d Regiment, under Lieutenant Colonel Barbee, on the right, the 45th Regiment, Colonel Brown[e], and Finney's Battalion, on the left."[237]

An account appearing in the *Lynchburg Daily Republican*, described the opening moments of the battle: "Reaching the summit of the hill which overlooks the town, our artillery commenced shelling the enemy beyond the town, (as we supposed with considerable effect,) which was in line of battle, and the only line of the enemy which could be seen at that time, but which afterwards proved to be only his reserve."[238]

Ohio Musician Charles Ramsey observed the artillery bombardment, commenting "there [sic] first shots hit in the town but they soon got range of the camp and the shot, shell and canister began to rain pretty thick around us. Some of the boys were badly scared and tore down there bunks and got things ready for a run. I concluded to wait until it became necessary and then if I had to go to take as little as possible. I got my cup of coffee and sat down over the brow of the hill and drank it and ate a few crackers. Some canister shot cut a small bush to pieces about ten feet to the right of me. One of the boys was eating under a bush and a piece of shell took the top of the bush off. It was musical to hear the different sounds of the missiles fired at us."[239]

One of the errant Confederate shots killed Charles L. Chewning, a private in Company H, 22nd Virginia Infantry, quite likely the first Confederate to fall that

JOHN WESLEY METHODIST CHURCH
Steve Cunningham

LOCATION OF CANNONBALL STRIKE AT
JOHN WESLEY METHODIST CHURCH
Steve Cunningham

---

237 *Richmond Whig*, Richmond, Va., May 28, 1862

238 *Lynchburg Daily Republican*, Lynchburg, Va., June 10, 1862 Letter signed "A Soldier" concerning 45th Va. Inf., most likely written by Captain Edwin H. Harman.

239 Ramsey Letter, May 23, 1862

morning, a victim of friendly fire. Other reckless shots struck in the town itself. One shot, said to have been fired from a position near the present day location of the General Lewis Inn (then the home of John Withrow), struck the corner of the Methodist Church on Foster Street. At least two other shots struck the Cary and Lipps homes in Lewisburg, and perhaps three others struck the McPherson home.

Louisa M. Cary, daughter of Ophelia Cary, lived in a brick home that stood along what is now Washington Street, near Sibold Lane. The teenager found herself between two contending armies. A cannon ball entered the home, scattering brick and mortar through the rooms. The family, a widow and four young daughters, fled to the cellar. It is related that Louisa helped carry pieces of burning wood out of the house to keep it from being consumed.[240]

Another brick home in the eastern part of Lewisburg also came under fire of the Confederate artillery. Mammie Lynn Lipps, a daughter of blacksmith John W. Lipps, recalled: "The Confederate general and his battle line was just behind our house. The Federals were on the opposite hill so we were between the fighting armies. We were hurried into the cellar when the cannon opened, and there we were cooped up with the two armies fighting on each side of us. The bullets rattled on the roof and the walls of our house and once a shrieking shell came through the roof and then down in the dark cellar."[241]

An account of the battle written by Captain William H. Dunham (Company D, 36th Ohio), commented on the Confederate artillery fire: "…just as we [were] getting into town they commenced throwing shot and shell at us which produced great consternation among the inhabitants, many took refuge in the cellers others fled in wild confusion. The citizens are very indignant at their friends for shelling their friends some houses were damaged by shot and shell but no citizen [was] killed or houses burnt. Col. [Joel] McPherson's house suffered the most having been penetrated by 3 shots. The family had a remarkable escape. It is certainly unprecedented in the annals of warfare to shell a town without giving its inhabitants warning but it is [in] keeping with all the acts of rebellion."[242]

Soon, the Confederate gunners adjusted their aim so that their shots targeted the main Federal camp on the western side of town. One Northern soldier noted that two batteries of three guns each were in operation. He described the firing: "…a red flame, a cloud rushing through the air, an explosion overhead was warning that bombs were coming thick and fast."[243]

Trooper J. M. Jones noted in his diary: "The enemy commenced shelling us from the brow of the hill above town throwing thare [sic] shell at the cavalry up

---

240 *Charleston Gazette*, Charleston, W. Va., August 28, 1932

241 *Charleston Daily Mail*, Charleston, W. Va., June 4, 1939

242 William H. Dunham Letters, U. S. Army Heritage and Education Center, Carlisle, Pa. (hereafter cited as Dunham)

243 *Springfield Republic*, Springfield, Ohio, June 2, 1862

on the hill on this side of town firing over the house tops. They were driving in our skirmishers & they saw the train moving & the cavalry falling back [and] they supposed that we were retreating. The unevenness of the ground & the buildings hiding our movements."[244] Trooper Jones added a little more information in a letter, stating that "They supposed we were leaving – the smoke of their battery and the undulation of the hill sides hid all our movements."[245]

At this juncture, the Confederates turned their guns upon this position. John T. Booth noted that the Confederates were firing a combination of shell and grape-shot at them. "This, to the great annoyance of the villagers, making them for the time less annoying to us. ... We could see men, women, and children, both black and white, running hither and tither, many of each class, just as they had arisen from their beds, -- but partially dressed. They were endeavoring to make their way out of town, or, to places of safety."[246]

The Union skirmishers continued to fall back toward the center of town, following a side street, all the while firing at the Rebels. After retreating about a "half square"[247], the men made a stubborn stand. John T. Booth wrote: "I could see them coming over the hill (ridge), as thick as grasshoppers in a stubble-field on a warm July day."[248]

As the two companies of skirmishers fell back, they went to the central cross street of town, and there held their position until Crook had formed the regiments. Each company then rejoined their respective units. Booth noted: "While here shot, shell and balls were flying thick and fast above and about us, one shell fell about a yard from where I stood, phized, and went out."[249]

Booth's reference (as well as other's) to the firing of grape-shot is incorrect. By the 1860's, the use of grape-shot was unheard of. In its place, the artillery now used canister. Considered to be the deadliest ammunition, canister consisted of a thin metal container filled with layers of lead or iron balls packed in sawdust. When fired, the container disintegrated, and the balls spread out like an oversized shotgun blast. The maximum range of canister was 350 yards, and within that range, it could knock great holes in a line of infantry.

After holding their ground for about twenty minutes, the two companies were forced to retire, to prevent their being cut off from the main force.[250] Each company then rejoined their respective regiments, which by now were forming in line of battle in the streets of Lewisburg.

---

244 Jones Diary
245 Jones Letters
246 *National Tribune*, Washington, D. C., June 24, 1886
247 A square is defined as one hundred square feet, so a half square would be 50 square feet.
248 Booth
249 Booth
250 Hale

May 23, 1862: 4:30 a.m. – 6:00 a.m.

As the two companies (Tulleys and Palmer) moved through town to the support of the pickets, the main part of the command turned their attention to the breakfast prepared by the cooks before roll call. "We had just fairly commenced eating when firing was heard on the hill east of town, & we were again ordered into ranks. We threw down our tins & spoons & were in ranks & loaded instantly. The firing was quite brisk, & we could plainly see the men, & the blue smoke rising."[251]

At the same time, Colonel Crook was getting his camp in order, in case he was forced to retreat. He ordered the baggage train to the rear, to stand by on the road to Meadow Bluff. Amid the confusion and bursting shells, the wagoner's quickly harnessed and hitched the horses to the wagons, and galloped to the rear.

Corporal Gilliam noted: "The cavalry were drawn up on the crest of the hill in full view of the enemy so as to hold their attention. They turned their artillery on us, but their marksmanship was not good."[252]

An account appearing in the June 5, 1862 issue of the *Troy Times* noted that most of the Confederate artillery shots seemed to be aimed at the commissary and wagon train, which were being put in order. The only damage was a mule killed by a shell, and another which passed through the stable and striking the commissary clerk's saddle. The saddle was shattered and a piece of the shell lodged itself in a feed trough. The clerk, who was putting the bridle on his horse at the time, was untouched by the shell.[253]

Crook also ordered Second Lieutenant John A. Palmer (Company G, 36th Ohio Infantry) to take a detail of men and remove the prisoners from the local jail and move them to the rear. Second Lieutenant John C. Allen (Company K, 44th Ohio Infantry) assisted Palmer. Palmer, one of the Officers of the Guard, recollected there were between 12 and 14 prisoners in jail at Lewisburg on the morning of the battle. "I accordingly went about it immediately, & as I had got them out, and ready to start, a brisk fire was begun, and kept up quite live for a short time as I was going out of town I met the rest of the 36th on her way to the fight as unconcerned, as if nothing was the matter."[254]

Lieutenants Palmer and Allen moved the prisoners to the hill west of town and halted. By this time, both the 36th and 44th Regiments – some 800 men – were moving forward to attack the Confederate line.[255]

---

251 Harrison Diary

252 Gilliam

253 *Troy Times*, Troy, Ohio, June 5, 1862

254 Salem Light Guard, p. 65

255 Salem Light Guard, p. 65

The greater part of the 2nd (West) Virginia Cavalry was ordered to remain in a position on the road, as a reserve force, while two companies were sent out on each flank to prevent a flanking maneuver by the Confederates.[256] Trooper J. M. Jones noted that the cavalry battalion formed on the hill west of town, in sight of the enemy. The Confederates soon directed their artillery fire upon the cavalrymen, forcing them to fall back about 300 yards. At the same time, Crook's wagon train was moving toward the rear.

A detail of men (size unknown) from the 36th and 44th Ohio, serving as a camp guard, did not participate in the battle. No mention is made of the disposition of the Mountain Howitzer's, other than the fact that through a misunderstanding, they were not brought into the action. Just what orders were misunderstood is not recorded. The regimental history of the 47th Ohio Infantry mentions that the howitzers were engaged and replied to the Confederate artillery.[257] Another account, appearing in an 1886 article in the *National Tribune* newspaper, notes that the howitzers were mounted on mules, and were thus useless.[258]

The activity on the western heights caught the attention of the Confederate officers, and it was immediately assumed they were retreating. One Northern newspaper correspondent wrote that "The enemy were so convinced of this, that they sent a regiment around to cut us off."[259]

Up till now, the fighting was restricted to the Confederate advance and the Union skirmishers under Captain's Tulleys and Palmer, accompanied by some artillery fire from the Confederate batteries. The overwhelming strength of the Confederate advance and the artillery fire, forced the Union skirmishers to fall back into the town. General Heth, as well as other officers, assumed that Crook's main force was before them, and was giving way. The blue-clad soldiers visible on the western slope were thought to be only a reserve force. Encouraged by this, and thinking they had the enemy on the run, Heth ordered his infantry and artillery to follow them into Lewisburg.

Upon receiving Heth's order, Captain Thomas A. Bryan and Captain George G. Otey protested[260], believing that their guns could do better service in their present position. Instead of listening to the advice of his subordinates, Heth insisted that both the artillery and infantry would follow the retreating Yankees into the streets of Lewisburg.

Corporal Charles C. Baughman, a member of Otey's Battery, wrote: "When we arrived at the top of the hill, we brought our pieces into position and opened

---

256 RE, Co. B, C, F, and I, 2nd W. Va. Cavalry; *National Tribune*, Washington, D. C., December 9, 1886.

257 Saunier, p. 78 – this is the only source suggesting the Federal artillery fired during the battle.

258 *National Tribune*, Washington, D. C., November 4, 1886

259 *Springfield Republic*, Springfield, Ohio, June 2, 1862. The writer must have seen the Confederate mounted cavalry on the far right (Union left) of the Confederate line.

260 McAllister, p. 30

upon the enemy who were in and around the town. After firing a few shots we were ordered to charge and down the hill we went at full speed. We ran into the town, the yankees [sic] pouring a hot fire into us from behind the houses and from the windows which killed several of our men (I don't mean of my company, but of our force). The town is situated in a hollow and as we came in to the town the main force of the enemy fell back to the hill at the back of the town and opened a very hot fire upon us."[261]

What followed was nothing short of chaos. Captain Sheffey, 8th Virginia Cavalry, recalled: "After cannonading awhile from the hill, the whole force, 45th, 22nd, W. W. Finney's Battalion and artillery, were allowed to dash down into the town, helter-skelter, pell-mell, without wings, without line of battle, without skirmishers, without any proper arrangement."

A correspondent of the *Daily Dispatch*, reported: "...after a few shots, the Federals retired down the hill, our men pressing on till they reached the farther edge of town ..."[262] Another correspondent of the Richmond newspaper put it this way: "But in an evil hour we were ordered to cease firing and charge the enemy."[263]

General Heth wrote: "I directed Lieutenant-Colonel Finney, commanding [the] battalion, to occupy a small body of oak timber. In doing this Colonel Finney had to cross a wheat field. The enemy, numbering only three companies, opened upon his battalion a very severe fire, which probably compelled his command to fall back. At this time the left of the enemy was in full retreat."[264]

Second Lieutenant William A. Smith, Company I, 50th Virginia Infantry, part of Finney's Battalion, wrote: "It was evident that the enemy's lines were several hundred yards from us. Consequently, we were ordered to advance, which we did over fences and across fields, till we came up 75 or 80 yards of the enemy's line, which was concealed behind a fence on a ridge."[265]

The *Richmond Whig* correspondent wrote: "They moved on steadily until they arrived within four hundred yards of the hill and had penetrated the heart of the town, when a terrific fire was opened upon them by the enemy, who were posted in houses, behind fences and in a thick orchard. The 22d Regiment drove the enemy before them up a hill, and had turned the left and centre of the enemy, when our forces on the left gave way, and despite the exertions of officers, could not be rallied."[266]

---

261 Baughman

262 *The Daily Dispatch*, Richmond, Va., May 31, 1862

263 *The Daily Dispatch*, Richmond, Va., June 3, 1862

264 OR, Series I, Vol. 12, part I, p. 812-13; post war accounts declare this last statement to be false, that the 36th Ohio did not retreat.

265 Smith Letters

266 *Richmond Whig*, Richmond, Va., May 28, 1862

Private Isaac F. Thomas, 45th Virginia Infantry, wrote: "When our men got in sight of town they saw the enemy in line of battle on the oposite [sic] side. Our men attempted to charge through town and attack them. When they got into town they were fired on from behind every house and fence. They stood the fire for some time, but at last had to retreat with a loss of 39 men killed, 61 wounded left on the field that fell into the hands of the enemy and 90 that were not wounded. We got several wounded men away, but I do not know how many."[267]

Captain Harman, 45th Virginia, wrote: "The town is so situated we could not see the movement of the enemy and advanced more than half way through [the town] when the left and right of our line was met with fearful odds, from behind houses, fences, trees, etc."[268]

Captain Harman, was on the left center of the line, and noted that his regiment got halfway through town before the enemy appeared. They "appeared in great force from houses and a skirt of woods not a hundred yards from our left and right ..."[269]

One of the few Confederate newspaper accounts, states: " ... the battle opened on our left, by Bryant's battery throwing shell into the lower portion of the town and upon a hill covered with a thick undergrowth of trees, where the enemy were thought to be posted. This cannonading continued for some time without the fire being returned by the enemy, when the order was given for the infantry to advance, which they did in good order, the 22d Regiment, under Lieutenant Colonel Barbee, on the right, the 45th Regiment, Colonel Brown[e], and Finney's Battalion, on the left."[270]

Cavalry Captain John Sheffey recalled: "Then the battle began in earnest. Suddenly the popping shots were condensed into one terrific crash, and the Belgian rifles of the enemy ... roared with ceaseless fury upon the right and left. The General [Heth] was near us when that peal of thunder broke upon us. It was something he had not anticipated. Our men were effectually ambuscaded, and for *that* General Heth alone was to blame."[271]

The *Lynchburg Daily Republican* account stated: "Edgar's Battalion, commanded by the gallant Finney and noble Edgar, was on the extreme left flank, the 22d on the right, and the 45th in the centre, commanding the streets and liable to be raked by the enemy's guns at any minute. Proceeding in this manner, the battalion received a heavy fire from a superior force of the enemy, who appeared

---

267 Isaac F. Thomas letter, Emory and Henry College, Archives, Emory, Va. (hereafter cited as Thomas) -
     Thomas was sick and did not take part in the battle, stopping some four miles from Lewisburg.

268 Harman, WVU

269 Harman, VT

270 *Richmond Whig*, Richmond, Va., May 28, 1862

271 Sheffey, p. 108

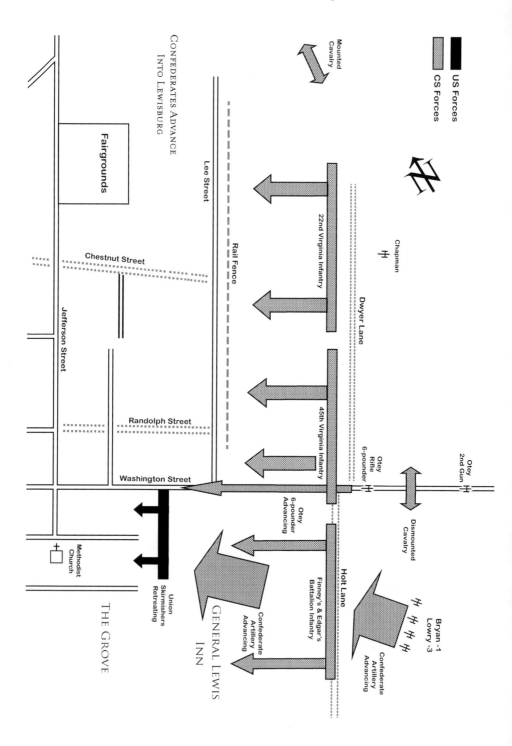

unexpectedly in their front on a hill, behind a fence, and protected by timber. The battalion, with the left of the 45th, returned the fire with heroic courage and daring bravery, the artillery changed position to the front. At that critical moment the infantry lost its support, and the battalion was compelled to fall back."[272]

272 *Lynchburg Daily Republican*, Lynchburg, Va., June 10, 1862 Letter written by "A Soldier" concerning 45th Va. Inf., most likely written by Captain Edwin H. Harman.

THE 36ᵀᴴ OHIO
ATTACKS

May 23, 1862

The route taken by the 36th Ohio is much more documented than that of the 44th Ohio. Lieutenant Colonel Melvin Clarke led his regiment along the main turnpike while under artillery fire, such as "might well try veteran troops".[273] Sergeant A. R. Phillips, Company E, noted: "Just as our company was passing into the cross-street a shell came whizzing down the main street, causing some men to dodge in a very undignified manner. When we turned off from the main road we were fairly hidden from the Rebel line of battle by a rise of ground."[274] At a cross street, they turned to the left and followed it to the outskirts of town, halting under the cover of a bluff or bank. While in this position, Captain Palmer's Company (G), which had been sent out in advance earlier that morning, rejoined the regiment. They were now in front of the 22nd Virginia Infantry, on Heth's right.

Captain Hiram F. Devol, Company A, 36th Ohio Infantry recalled a close call while passing through town. One of the shells fired by the Confederates exploded nearby and a fragment clipped the brim of his hat, but did not touch him. The officer picked the fragment up and kept it as a keepsake.[275]

Although in command of a brigade, Colonel Crook accompanied the 36th Ohio as it advanced into its maiden battle, which Crook later referred to as "... the neatest little stand-up fight of the war." As the regiment was forming, Crook's

273 Booth; This is now the Randolph Street area of Lewisburg
274 *National Tribune*, Washington, D. C., November 4, 1886
275 Devol, p. 31

horse "became unmanageable and plunged with him into a mud-hole, near a tannery. He dismounted and left him, going in with us on foot."[276]

Lieutenant Colonel Melvin Clarke reported that: "… at the foot of a steep declivity, having an elevation of some 50 feet, and along the brow of which were several houses surrounded by inclosures [sic], beyond which the larger portion of the enemy's infantry, commanded by General Heth in person, were formed."[277]

The day after the battle of Lewisburg, Captain Hiram F. Devol drew a highly detailed map of the battleground. One of his notations shows a company of sharpshooters positioned in the fairgrounds, on the extreme left of the Union battle line.[278]

Once the regiment was in position, Crook gave Clarke permission to proceed. Clarke reported: "… I at once marched my battalion to the top of the steep declivity, and passed the houses over numerous fences found myself in front of the enemy, who was posted behind a fence, and immediately opened a brisk fire upon us, which was returned with promptness and alacrity."[279]

Private George Hechler recalled the movement of the regiment up the bank: "A shout rolled down our line, but the Rebels did not fire, the distance yet being too great for them. When within about 150 yards of them we were commanded to halt. They had saved this opportunity to deliver their fire, and we were not slow to reply."[280]

After gaining the top of the bluff, the 36th Ohio halted briefly, as the terrain became less steep. Colonel Crook now ordered Captain Palmer's Company (G) to go out as skirmishers in advance of the regiment. Captain Palmer gave the command immediately: "Company – as skirmishers – on the right file – take intervals – double quick – march."[281]

The skirmishers advanced only a short distance until they came in contact with the Confederate lines, which were ready to meet them. The skirmishers fired several rounds, advancing all the while. As soon as the firing commenced, the regiment was ordered forward to support the skirmishers, which fired several times before the regiment joined them. The men would fire, then drop to the ground, load, rise, and advance a few yards, fire and drop to the ground.[282] The enemy fire cut the air all around the men of the 36th, many of the shots missing because of the distance between the two lines. Some, however, came too close for comfort.

---

276 *National Tribune*, Washington, D. C., November 4, 1886; W. H. Beers & Co. The History of Clark County, Ohio. Chicago: W. H. Beers & Co., 1881, p. 1059.

277 OR, Series I, Vol. 12, part I, p. 808

278 Devol; a copy of his map appears in the front of this volume.

279 OR, Series I, Vol. 12, part I, p. 808

280 Hechler, p. 60

281 Hechler, p. 63

282 Booth

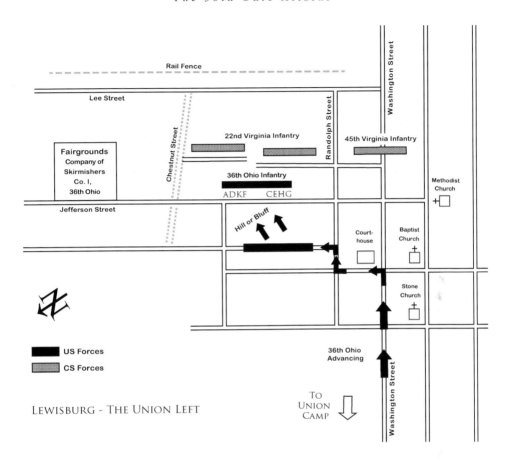

LEWISBURG - THE UNION LEFT

Sergeant A. R. Phillips, Company E, 36th Ohio commented: "The main line [of the enemy] was posted behind a rail fence on top of the hill, beyond a cornfield, with skirmishers thrown to the front. Their flank reached far beyond our left, and there were the cavalry bearing down on us across the undulating fields still farther to the left, and only held in check by the skirmishers of Co. G."[283]

The sergeant also noted that Colonel Crook noticed the men lying down to load, rising, and after advancing a few yards firing. To hasten the advance of the men, Crook loudly ordered the men to "Load as you go!"[284]

Colonel Clarke reported: "I continued to advance until the line of the battalion was within 40 yards of that of the enemy, when they fled in confusion. The firing ceased only when the enemy had got beyond our range ... A number of

---

283 *National Tribune*, Washington, D. C., November 4, 1886

284 *National Tribune*, Washington, D. C., November 4, 1886

their dead and wounded lay behind the fence where they were first posted and scattered through the fields beyond."[285]

Captain William A. Walden, Company K, recalled: "We marched through a town lot, about the width of a company front. It was enclosed by a high rail fence; Rebels posted behind the fence for about a third of the way down.[286] Despite loosing three men killed and nine wounded in a very short time, Walden's men kept advancing. Rebel dead and wounded filled the fence corners.

Pressing onward up the slope, the 36th Ohio forced the Confederates to fall back. Private John F. Booth recalled: "The enemy slowly at first yielded, yet disputed, desperately, every particle of ground, taking advantage of every fence or other cover, fancied or real to halt, to rapidly fire, and bravely endeavor to hold. Here their dead lay thick, piled one upon another."[287]

Private H. A. Shoemaker, Company I, 36th Ohio Infantry, on the flank of the 22nd Virginia Infantry, noted that they were "mowing the Rebels down like wheat."[288]

During the heavy fighting, Colonel Crook was moving through the ranks of his men. Ohio Private Oliver Parker recalled that Crook "came around during the hottest ingagement [sic] and saw one boy out of Com[pany] C wonded [sic]; he took him up in his arms and laid him down in a fence corner then took his cartridge box and gun and fought in the ranks."[289]

PRIVATE OLIVER PARKER
Copy in possession of Terry Lowry

Captain Hiram F. Devol's Company A, suffered heavier losses than the rest of the command, mostly while crossing a clear pasture field, toward the Rebel line sheltered behind a rail fence. Ten of his men fell wounded, two of whom later died of their wounds.

Captain John Beckley, Company C, noted that the fighting was intense, and that Companies D, K, I and C were in the hottest part of the battle. "The balls flew around us like hail. I was turned almost around by a grape shot, but was unmarked … God was with us."[290]

---

285 OR, Series I, Vol. 12, part I, p. 808
286 Another Day, p. 242
287 Booth
288 *Gallipolis Journal*, Gallipolis, Ohio, June 12, 1862
289 Oliver Parker Letters, copy in possession of Terry D. Lowry (hereafter cited as Parker)
290 *Athens Messenger*, Athens, Ohio, June 5, 1862

The Union troops reached the summit of the eastern ridge about 6:30 a.m., just over an hour and a half after the fighting began. The Rebels, reported Private Booth, were in full retreat. From the time that the 36th Ohio formed in front of the Rebel position to their arriving at the summit of the ridge took only about thirty minutes.[291]

Major E. B. Andrews, 36th Ohio, noted: "The fight, was desperate & deadly while it lasted but the 22nd [Virginia] gradually yielded leaving nearly 50 dead & mortally wounded & as many others less wounded. After driving them back nearly ½ a mile they all broke & fled in utter rout & our part of the field was won. The time occupied was about twenty minutes."[292]

From the Confederate Right

As the Confederate forces rushed headlong into the town, cavalry Captain John P. Sheffey, recalled: "The houses were filled with the enemy. So was the street at the farther end of the town, and the force upon the enemy's right and left must alone have been superior to ours. A reserve was drawn up beyond all these. Our reserve was then ordered to follow close upon the heels of the main body and halted in the town at a point where the fire from both wings of the enemy concentrated. Here many of our men would have been killed had not Lt. Col. [Cook] allowed them to kneel upon their knees while we were awaiting further orders. The men were as cool and determined as any set of men I ever saw."[293]

Private Joseph A. Brown, one of the 22nd Virginia Infantry, wrote of his observations on the Confederate right: "From the crest of the hill over-looking the town the rattle of musketry was a sure sign of a death-dealing struggle. A few steps from me my friend, Henry Radford, received a fatal wound. In our enthusiam [sic], Henry MacFarland and I pushed on among the dwellings and secured a position of vantage close to a stable corner. Here we were intensely engaged in the fight, protected somewhat by a portion of the stable."[294]

First Lieutenant William F. Bahlmann, Company K, 22nd Virginia Infantry, noted the ferocity of the battle on Heth's right: "We were under a heavy fire and men falling like ten-pins in a bowling alley."[295]

---

291 Booth

292 State Archives Series 147, Correspondence to the Governor and Adjutant General of Ohio, 1861 – 1898, Letter of Major E. B. Andrews, 9 June 1862: Ohio History Connection, Columbus, Ohio (hereafter cited as Andrews)

293 Sheffey, p. 107-8

294 Brown, p. 19-20

295 Bahlmann, 60

Private Oliver Parker, Company I, 36th Ohio, noted that he "…saw thare [sic] flag shot dow[n] 3 times." A Rebel undoubtedly recovered the flag, as there is no mention of any colors being lost at Lewisburg.[296]

Private H. A. Shoemaker, Company I, 36th Ohio, in an account published in the *Gallipolis Journal*, noted that when the 36th Ohio reached the crest of the hill, that two regiments of the enemy poured a galling fire into their ranks. The Northern troops drove the enemy back, where they rallied briefly behind a fence. The Ohioans quickly drove the Southerners out of this position.[297]

Although not present at Lewisburg, Private John E. W. Morgan, a member of Chapman's Battery, commented on the battle: "The Yankees that had showed themselves, retreated down to town, Edgar's battalion after them. The artillery followed. When they got fairly in, the Yankees rushed from house, stable and cellar to the amount of 9000 [men]. Closed on our men from both sides and poured in upon [them] a galling fire. Our men dropped upon their knees and fought for a few minutes. They were ordered to retreat. …"[298]

Private Morgan mentioned Chapman's 24-pounder, stating: "We were closed upon three times but held on to her [the gun] …"[299]

---

296 Parker

297 *Gallipolis Journal*, Gallipolis, Ohio, June 12, 1862

298 Harry L. McNeer. The Letters of John and Susan Morgan: A Story of Everyday Life, Love and Loss in the Civil War Years. Wolf Creek Publishing, 2006, p. 15 (hereafter cited as Morgan)

299 Morgan, p. 15

THE 44TH OHIO ATTACKS

May 23, 1862

Within a short period of time, the men of the 44th and 36th Ohio were in ranks and ready to advance to meet the Confederates. Private John E. Harrison, Company G, 44th Ohio recalled: "It was soon apparent to all what the movement meant, for we had been in ranks but a few minutes when we could see men in the road on the hill east of town running this way, which we supposed to be our pickets."[300]

Colonel Crook determined not to wait for the Confederates to come to him, but to take the attack to them. Forming his plan of attack, the colonel rode down into the town to ascertain the Confederate position. Upon his return, he ordered Lieutenant Colonel Melvin Clarke to take the 36th Ohio and advance on the left of the main turnpike (now Washington Street), and ordered Colonel Samuel Gilbert to take the 44th Ohio and move against the enemy on the right side of the turnpike. This order threw the 44th Ohio against the bulk of the Confederate artillery, which Crook instructed them to capture if possible.[301]

The 44th Ohio moved down the hill toward their assigned position, under the fire of the Confederate artillery. A 24-pound shot struck the ground in front of Company I, 44th Ohio, bounced over their heads, covering them with dirt.

Samuel C. Leavell, Company B, 44th Ohio, noted that "Just as we came to a graveyard a shell passed thru my company, and killed Serg't. Alt, of Co. F." Adam

---

300 Harrison Diary
301 Hechler, p. 60; *Springfield Republic*, Springfield, Ohio, June 2, 1862

S. Alt, who was standing on a rock in the rear of his company, was struck in the abdomen by a rebel shell. Though badly mangled by the projectile, Alt clung to life for nearly an hour before he died.[302]

"One shell burst in the air just in front of us" wrote Private John E. Harrison, adding that "a piece passed whizzing directly over our company – the men involuntarily dodging."[303] Harrison also noted: "The shell & shot commenced lighting in our camp behind us, & I looked back & saw one of our companies just starting out, & a shell struck down among them while I was looking & I saw them dodging but could not tell whether any were killed or not."[304] Another of the 44th Ohio, noted in his diary: "The "'bum shells"' and cannon "'bawls"' flew fast and thick."[305]

Lieutenant Palmer, who remained in the rear with the prisoners, noted that the Confederate artillery overshot the Union camp most of the time.[306] He wrote: "I tell you tis [sic] a grand sight to see them shells coming squealing and hissing through the air (rolled up in a roll of smoke about as big as a 2 bushel basket) at you, as if all the Fiends of Hell had been turned loose."[307]

The route taken by Colonel Gilbert's 44th Ohio is described in the June 2nd issue of the *Springfield Republic*: "The 44th marched by the right flank direct to a stone church, filed to the right to the road. A little further on, they filed to the left, then again to the right and formed in line behind cover of the hills."[308]

Along the way, Captain Tulleys rejoined the regiment with his company (D), and continued to act as skirmishers.

Lieutenant James Shaw recalled the move into position on the left: "Meanwhile shot and shell were screaming through the air, plunging through the camp, and bursting on all sides; but our boys marched to slow time right through the storm. When we got down in the road, they [Confederates] depressed their pieces so that the projectiles passed about 1 ½ feet above our heads. The first shell passed at that distance over the left of our company, the next exploded in the air at a distance of thirty feet from our lines, and the next about the same distance to our rear – the pieces flying around us in a scary manner. The boys of our company dodged their heads a little at the first shell, but on being spoken to by one of their officers, they held their heads upright and steady, and paid no more attention to the "screeching devils." One shell came through the fence and passed through one man of Co. F,

---

302 *Springfield Republic*, Springfield, Ohio, June 2, 1862; *National Tribune*, Washington, D. C., September 12, 1912

303 Harrison Diary

304 Harrison Diary

305 Pearson diary

306 Salem Light Guard, p. 62

307 Salem Light Guard, p. 62

308 *Springfield Republic*, Springfield, Ohio, June 2, 1862

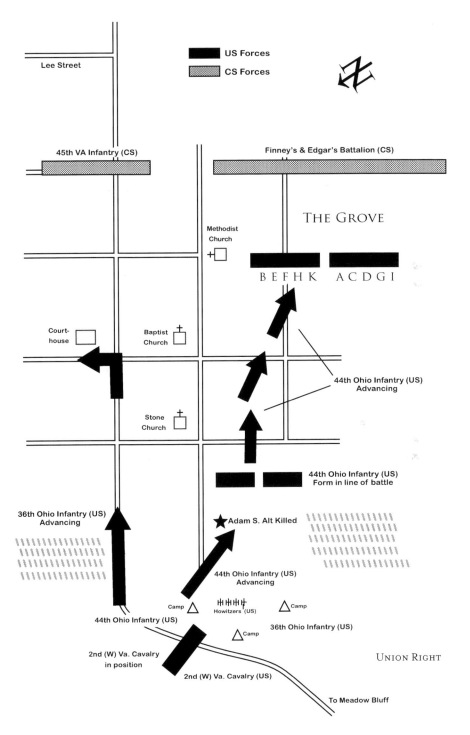

US Forces

CS Forces

Lee Street

45th VA Infantry (CS)

Finney's & Edgar's Battalion (CS)

THE GROVE

Methodist
Church

B E F H K   A C D G I

Court-
house

Baptist
Church

44th Ohio Infantry (US)
Advancing

Stone
Church

44th Ohio Infantry (US)
Form in line of battle

36th Ohio Infantry (US)
Advancing

★ Adam S. Alt Killed

44th Ohio Infantry (US)
Advancing

Camp △

Howitzers (US)

△ Camp

44th Ohio Infantry (US)

36th Ohio Infantry (US)

△ Camp

2nd (W) Va. Cavalry
in position

UNION RIGHT

2nd (W) Va. Cavalry (US)

To Meadow Bluff

that the Confederate line seemed to be well preserved at this point, and the men steadily advanced, returning the fire.[314]

Captain Israel Stough (Company F) observed the Confederates attempting to move an artillery piece into position to rake[315] the left wing of the regiment. Stough ordered his men to direct their fire on the artillerymen. Captain Robert Youart (Company K), directed his men to fire on the caissons, and succeeded in taking out three cannoneers and three horses.[316]

Another account describes the action: "The enemy are thunder struck; they waver and as we pour into them our murderous fire they stagger and reel like drunken men. The order is given: '"charge bayonet"' – with a spring and a ringing shout that shook the hills, they rush forward sure of victory. The enemy can't stand cold steel. They break and fly and the boys of the 44th seize a cannon, loaded with canister, before they can touch it off."[317]

The order to fix bayonets seems to have been only partially obeyed by the men of the 44th Ohio. This order was quickly followed by one from Major A. O. Mitchell, who ordered the left wing of the 44th Ohio to charge the cannon. Lieutenant Evans (known as Zouave, the *Springfield Republic* correspondent) noted that the men "Ramming in a load and not stopping to fix bayonets, ... started on the double-quick."[318]

On the right wing, however, the order to fix bayonets must have been obeyed. An account in the *Troy Times* notes that the 44th Ohio "charged bayonet" and took four guns. At least one Confederate was wounded in the back by a bayonet, which later cost him his life.[319]

Company B of the 44th Ohio, positioned on the extreme left of the battalion, did not come into close contact with the rebel artillery, it being about two hundred yards away. Private John A. McKee noted that the artillery was opposite the center of the battalion. According to McKee, one rebel gun was loaded with grapeshot and aimed at the right of the battalion. As the gunner was preparing to fire, Captain Stough (Company F) shot him.[320]

---

314 *Dayton Weekly Journal*, Dayton, Ohio, June 10, 1862

315 Rake – to direct gunfire along the length of a target; instead of meeting the men of the 44th Ohio straight on, the Confederates attempted to turn at least one cannon in order to fire into the side of the advancing force.

316 *Springfield Republic*, Springfield, Ohio, June 2, 1862

317 *Gallipolis Journal*, Gallipolis, Ohio, June 5, 1862

318 *Springfield Republic*, Springfield, Ohio, June 2, 1862

319 *Troy Times*, Troy, Ohio, June 5; Ingram Stone was wounded in the back by a bayonet while in a fence corner, taken prisoner, and later died of the wound.

320 McKee, p. 40

The men of Company F reached the guns first. Captain Stough, laying his hand on one of them said "I take this gun in the name of Company F." It was here that Private Francis M. Runyon fell, taking two balls in the breast.[321]

Captain Stough recalled: "As soon as I came in range of the battery, I directed the fire of my company upon it, and charged, and I rejoice that Company F succeeded in carrying one splendid gun, caisson, ammunition, and ten horses, from the grasp of their owners, and they now stand in pride before our quarters."[322]

Captain Stough later wrote: "Our advance now became so determined and fire so deadly that the three first guns were abandomed [sic] when it was observed they were making an effort to get a 10 pounder (rifled) in position to rake our flank, when I directed the entire fore of my Co. upon it killing a few and them immediately commanding a charge which proved an entire success. First a Caison [sic] & 6 horses & then the gun fell into the hands of Co. F."[323]

Captain Woodward recalled that when the men were within 200 yards of the enemy guns, the "boys" gave a whoop and with a yell, leaped the fences and went after the rebels. The Ohioans soon drove back the battery support, and the guns were taken.

Private Joseph Pearson, Company F, noted in his diary: "We pushed on to the battle ground and we fought hard. Took one piece of cannon and the horses we shot three horses and stop the cannon. I shot one."[324]

While the left wing was charging on the battery, Finney's men poured a galling fire on the right wing of the 44th Ohio. "Heedless of it as hailstones," recalled one witness, "the boys gave them a Roland for every Oliver."[325]

Private John T. Booth, historian of the 36th Ohio, recorded that Colonel Gilbert ordered the men of the 44th Ohio to hold their fire until they were within 40 yards of the enemy. The rebels, observed Booth, used the same tactic, and at the same instant, both fired a volley into each other. The second volley of the 44th Ohio completely broke the rebel ranks. A few fought stubbornly from what cover they could find. Try as they might, the rebels were unable to rally and reform the line. The 44th advanced so rapidly that the Confederates had no chance to remove their artillery. "A well directed and opportune volley from one or two companies had killed or wounded so many of the artillerists, and horses that there was not a sufficeint [sic] number of them left to remove the pieces".[326]

---

321 *Springfield Republic,* Springfield, Ohio, June 2, 1862

322 *Springfield Republic,* Springfield, Ohio, June 4, 1862; this is the "relic" gun that was later sent to Springfield, Ohio.

323 Stough

324 Pearson Diary

325 *Springfield Republic,* Springfield, Ohio, June 2, 1862. The phrase "a Roland for every Oliver" refers to two legendary knights in the time of Charlemagne, who were of equal strength, exchanging blows; an eye for an eye.

326 Booth

Lieutenant James Shaw recalled: "… we took their battery of four pieces, which did the mischief at first. We shot nearly every man at this battery, a few running away. They had just loaded a fine 12 pounder with canister and trained it obliquely on our regiment, and the gunner had the lanyard wrapped around his hand about to pull, when we shot him, thus saving two or three of our company from annihilation."[327]

After the Confederate artillery was captured, Company A was ordered to relieve Captain Tulleys Company (D) as skirmishers. An account recorded by a member of Company A tells what happened next.

"This was done and our boys on raising the crest of the hill were met by the fire of the Grey bucks [backs]. Captain [A. S.] Moore gave the command to commence firing which the boys did with a will. We had been under fire a few minutes when the Battalion commenced firing, and such a whistling of bullets can only be imagined by those who have [never] heard it. We were exposed to a heavy fire which came from our left. At this time the yells of both Federal and Secesh with the shrieks and groans of the wounded and dying made an impression on my mind that will never be erased. The hottest part of the battle lasted about 30 minutes when the enemy broke and ran like the Secesh can only run, …"[328]

Major E. B. Andrews, 36th Ohio, noted the following about the advance of the 44th Regiment: "The 44th marched firmly up the hill reserving its fire until within about 40 yards of the enemy's line of battle where it poured a terrible volley in upon the rebels line which was formed behind a rail fence on the top of a wooded knoll. This volley broke apart the line & the second volley which was also well directed broke it completely & from that time Gen. Heth's left wing was routed & could not rally & a volley from one or two companies so killed & wounded the artillery men & horses at their batteries, (no longer supported by the infantry) that the 4 guns (two of them rifled) all they had brought upon the field were captured & that side of the field gloriously won. The time occupied was not more than ten minutes from the time the 44th began their march up the hill till the field on the right was won, cannon and all, so rapidly & bravely moved on the gallant 44th."[329]

Colonel Samuel A. Gilbert described the activity of his regiment: "On emerging from a small grove we came suddenly upon a battery of the enemy, consisting of two rifled 10-pounders and two 12-pounder field howitzers, which was charged with such impetuosity that the gunners had no time to fire. Here some

---

327 *Darke County Democrat*, Greenville, Ohio, June 11, 1862
328 *Troy Times*, Troy, Ohio, June 10, 1862
329 Andrews

20 of the enemy were killed, as many more wounded, and many prisoners taken; also about 200 stand of small-arms taken."[330]

Northern correspondent "Zouave", noted that when the rebels saw their battery taken, and that the right wing of the 44th Ohio out-flanking them, started to retreat on the double-quick. "Then for the first time our boys gave a yell and pitched in."[331]

Private William G. Felton, Company A, 44th Ohio, noted that when the rebs started running, the band of the 44th started playing, referring to the sound as noise. Felton recalled the chase after the fleeing Confederates: "This was the first rebs we had seen. Soon I came to a wounded one. I asked him if he was hurt much. He said yes, I am going to die – give me a drink of water. I took my canteen off, bent down & was giving him water when I cast my eye to the right about thirty yards. I seen a wounded reb drawing a bead on me. I fell down by the side of the wounded reb. I yelled out "throw that down or you will be a dead rebel. He throwed [sic] it [down] & threw up his hands. I went over to him & took the gun & started on double quick to join my comp[any]."[332]

Private John E. Harrison recorded in his diary: "About this time they commenced retreating, but kept up their fire. Nearly our whole reg. were now going for them in earnest. We next had to pass through a patch which had been plowed & harrowed, & the bullets struck the ground right amongst us, one or two striking close to my feet. We went for the fence double quick, & was soon over it & into a small piece of woods. We could see the rebels running & we fired with as much precission[sic] as possible considering we were firing at moving objects. I was looking at one fellow, & saw him fall, & we soon passed him as he lay on his belly – his knapsack on his back, our Adjutant went to him & picked up his gun which was lying by him, and broke it over a stump & passed on."[333]

Lieutenant Shaw also recorded the chase, writing: "*Not a man* held back, but onward and upward, over fences, through ditches and undergrowth, to the brow of the ridge on which the enemy were posted, did they go, the fire becoming fiercer, the balls flying thicker, until when within fifty yards of their lines, we poured in such a galling fire that in the language of Major Edgar (whom we captured), "'No mortal could withstand it,'" so they broke and run, leaving their dead and wounded strewn over the field."[334]

---

330 OR, Series I, Vol. 12, part I, p. 809

331 *Springfield Republic*, Springfield, Ohio, June 2, 1862

332 Life and Adventures of William G. Felton, Huntington Library, San Marino, California. (hereafter cited as Felton)

333 Harrison Diary

334 *Darke County Democrat*, Greenville, Ohio, June 11, 1862

The Confederate Left

The men of Finney's command took note of the retreating Union skirmishers, who according to *Richmond Dispatch* corresponded Filurius "After a few shots, the enemy retired down the hill."

This prompted an order to advance, and according to Second Lieutenant William A. Smith, Company I, 50th Virginia Infantry, "we did over fences and across fields, till we came up 75 or 80 yards of the enemy's line which was lying concealed behind a fence on a ridge."[335] Smith's company formed a part of Finney's Battalion, and was on the extreme left of the Confederate line.

Advancing toward a wooded knoll on the outskirts of Lewisburg, Finney's command soon ran into trouble. "Filurius" noted: "The confederates pressed on until the farther edge of town was reached, and then the engagement became fierce and general. The Federals shot from behind a fence and fired while our men stood in line on the open field."[336]

Lieutenant Smith recalled: "We were in a flat hollow below them, in open field when they poured in a volley upon us which cut our men down like grass. We remained there 15 or 20 minutes under a galling fire and fought the best we could."[337]

Correspondent "Dane", in his account, stated that most of Finney's men had never been under fire. He described the action: "But in an evil hour we were ordered to cease firing and charge the enemy. As our brave men rushed down into the town, to the command, they encountered a most galling fire. sheltered in the houses behind fences, from every direction the enemy literally mowed down our men." "Dane" continued: "At each discharge from the enemy's guns they fell by scores; …"[338]

The men of Finney's battalion fought stubbornly until Major George M. Edgar was shot. Soon afterward the men became dispirited and "no longer able to stand the heavy fire of the enemy, and fled."[339]

The Yankees poured a destructive fire into the left of Heth's line, held by Colonel Finney's Battalion. The 44th Ohio, split into two wings, managed to get onto the flanks of Finney's men. For a brief period, Finney's raw troops held their ground, but the Union musketry became too great to bear. Captain Harman, in position next to the battalion, noted "our men were cut down like grass."[340]

---

335 Smith Letters

336 *Richmond Dispatch*, Richmond, Virginia, May 31, 1862

337 Smith Letters

338 *Richmond Dispatch*, Richmond, Virginia, June 3, 1862

339 *Richmond Dispatch*, Richmond, Virginia, May 31, 1862

340 Harman, VT

One company of the 45th Virginia remained outside the town, on the left of the regiment, where it joined with Finney's Battalion. The other companies of the regiment were in the town, sheltered somewhat by the houses. Captain Harman was with his company (H), and witnessed the devastating fire on Finney's men: "I never witnessed such slaughter as was in the battalion."[341]

When General Heth observed Captain's Tulleys' and Palmer's skirmishers falling back, he believed that Crook's forces were on the run. Anxious for a victory, he ordered his infantry and artillery forward into Lewisburg. Captains Otey and Bryan protested, stating that the artillery could do better service where they were, but Heth insisted that the artillery advance as well. Here was the fatal error.

An account appearing in the *Richmond Whig* on May 28, 1862, noted that the enemy repulsed us "owing to mismanagement and blunders. ... The battle commenced at 7 – at 8 we had whipped them, driving in their centre and turning their left wing – our left gave way, owing to the heavy fire directed upon them by the enemy, who were under cover of trees, fences, houses, &c. The artillery was ordered to cease firing and change position at a time the most critical. During the time occupied by this, the enemy came from under cover, and from their position on a hill poured a furious and galling fire upon our men. They withstood it for some time, but it was too much for human endurance, and they gave way and fled precipitately."[342]

Reverend George Boardman Taylor, a member of Otey's Battery, wrote: "Our *rifle gun* was ordered down into the town, not two hundred yards from the enemy, and no sooner had we reached *this* position than the regiment supporting us broke and retreated in the greatest confusion. We had no officer with us, and not wishing to retreat without orders we stood by our gun till nearly every infantryman had passed us, when we saw that retreat was all that remained; but being in a very narrow lane, it was only with greatest difficulty we could turn the horses around. We tore down the fence and reversed the limber amid a storm of bullets, but had we then stopped to limber up the gun we would certainly have taken a trip to Columbus. The Yanks were not over thirty yards from us when our sergeant ordered us to leave. I cannot express to you my feelings when I was thus forced to turn my back upon my country's foe. Men, white with terror, were seen panting as they ran, and every scene of the day tended to shake our faith in Southern chivalry or Yankee cowardice."[343]

The *Richmond Whig* correspondent, wrote: "During this time five pieces of artillery, two of Otey's Battery and three of Bryant's, had been ordered to change

---

341 Harman, VT

342 *Richmond Whig*, Richmond, Virginia, May 28, 1862

343 George Braxton Taylor. Life and Letters of Rev. George Boardman Taylor, D. D. Lynchburg, Virginia, J. P. Bell Company, Printers, 1908, p. 70-1 (hereafter cited as G. Taylor).

position and move forward to the front. Every piece of artillery was thus with-drawn and our infantry was left without any protection. Otey's Battery came into position under galling fire, and while the 45th and 50th was retreating, the enemy, seeing the confusion, advanced, killing nearly all the horses attached to Bryant's Battery and capturing the guns – the third piece of Otey's Battery, under Sergeant E. O. Gordon, became entangled in a fence, and despite the exertions of himself to extricate it, had to be left behind. The fourth gun was limbered up by the Captain and five of the gun detachment, and carried from the field under a heavy fire from the enemy, who were only a hundred and fifty paces from them."[344]

According to an account appearing in the columns of the *Richmond Dispatch*, when Finney's (Edgar's) men broke, the batteries of Otey and Bryan were left without protection. "Captain Otey, though wounded, stood by his men, while they strove amid iron hail to get their gun from the field. ... the artillerymen stood by their guns till the enemy were not more than forty yards distant, when they were ordered to leave." Captain Otey's horse had been shot down earlier, and Otey had to be ordered from the field to have his wound attended to.[345]

To complicate matters, the men of the 22nd and 45th Regiments were forced to lie down to get out of the line of fire of the artillery behind them.

Another correspondent in the *Richmond Whig* which signed himself "A. A.", noted about Otey's Battery: "My gun was near them, and they fled by us, the enemy in pursuit. I never heard such a whiz of bullets in my life. ... Capt. Otis [Otey] was slightly wounded, and we lost the third piece, a rifle gun."[346]

Edward Smith, Commissary Officer for the 45th Virginia Infantry, noted that "our guns were lost (Bryant's [sic]) by being moved down in a hollow, whence it was impossible to retreat with any speed. Thirty-eight horses of his battery were lost."[347]

Cavalryman John Sheffey also commented on the loss of the artillery, writing: "Detachments of batteries had been indiscreetly rushed down into the street and upon the left and the horses were shot down. Four of our best pieces of cannon were captured."[348]

No mention of the artillery of Chapman (on the right) and Lowry (on the left) is made by any of the accounts. It is probable that since Lowry's and Bryan's Batteries were position together on the Confederate left, that it was assumed all of the guns belong to Bryan.

344 *Richmond Whig*, Richmond, Virginia, May 28, 1862
345 *Richmond Dispatch*, Richmond, Virginia, June 3, 1862
346 *Richmond Whig*, Richmond, Virginia, May 28, 1862
347 Duncan
348 Sheffey, p. 108

CHAPTER TEN

LEWISBURG LOST

May 23, 1862 — About 6:30 A.M.

As the men of the 44th Ohio steadily and stubbornly moved forward, pouring a heavy fire into the Confederate line before them, it became too much for the untried men of Finney's battalion. The Ohioans enveloped Finney's men, breaking the Confederate line. Panic stricken, the men of Finney's command began to give way. Each man seeing his comrades turning back, gave in to the terror within, and joined the mad rush to escape.

Lieutenant William Smith, 50th Virginia Infantry, wrote: "The command was then given to fall back, and instantly obeyed. Our men left the field in confusion; the rout soon became general, the enemy followed and fired upon us, cutting down our men till we had run about 400 yds. Each man made his escape the best he could."[349]

Captain John Sheffey, 8th Virginia Cavalry, recorded: "Finney's Battalion, after fighting bravely, mistook an order of their commander and began to retreat. The 45th saw this and followed the example, many of them flying in the wildest confusion."[350]

The cavalryman next related General Heth's reaction to the break: "Genl. Heth ordered the reserve which was as yet unbroken to form a line in the field upon the left and stop that flight. Under the fire of the enemy, our men obeyed every order to the letter, but we might as well have tried to stop the wind as to check that disgraceful rout. Up to this time, we [the cavalry] had not been allowed to fire a gun. It is useless to give the further details of this disgraceful affair. It was disgraceful in the extreme whether the fault be upon the shoulders of the general

---

349 Smith Letters
350 Sheffey, p. 108

or the men. ... The affair is the most disgraceful of the war and can only be wiped out with blood."[351]

From his vantage point on the right of the Confederate line, Private Joseph A. Brown (22nd Virginia), recalled hearing a shout "Lord, boys look at the 45th."[352] Brown glanced to his left, and saw a large number of gray-clad soldier's running back toward Greenbrier River Bridge. He, like many others, believed the fleeing soldiers to belong to the 45th Virginia. Instead, it was Finney's and Edgar's battalion that broke; the 45th stood fast.

The next to break was the veteran 22nd Virginia Infantry, on the right of the line; the first time in their history to be beaten. The men of the 22nd were slow to yield at first, but as the 36th Ohio pressed forward, pouring a heavy fire into the ranks of the Virginians, their line finally broke in confusion. A wild panic seized the Confederates and they discarded anything that would slow their retreat. Private George Hechler (36th Ohio) wrote: "After a few rounds, the enemy fled in confusion and in every direction, leaving behind cartridge belts, some with the belts cut, guns, horses, sacks, with a little ration in some, biscuits, canteens, overcoats, blankets, drawers, pants, vests, shorts [shirts] and other articles strewn along the road."[353]

Private John A. McKee, 44th Ohio Infantry, confirmed Hechler's account: "a great many in their haste did not take time to take their accoutrements off, but just took out their knives and cut the straps in two letting them drop in the road."[354]

Despite being alone and in an advanced position, the men of the 45th Virginia held fast. The fire of the two Northern regiments was now directed toward them. Captain Harman, remained mounted, directing his men on the left of the regiment. Musket balls flew thick around him. Several struck him, but did not draw blood. One grazed the inner part of his left leg, about the top of his boot, but did not break the skin. Another tore through his gum overcoat and cape about his right breast, striking his right arm, inflicting a nasty looking, blueish bruise.[355]

The captain later wrote: "Kind providence spared me. I feel very thankful, though when I found that the battalion on our left were running and we would be forced to retreat, without being really into the heat of the engagement, I felt like I would prefer to be killed."[356]

Colonel Brown's after action report of Lewisburg has been lost, however, a portion of it has survived, thanks to Captain Edwin H. Harman's use of a portion

---

351 Sheffey, p. 108-9
352 Brown, p. 20
353 Hechler, p. 60
354 McKee, p. 35
355 Harman, VT
356 Harman, VT

of it in one of his letters. The surviving portion of Brown's report gives a look at the last moments of the fight at Lewisburg. "After a severe fire the battalion [Finney's] gave way, and the enemy followed, passing the line of my regiment on the left at least one hundred yards. The 22nd suffering severely commenced wavering and breaking at points along the line, and the enemy pressing heavily upon their right. Its falling back then became general, and so far as my regiment is concerned, it did so with my consent, intending to occupy the hill in our rear. A caisson and limber were run into my line, against the posts of a fence, which Capt. Fudge with his company tried to extricate and did get off the limber and would have succeeded with the caisson had not some of the horses of the team been killed, which rendered it impossible, and this after the cannoneers had left the field. The enemy then had nearly entirely surrounded them, and this company came from the field in good order, the last from Lewisburg. This caisson and limber were

the only parts of artillery along my line during the engagement. My regiment could have been reformed on the hill mentioned, but it was believed that it was your [Heth's] desire for the regiment to move on in the rear, which it did slowly and in good order."[357]

Corporal Charles C. Baughman, Otey's Battery, recalled: "The fire was kept up for about fifteen minutes when our infantry broke and ran and left the artillery without any support. The enemy then charged on us and a good many of our men ran, there were only five of us left to limber up our gun and the Capt. was one of them, he was wounded just before we succeeded in getting our gun limbered up. He was at the trail end, I was just before him so that if the ball had not struck him it would have hit me. When we got limbered up the

CAPTAIN CHARLES A. FUDGE
History of Tazewell County and Southwest Virginia

enemy were within about forty yards of us, taking deliberate aim and firing at us. We took two guns into the action and lost one of them, our rifle piece, our other two guns were at Rocky Gap."[358]

With both flanks of the Confederate line in retreat, the 45th Virginia was left alone in the center, but for only a short while. General Heth and other officers tried in vain to rally the rapidly disintegrating line, but to no avail. Lewisburg was lost.

357 Harman, VT
358 Baughman

Captain Harman, 45th Virginia, remained in the rear of the retreating column, along with Major Robert Augustus Bailey, of the 22nd Virginia, and a guard of twenty men from each regiment.[359]

2ⁿᵈ (West) Virginia Cavalry Pursues

As the Confederate line broke apart under the heavy fire delivered by Crook's two regiments, the order was given for the cavalry to swing into action. The cavalry had to travel at least a mile to reach the position occupied by the Confederates. When they did, their quarry was long gone.

Corporal Gilliam noted the order to charge came just after the 44th Ohio succeeded in taking the artillery on the Confederate left. "Now came the order for the cavalry to charge and we descended the hill on the jump, but before we could reach the enemy they were in full retreat."[360]

COLONEL WILLIAM M. BOLLES
A History of Scioto County, Ohio

Adjutant E. F. Gillen, who was with Colonel Crook during the fighting, upon being ordered to return to his regiment, noted that he found them "on a charge on the enemy center, which was in confusion. We pursued them to the bridge, which we found on fire, and, as Greenbrier River was too deep to ford, the pursuit was discontinued. Our own loss was small – a few wounded and some two or three missing."[361]

Colonel Crook, stated in his report: "Colonel Bolles, of the Second Virginia Cavalry, who had been held in reserve, was ordered forward in pursuit, but their retreat was so rapid and the ground so unfavorable for pursuit, the road passing through narrow and rocky defiles, that they crossed Greenbrier Bridge, burning it behind them, before they could be overtaken…"[362]

The cavalrymen pursued the fast moving Confederates as far as the bridge, when they were recalled by order of Colonel Crook. The colonel was apprehensive

---

359 Harman, VT
360 Gilliam
361 *National Tribune*, Washington, D. C., December 9, 1886; those wounded have not been identified.
362 OR, Series I, Vol. 12, part I, p. 807

of a rear or flank attack, and sent detachments of the recalled cavalry out on every road to guard against a surprise.[363]

Colonel Crook, in his after action report, wrote of the 2nd (West) Virginia Cavalry: "The 2d W. Va. Cav. had the most difficult part to perform, that of being under fire and not being able to actively engage in the battle."[364]

44th Ohio In Pursuit

After relieving Company A as skirmishers, Company I followed the fleeing enemy, "gathered a great many guns, accoutrements and prisoners. A sudden turn in the road showed the bridge in flames, and the Rebels drawn up on the other side of the line, with cannon planted to command the road. The captain reported this to the colonel, and before the colonel could reach the front, the Rebels retreated."[365]

Private John E. Harrison, 44th Ohio, noted in his diary: "We halted in a clover field & reformed our line of battle which had been broken up in passing over hills & fences. We here rested an hour or more, but we had several scouting parties out, scouting the surrounding ravines & clump of bushes for a considerable distance. When we had been here about an hour we saw a smoke rising in the direction of Greenbrier Bridge, & immediately started for the road, where we formed in line by the right flank, & waited until our cav. passed up on double quick, when we moved on towards the bridge. We did not reach the bridge until we met some of our cav[alry] which informed us that the bridge was burned. We then about faced & started for town."[366]

Zouave, the faithful correspondent of the *Springfield Republic*, reported an incident of the pursuit: "When Com[pany] I was following the retreat as skirmishers – Capt. Cummings halted a moment with the reserve to examine a house. The old lady and girls were huddled together in front. The old lady stopped him a moment [and] the conversation was naturally on the Battle. Says she, '"I had two sons in the army, would you hurt them if you should find them?'" The Captain assure[d] her if they were overtaken and made [no] resistance, they would be treated as prisoners of war ought to be. Without saying another word the old lady stepped behind the house and reappeared with two stalwart sons, their faces stretched in a broad grin glad to fall in the hands of the Federals when assured of safety."[367]

---

363 Gilliam

364 OR, Vol. 12, part I, p. 807

365 *Springfield Republic*, Springfield, Ohio, June 2, 1862

366 Harrison Diary

367 *Springfield Republic*, Springfield, Ohio, June 6, 1862; the identity of these two soldiers is unknown.

COLONEL SAMUEL A. GILBERT
Terry Lowry

On the Union right, Colonel Gilbert described the pursuit of the fleeing Rebels: "Leaving small guards over the artillery and prisoners we pushed to the top of the hill, where the enemy had first formed into line. Here we reformed our line and relieved our companies that had been deployed as skirmishers; ordered the new line of skirmishers, composed of two companies, to continue the pursuit, feeling their way carefully through the dense woods that cover the greater part of the slope toward Greenbrier River."[368]

On November 23, 1865, Gilbert wrote an account of service for the files of the U. S. Coast & Geodetic Survey (now National Oceanic & Atmospheric Administration), where he had been employed before the war. He wrote: "Leaving sufficient guard for the guns and prisoners, without waiting swept around upon the flank and rear of the force opposed to Crook's regiment. The forces speedily gave way and the victory was ours within a half hour of the time the fight commenced."[369]

Colonel Gilbert was reluctant to allow his men to pursue any further, fearing they would rush into a trap - a second line of battle. He gave the order to return to camp.[370]

36ᵗʰ Ohio In Pursuit

On the left of the Union line, the 36ᵗʰ pursued only a short distance, the ground being very rough and hilly. Two companies of skirmishers (Companies A and K) followed the retreating enemy to the Greenbrier River bridge, which was burning.[371]

Captain Walden's company (K), followed the fleeing Confederates for about a mile, then returned to camp. Captain Devol's company (A), followed Heth's men

---

368 OR, Series I, Vol. 12, part I, p. 809

369 NOAA History, A Nation at War: Civil War: War Record of Samuel A. Gilbert, http://www.history.noaa. gov/stories_tales/samgilbert.html, last visited April 2016. (Hereafter cited as NOAA)

370 *Springfield Republic*, Springfield, Ohio, June 2, 1862

371 Hechler, p. 60

to the Greenbrier River Bridge. The captain noted in his recollections that he did not return to camp until nightfall.[372]

Private John T. Booth noted that the road was very unfavorable for a rapid pursuit, however, the 36th Ohio followed them as fast as circumstances allowed. They were unable to overtake the Confederates, "Their incentive to get away was far greater than ours to follow."[373]

Booth described the scene: "The entire field and road was strewn with muskets, bayonets, bayonet scabbards, cartridge and cap-boxes, knapsacks, and haversacks, rations, canteens, blankets, overcoats, pantaloons, jackets, books, packets, letters, letter-paper, envelopes and other etceteras [sic], too numerous for enumeration, but unquestionable evidence of a total rout and stampede of the enemy."[374]

He also recorded sights and signs of the struggle: "We could tell where the surgeons had been at work, by the large puddles (pools) of blood, along the road could be traced the trail of blood that had ran from the wounded that had been carried away by the cavalry-men; in the ambulances and on stretchers; and from those who had walked or limped away; also, by the clothing that had been thrown down by the wounded, or their attendants, or, possibly both."[375]

The Greenbrier River Bridge

Private Joseph A. Brown, 22nd Virginia Infantry, recalled the retreat and destruction of the bridge: "We demoralized soldiers, most of us without arms, reached the bridge. My companion and I, debated if best to risk running through the burning bridge, which the Confederates had set on fire. After a moment's hesitation we decided to risk running through. We did so successfully, and without very serious burns. The bridge was blazing on both sides and on reaching the end of the two hundred yards, we fell exhausted and sprawling on the ground. The army who so proudly occupied the same spot at the "morn's early dawn" was now struggling in hopeless confusion along the road-way that led to the town of Union in Monroe county. The bridge destroyed, prevented disastrous pursuit and the defeated Confederates were permitted without interruption to brood over their disgraceful defeat."[376]

Private R. Byrd, 36th Ohio, commented on the retreat, stating that when the guns were silenced, "they began to retreat but made another stand. Our men

---

372 Devol, p. 31
373 Booth
374 Booth
375 Booth
376 Brown, p. 20

never stoped [sic] but poured in such a heave and constant cross fire on them that they were soon obliged to retreat and they became confused and away they went throughing [sic] knapsacks, blankets and a great many through there guns and everything and then took to there heels. They retreated back about three miles to the river crossed it and then burned the Bridge a beautiful bridge. (Oh what cowards.)"[377]

Several incidents that occurred on the retreat were recorded by Heth's men. Private Brown, 22nd Virginia Infantry, wrote: "We threw our arms and accoutrements all along the road side. Several ludicrous incidents happened on the run down the hill. One of the Confederate boys seeing the "big bass" [drum] abandoned on the road side, collected and composed himself sufficiently to yell, "You'll never wake me up again in the morning," and jumped on it with both feet to its complete ruin."[378]

Captain Harman recalled that Lieutenant Colonel Finney "…would not run and swore if his battalion would not halt, he would fight alone, and we could not persuade him to come away with us. He drew out his pistol and said he would sell his life as dearly as possible and sat down to await his doom."[379]

A small clipping in the Cadet File of William W. Finney (VMI, Class of 1848), recorded a similar version of Finney's capture: "In the battle of Lewisburg, according to an officer of General Heth's staff who witnessed the incident, Colonel Finney's conduct was most conspicuous. Deserted by his '"squirrel rifle and bird gun"' equipped recruits who ignominiously fled before the Yankee attack, the former cadet, after appealing to his men with all the force of his soul, denounced the whole crowd as cowards and declared he would not turn his back upon the enemy. Then he marched straight into the Union lines, fired his pistols in their faces and was taken prisoner."[380]

At the Greenbrier River Bridge, the rear guard waited until the enemy were within 200 yards of it before setting the lengthy structure on fire. This differs greatly from the statement by Joseph A. Brown, who stated the bridge was already burning when he and some companions crossed it. Brown's statement is supported by Private John T. Booth, historian of the 36th Ohio, who noted that the bridge was burning before the last of the Confederates had passed over it.[381]

Private William G. Guerrant, a member of Captain Otey's Battery, claimed to have lit the fire that destroyed the bridge at General Heth's order. "I was ordered by Gen. Heth to burn the bridge across the Greenbrier River & save the fleeing

---

377 VFM 1727, Sidney C. Baker Correspondence, Letter 21, R. Byrd to Carrie Baker, 25 May 1862: Ohio History Connection, Columbus, Ohio (hereafter cited as Byrd Letter).

378 Brown, p. 20

379 Harman, VT

380 VMI Cadet File, William W. Finney (1848), Virginia Military Institute, Archives, Lexington, Virginia

381 Harman, VT; Hale; Booth; Brown, p. 20

troops. I had seen enough of Crook to know he would let no opportunity slip to capture Heth's command & knowing there was a ford below the bridge a mile or two, called Gen. Heth's attention to that fact and that Crook might take that route with a strong column and strike his retreating army in flank. He [Heth] sent a body of cavalry at once to hold the ford. I had the bridge ready for firing and rode out to Gen. Heth and told him it was ready. I had the bridge blocked with rails to prevent a charge in case one was attempted by the enemy before I could get ready for firing. In the meantime, Col. [Major] King had a piece of artillery placed on a bluff on the left of the bridge. He directed me to apply the torch. It was done and soon the great volume of smoke & flame announced the loss of a fine bridge in connection with our loss of a victory. The Yankees were on the bluffs watching us when the bridge was burning. I could see them in the woods – their belt buckles shining in the sun."[382]

After crossing over the burning bridge, Captain Edwin H. Harman stood on the river bank watching the Northern troops approach on the opposite side. Lieutenant Joseph S. Moss, 8th Virginia Cavalry, was with Harman, and, according to Harman, fired on the enemy with his carbine, killing one. Lieutenant Moss reloaded his weapon and handed it to Captain Harman, who also fired, killing another "blue coated yankee". Harman here stated that this was "the only time I had shot during the day."[383]

Heth's demoralized men fell back to Union, in Monroe County, and finally halted at Salt Sulphur Springs to lick their wounds.

---

382 Michael A. Cavanaugh. The Otey, Ringgold and Davidson Artillery. H. E. Howard, Inc., Lynchburg, Virginia, 1993

383 Harman, VT; Northern accounts do not support this claim, no loss has been documented to have occurred at the bridge after the battle.

VICTORS RETURN TO CAMP

May 23, 1862 – 7:30 A.M.

The victorious Northern troops straggled back to camp over the next several hours. Many had returned to camp by 7:30 a.m., and resumed their interrupted breakfast. Others did not arrive back in camp until around 11 a.m. that morning, and at least one company at dark.

Private John E. Harrison, 44th Ohio, noted some observations on his return to camp. "When we got close to town we saw the sickening part of the scene as here was where the fight commenced. There we saw the dead & wounded lying at the roadside, right & left. On my right I saw a dead Rebel lying flat on his back – on my left, & just over a board fence lay another on his side, pale & dead, his face & ear in a smear of blood. The ambulance wagons were running in with the dead & wounded. One I noticed in particular, as it was loaded with wounded Rebels which our men had picked up. They were groaning most lamentably."[384]

The work of collecting the dead, wounded, prisoners and abandoned property commenced almost immediately. It must have been a grisly task. Musician Charles Ramsey, 44th Ohio, wrote that after the Rebels were driven from the field "…the band started for the battleground to attend to the wounded. We each filled two or three canteens with water to bathe the wounds and for the wounded to drink. When we arrived on the field it was awful to witness. On all sides of [us] was the wounded, dead and dying."[385]

---

384 Harrison Diary
385 Ramsey Letters

Private John E. Harrison, 44th Ohio, wrote in his diary: "The boys now commenced gathering up the guns, blankets, knapsacks & clothing of almost every description, which the Rebels had thrown away in their flight. Col. Wilson got a splendid sword; also several revolvers were picked up, but I did not have the luck to get one myself."[386]

Private Joseph Pearson, 44th Ohio, was among those gathering up the dead, and noted in his diary that they "surched [sic] the houses [and] found lots of things."[387] Pearson does not note what "things" were found.

Several Northern soldiers recorded their observations of those killed and wounded in the fighting. Private R. Byrd, 36th Ohio, wrote that, "The killed were a horrible looking sight. The most were shot in the Breast and head, some had two or three holes shot in them."[388]

Cavalryman George Jenvey noted that they had spent the morning gathering up the dead, and there were still at least twenty more to remove. He noticed that, "Behind a fallen log, 3 dead lay, just as they were shot – in the head or breast, while in the act of firing. In another place a gunner lay in a bed of clover – matchlock in hand – shot through the head twice – he fell trying to discharge the largest piece they had. Most of the wounded were shot through the arms, fingers, or legs. One wounded in the breast, just over the heart, the ball did not have force enough to penetrate the heart, having passed through his cartridge box straps and clothing into the flesh."[389]

The cavalryman also described the scene that met his eyes when he entered one house and found 12 wounded Rebels inside, and one of our men, shot through the heart. "I looked at the wounded as they lay on the floor. The first one was wounded through the stomach, and his shirt was saturated with blood. He was on that dividing line over which no man returns, passing into that other land, as his face clearly indicated."[390]

Ohio musician Charles Ramsey was among the first on the battlefield to tend to the wounded. He recalled: "When we arrived on the field it was awful to witness. On all sides of [us] was the wounded, dead and dying. Our men escaped wonderfully. I do not think (and I speak after making numerous enquiries) that there was over twelve killed on our side and very few seriously wounded. The most of the wounds are flesh wounds either in the arms or legs. ... Several ladies of the place were out on the battlefield attending to the wounded Rebels doing

---

386 Harrison Diary
387 Pearson Diary
388 Byrd Letter
389 *Home News*, Marietta, Ohio, June 6, 1862
390 *Home News*, Marietta, Ohio, June 6, 1862

what they could for them. Some real handsome ones. One young lady found her brother among the wounded. She took it right hard. I pittied [sic] her."[391]

The Union soldiers were not the only ones roaming about the battlefield as noted above; they were joined by many of the residents of Lewisburg. Private George Hechler, 36th Ohio, wrote: "After the battle we saw more of the inhabitants than we had before, especially women. Some came to hunt up husbands, other[s] brothers and friends. Alas, only too many found the lost dead, wounded or taken prisoner. Some of them showed remarkable intelligence and knowledge, but others are rough and almost ignorant. (I speak of the women for the men are nearly all gone.)"[392]

One Northern account described the Confederates, stating they were "… composed of all ages from 14 to 50, wearing no uniforms, no two being dressed alike; their arms comprising every variety of shooting-irons that the ingenuity of man has invented since the commencement of time."[393]

Musician Charles Ramsey, noted in one of his letters: "On some of the dead bodies were found passes issued but two days before by Colonel Crooks [sic] and the body of a man was found who had been brought to camp Piatt a prisoner and had taken the oath of allegiance. He represented himself there as a minister. That shows how much reliance can be placed in the oath of a Rebel. He met his reward, will never violate his oath again."[394]

When time permitted, the men of Crook's command wrote numerous letters to let their loved ones and friends know what had transpired in their first taste of battle, and whether they were safe or not. The battle was much discussed among the men. One topic was how each felt to be under fire. Private John A. McKee, 44th Ohio, wrote: "I do not know whether I hit anyone or not but I had several fair shots at the distance of about one hundred yards and do not think I was any more excited than if I were shooting at a squirrel."[395]

Private William G. Felton, also of the 44th Ohio, admitted his fright, writing: "Now as I have often heard remarked oh no I did not fell [feel] the least afraid not a bit excited. I can't say how they all felt, but for myself, I was pretty badly frightened & had ten thousand quare [queer] felling [feeling] my hair was strait up like to pushed my cap off."[396]

On the afternoon of May 23, Colonel Crook sent a brief statement to General Cox's headquarters. After giving a few details of the battle, Crook wrote: "I regret to have to report that our wounded men passing to the rear were fired on from the

---

391 Ramsey Letter
392 Hechler, p. 61
393 *Public Ledger*, Philadelphia, Pa., June 5, 1862
394 Ramsey Letter
395 McKee, p. 35
396 Felton

houses and some killed. I have instituted a search & shall burn all the houses from which was firing from and shall order a commission on those who are charged with firing & if found guilty will execute them at once in the main street of this town as examples."[397]

General Cox's reply came the following day: ""I congratulate and thank you and your command for your brilliant conduct, and shall immediately transmit the intelligence to department headquarters. ... Your retaliation upon the citizens who fired on your wounded will be approved."[398]

The shooting of the wounded men referred to by Crook, occurred during the latter stages of the battle, and perhaps even after it was finished. While several wounded men of the 36th Ohio were making their way back through town to have their wounds treated at the hospital, they were fired upon and one of the men killed. The shooter is alleged to have fired from inside a house, and was reported to be a civilian. It was later determined that the fatal shot was fired by a soldier visiting his family.

Private George Venters, 36th Ohio Infantry, recorded in his journal: "After the battle had ceased, myself and several others of the wounded who were able to walk, started [off] the field to go into the town to the hospital to have our wounds taken care of. We had reached the edge of town and were going down an alley. [George] Shearer [Sherer] was the only man who had a gun, but was unable to use it as one of his hand[s] was nearly shot off. When we were passing a barn on the alley a man stepped out and said to Shearer [Sherer], give me that gun you Yankee son of a bitch. Instead of complying with the command he [Sherer] started to run. The man pulled up the shotgun and at range of not more than ten feet shot him between the shoulders and he pitched forward on his face dieing [sic] instantly. The man grabbed Shearer's [Sherer's] gun, and ran back into the barn. ... So far as I know the man who did the dastardly deed never was caught."[399]

Colonel Crook later wrote: "During the fight, while one of our wounded men was on his way to the hospital, he was murdered by one of the Confederates who had slipped into the town to see some of his friends. The soldiers were much worked up about it, and it was with some difficulty I could restrain them from doing violence to the town under the belief that the dastardly act was committed by some of the inhabitants."[400]

---

397 OR, Series I, Vol. 12, pt. 1, p. 805-6

398 OR, Series I, Vol. 12, part 1, p. 805

399 Kenneth P. Werrell. Crook's Regulars: The 36th Ohio in the War of Rebellion, Christiansburg, Va., KPW, 2012, p. 44-5; This account differs somewhat from the official casualty list, which states that Sherer was originally wounded in the hand, and was shot in the heart from a house in Lewisburg. (Casualty Rolls, File A, RG-94, National Archives, Washington, D. C.)

400 Schmitt, p. 90-1

Among those angered by the shooting was Sergeant James Haddow, Company F, 36th Ohio, who predicted, "A fearful day of reckoning waits those guilty of such barbarism. ... The whole place should be destroyed as there are no Union people in it ..."[401]

An account written by J. M. Clark, 36th Ohio, noted that two of the wounded were shot in the streets by citizens. Historian Tim McKinney also reports two of the Northern soldiers were killed in the streets of Lewisburg.[402]

Trooper George Jenvey reported that, "Another solder told me he was shot through the leg while marching up to the fight, by some one behind a house. He turned around quickly, but could not discover his dastardly foe."[403]

The English-born musician noted that, "...another citizen raised his gun to shoot another boy, who was already wounded in the face. His gun missed fired, the boy cooly [sic] took note of the house and the features of the man, later in the day [he] pointed out to Colonel Crook the man and the house. The man, so rumor says, is dead."[404]

Private Milton Phillips, 36th Ohio Infantry, is also said to have been shot in the back by a citizen with a squirrel rifle. He may be the second man mentioned above. Colonel Crook's wound to the foot is also reported to have been fired from a window in the town.[405]

There are several reports concerning the shooting, or attempted shooting, of Union men making their way to the rear after being wounded. Lieutenant Levi Barber, Quartermaster of the 36th Ohio, is said to have observed "one of the villains in the act of trying to shoot one of our soldiers, standing within his own door, Barber quickly riding up, drew his revolver, shot and killed the dastard."[406]

The quartermaster related a different story in a letter to his hometown newspaper, an account which appears much closer to the truth: "In one case a wounded man from Co. D, who was coming from the field shot through the body, when a Rebel came out of the house, shot him dead in the street, took his gun and fled to the woods. We have not yet found him, but last night [24th] Col. Crook told me to take a squad of men and burn the house, which I did, and will burn all the balance if we can only find them out. I have no sympathy for any of them."[407]

Captain Lysander Tulleys, Company D, 44th Ohio, wrote of the shooting: "As our wounded were carried back through the village to the Hospital some of

---

401 "Sergeant Haddow Writes Home", *Journal of the Greenbrier Historical* Society, Volume 6, No. 6 (1998), p. 51 (hereafter cited as Haddow)

402 *Gallipolis Journal*, Gallipolis, Ohio, June 5, 1862; McKinney, p. 185

403 Another Day, p. 246

404 Another Day, p. 246; this is probably only a rumor.

405 Hanging Rock Iron Region, p. 467-8; Another Day, p. 243

406 Another Day, p. 243.

407 *Home News*, Marietta, Ohio, June 13, 1862

them were fired upon from the windows of a large brick residence. The cowardly miscreants made their escape, but, as a punishment for harboring them, Crook determined to destroy the building."[408]

The Ohio officer noted that the house was burned on the evening of May 23rd, which is not supported by other accounts. He stated that "the two regiments were marched to a point in full view of the fated building, and it was fired. Judging from the indignant remarks made by the men while the flames leaped high, if the guilty parties had been captured, they too would have gone up in smoke with the building."[409]

Only one wounded Northern soldier has been documented as being killed in the incident, Private George Sherer, 36th Ohio Infantry. According to historian Tim McKinney, the man who shot Sherer was named Abraham H. Strealey (Straley), and belonged to Company A, 22nd Virginia Infantry. After taking part in the fighting at Lewisburg, and before retreating, Strealey secretly visited his grandmother-in-law to get some clean clothing. While in the home of Mrs. Phoebe Welch, a 62-year old widow, Strealey saw Sherer pass by, and not aware that he was wounded, shot him. Strealey then hid in a wood shed by climbing up onto a wide plank on the rafters, remaining there until the danger had passed.[410]

Near dark on May 23rd, the Union camp was alarmed by a report that the pickets on the Frankford Pike had been fired into. The Brigade quickly fell into line, and Companies A and G, 36th Ohio were sent out to reconnoiter the road. The two companies went out about three miles, but did not encounter any enemy, and returned to camp. As a result of the alarm, the Northern troops spent the night sleeping on their arms, ready to meet any threat that might come against them. The night, however, passed peacefully by.[411]

---

408 Tulleys
409 Tulleys
410 McKinney, p. 186
411 Another Day, p. 241

CARING FOR THE DEAD AND THE WOUNDED

May 24 – 28, 1862

The day following the battle, May 24th, was spent in caring for the wounded men, preparing the dead for burial, sending wounded men, captured weapons and prisoners to the rear. About fourteen of the Union wounded were sent to Gauley Bridge by wagon, and placed in a hospital there; others were sent on to Charleston. Approximately 140 Confederate prisoners were sent to the rear at the same time, under guard of the 2nd (West) Virginia Cavalry, who turned them over to the 47th Ohio Infantry the next day at Meadow Bluff.

Among the prisoners sent to the rear were about 25 wounded, who were considered well enough to withstand the trip. Lieutenant Bahlmann, 22nd Virginia Infantry, noted that "Those wounded in the lower limbs were carried to ambulances, those wounded in the shoulder and arms walked."[412] These wounded prisoners were sent on to Charleston, where they remained for eleven days, and then moved to a hospital at Gallipolis, Ohio, where they arrived about June 10th.

Colonel Crook reported: "The rebels left, 38 dead on the field, and 66 wounded that we have found, besides carrying a good many of their wounded with them. Besides the four pieces of artillery we have collected some 300 stand of small-arms, have no doubt many are still lying in the brush. We took 100

---

412 Bahlmann, p. 61

prisoners. Our loss was 13 killed, 53 wounded, and 7 missing. I send prisoners and some of our wounded and small-arms to Gauley to-day."[413]

At 4 p.m., the 36th and 44th Ohio Regiments turned out and conveyed their dead to their resting place. The fallen soldiers were buried on a little knoll northwest of Lewisburg, and immediately west of the turnpike in a beautiful grove of trees. Each regiment tended to the burial of their dead, placing them in crude coffins, and gently laying them to rest in individual graves. The men of the 44th Ohio were place in one row, while those of the 36th were laid to rest in another row, adjacent to those of the 44th.

The Chaplain gave a few remarks, and offered a prayer, which was followed by the firing of a military salute. It was a solemn scene, and made a lasting impression on those attending the ceremony.

Once the ceremony was over, the graves were sodded over, and marked with the name, company and regiment of each. The final touch was the erection of a white picket fence around the graves.

Once completed, the Northern troops returned to their camp, where a dress parade was held. During that time, black smoke could be seen rising from a house in the eastern part of Lewisburg, and "soon the flames shot forth."[414]

The parade over, the men returned to their quarters, where Private Harrison learned that the burning house was set on fire by order of Colonel Crook. "It was the house from which the firing had been done at our wounded as they passed through town during the battle, & was burned as an example to show the rebels that they could not commit such enormities with impunity."[415]

The destruction of the Welch home was carried out by Corporal Melvin C. True, with twenty men from Company D, 36th Ohio, accompanied by Lieutenant Levi Barber. The house of Mrs. Welch, located in the eastern part of Lewisburg, is the only house documented to have been burned in retaliation for the shooting of wounded soldiers. Had there been others, there would likely have been mention of them in some of the newspapers, particularly in *The Yankee*, published by some enterprising men of Crook's command on May 29, 1862. Among the various accounts of the battle, lists of casualties, the following story appeared: "Mrs. Welch's dwelling in the east part of town was burned last evening, by order of Col. Crook, because one of the wounded of the 36th O. V. was shot from it. The poor fellow was shot by Mrs. Welch's grand son-in-law. He had returned home a few days before the battle, and too cowardly to meet his foes on the field, he murdered them when disabled. He saved his neck by "skedaddling." Enlightened

---

413 OR, Series I, Vol. 12, part I, p. 806; after Crook's statement, one additional soldier died, bringing the total to fourteen.

414 Harrison Diary

415 Harrison Diary

usages of war require that all who fire on wounded men from houses, should be killed and their property committed to the flames."[416]

Colonel Crook mentioned his intention to hold commissions and execute any found guilty of firing on the wounded soldiers. If any investigations were held, there is no record of it, nor is there any evidence of any executions.

The Confederate Dead

The Confederate dead were laid out in the vestibule of the Old Stone Church after the battle, where they remained until the next day, joined periodically by others who died of their wounds. Colonel George Crook would not allow the citizens of Lewisburg to bury the slain Confederates, but apparently allowed some to claim the remains of their family members for burial elsewhere. About a dozen dead Confederates were claimed and removed by their families.

OLD STONE PRESBYTERIAN CHURCH
Steve Cunningham

Sometime during the day, the Northern soldiers dug a trench some 50 feet in length in the cemetery adjacent to the Presbyterian Church, where "without coffins, unknelled and unblessed, without ceremony, they were laid away."[417] John T. Booth, in his recollections, noted that several trenches were dug beside the church.

Lieutenant Shaw, 44th Ohio, recalled: "The burial of the rebel dead was in a style that might shock the delicate senses of some [of] our fancy undertakers. A long trench 2 ½ feet deep and wide enough and long enough to admit the requisite amount of dead Secesh, was dug in the burying ground near town. They were placed in the trench side by side, no coffin, box or any thing else to keep the dirt

---

416 *The Yankee*, Lewisburg, Va., May 29, 1862. The men credited with publishing the newspaper were named Watt, Frye, Oldham, Sykes, and Raymond. (Ohio Civil War Genealogy Journal, Volume XIII, 2009, p. 6)

417 Rose W. Fry. Recollections of the Rev. John McElhenney, D. D. Richmond, Va.: Whittet & Shepperson, Printers, 1893, p. 180. Unknelled – no bell rang for the dead

off of them. Their caps were usually placed over their faces, the dirt thrown in, and that perhaps will be the last that either Union or Secesh will think of them."[418]

Corporal Samuel J. Harrison, also of the 44th Ohio, noted that they buried 40 men in one grave, including a captain and chaplain. "It was the hardest looking sight ever I saw sure. They were laid in close order side by side with their close [clothes] all on & dirty & muddy & the dirt throwed in on them just as we would bury a dog."[419]

Harrison's brother, John, noted in his diary: "During the day our men buried some 39 rebels in one large grave. Some 10 or 12 were buried in other places..."[420]

Other soldiers noted that the Confederate dead were "carefully interred" and that the depth of the trench was four feet, and six or seven feet wide.[421] Yet another noted the depth of the grave was about 2½ feet, due to the ground being very stony and hard to dig up.[422]

Care of the Wounded

After the battle, the grim task of collecting the dead, dying and wounded of both armies from the battlefield was undertaken. The wounded Confederates were at first cared for in public buildings and private homes in Lewisburg, but were soon moved to the Virginia Hotel, which was converted into a hospital.[423] The residents of Lewisburg were quick to offer their assistance in caring for the wounded soldiers. The army surgeons treated the wounded men, the Union men first, then the Confederates. All received the same kind of care. Two men from the 36th Ohio Infantry, Privates Montgomery and Schaefer, were detailed as nurses to care for the wounded rebels.[424]

Treatment at the time consisted of cold water, bandages and the administration of pain killers. Amputations and removal of bullets from the wounds were extremely crude, and often did as much damage as the wound itself.

A number of the wounded Confederates died of their wounds while at Lewisburg. The Yankees prepared a list of the wounded Confederates in their hands after the battle, noting one man without a name. Likely the soldier was unconscious and died of his wounds without his name ever being known. Others

---

418 *Darke County Democrat*, Greenville, Ohio, June 18, 1862
419 S. Harrison letter
420 Harrison Diary
421 Booth; Ramsey Letters
422 *Public Ledger*, Philadelphia, Pa., June 5, 1862
423 Bahlmann, p. 61
424 Bahlmann, p. 61

on the list cannot be found in the Compiled Service Records, and it is likely they died as well.

Lieutenant Evans, 44th Ohio, noted in one of his many letters to the *Springfield Republic*, that by May 28, 1862, twelve of the wounded rebels had died of their wounds.[425]

There are some mention of atrocities committed against the wounded Confederates; whether true or not, cannot be determined. One wartime account, attributed to Captain Thomas A. Bryan, states that the captain personally saw several men run through with bayonets after they had fallen wounded. "One poor fellow, after hard fighting, completely exhausted, cried for quarter as a Yankee soldier approached, 'I'll give you quarter,' he replied, and, raising his rifle, blew his brains out."[426]

Another account of mistreatment of the Confederate wounded appeared a hundred years later, in the *Beckley Post-Herald*. Charles Welch Hanger, grandson of John Harvey Hanger, related the following about the battle at Lewisburg, told to him by his father, William Harvey Hanger. He reported that after the battle, "when the graves detail searched the battlefield after the battle had ended and came upon a man who appeared to be [so] badly wounded that he could not recover they knocked him in the head and put him out of his misery!"[427]

Major George M. Edgar, commanding a battalion on the left of Heth's line, was seriously wounded in the battle. The major was shot through the body, near one of his lungs, and the wound was thought to be mortal. Upon learning of the major's wound, Mrs. Mary Creigh, a sister of Captain Alfred M. Edgar (cousin to the major), started for Lewisburg in the company of a Mrs. Robinson, whose husband was thought to have been in the battle. When they reached Lewisburg, they found the major still clinging to life. He was being cared for at the home of cousin John Withrow (now a part of the General Lewis Inn), and

GENERAL LEWIS INN
Steve Cunningham

425 *Springfield Republic*, Springfield, Ohio, June 6, 1862

426 *Richmond Whig*, Richmond, Va., June 11, 1862

427 *Beckley Post-Herald*, Beckley, W. Va., August 21, 1963

was being attended by Dr. [William N.] Anderson and two Federal Surgeons.[428] Major Edgar eventually recovered and returned to service.

Removal of Confederate Dead and Wounded

It has long been speculated at the number of wounded men that were removed from the field of battle by the Confederates when they fled Lewisburg on the morning of May 23, 1862. The actual number of men wounded and carried off will never be known. It is, however, known that some were removed; just not how many.

Wartime writings indicate that the Confederates removed a number of their dead, especially during the early part of the battle. I believe this to be fiction, since the Confederates had not the means to remove the dead, and there is no record of any mass burials after the battle, other than the one in Lewisburg itself.

J. M. Clark, in an account appearing in the *Gallipolis Journal* on June 5, 1862, noted that the "enemy admit to taking six wagon loads of wounded away," and that he (Clark) heard of six deaths on the road.

John T. Booth, 36th Ohio, noted that a subsequent raid to Union revealed that General Heth had brought more than a hundred men from Lewisburg, and place them in hospitals there. Many of these men died of their wounds, as well as a number that died while being conveyed to their homes.[429]

A newspaper account of the expedition to Union states "It was ascertained that after the battle of Lewisburg, General Heth carried 64 of his wounded to Salt Sulphur Springs, 20 to White Sulphur, and that he buried many of his dead after crossing the Greenbrier River."[430]

Visiting the Wounded Rebels

Another activity that seemed popular on the 24th was visiting the wounded Confederates. Among those doing so, was Captain Hiram F. Devol, 36th Ohio Infantry. At the hospital, he was spoken to by Captain John K. Thompson, Company A, 22nd Virginia Infantry. Thompson said to Devol: "Captain, I tried to kill you yesterday as you were nearing the fence. I had shot at you three times with my revolver when one of your men's balls came through a rail and mashed this eye out. It did not seem to make a dammed [sic] bit of difference whether

---

428 Alfred Mallory Edgar. My Reminiscences of the Civil War. 35th Star Publishing, Charleston, W. Va., 2011, p. 114 – 116 (hereafter cited as Edgar)

429 Booth; there are no records to support this claim.

430 *Albany Evening Journal*, Albany, NY, July 8, 1862, copied from the *Cincinnati Gazette*, account dated Meadow Bluff, June 25, 1862.

your balls came through the cracks or rails, they were sure to kill or wound some of us."[431]

Captain Devol noted in his recollections that he had Thompson's sword, and in 1880, returned it to him.

Quartermaster Barber was also among those who visited the wounded rebels that day. He wrote: "Their wounds are awful to look at. Our Enfield's make a terrible wound, tearing a man all to pieces. It makes the heart sick to go among them, and to look at the poor suffering creatures and hear them groan and cry."[432]

Private William G. Felton, 44th Ohio, noted that there were a number of vacant buildings in Lewisburg, some of which were used as a dead house and others as hospitals. He wrote that "I went out in several places & it looked like a slaughter house, cutting legs [sic] & arms off, throwing them in one corner."[433]

CAPTAIN HIRAM F. DEVOL
Ohio History Connection,
Columbus, Ohio

Private John T. Booth, who recorded much about Lewisburg, noted about his visit to the hospital: "Going through the Ward of the hotel, with a comrade or two, we noticed one patient, who, whenever we would come near him, would cover his face as completely as he could. I stopped where I could see his face when he uncovered it, he proved to be our Ex-Guide, who gave us the slip that dreadful cold and stormy night, on "Cold Knob," and warned the enemy, Captain Burkhardt, of our proximity. Yes, it was Rhodes, all right, wounded unto death, he died next day."[434]

Hard Feelings

Several of the Northern soldiers expressed hard feelings against the residents of Lewisburg, likely brought on by the suspected snipping by citizens. Quartermaster Levi Barber noted in a letter home: "Lewisburg is rotten secesh – every family with perhaps two or three exceptions. The citizens knew the day before that we were to be attacked that morning, and had in a great many houses large amounts

---

431 Devol, p. 31-2

432 *Home News*, Marietta, Ohio, June 13, 1862

433 Felton

434 Another Day, p. 269; The incident referred to by Booth occurred in March 1862. No further identification or record has been found for Rhodes.

of victuals cooked, and a warm breakfast for the rebels prepared, assured that Gen. Heth would have an easy victory."[435]

Colonel Crook, in his autobiography, noted that "The residents of Lewisburg, except one, are secesh, and were well aware that we were to be attacked; had breakfast ready for the men." Crook made good use of the prepared meals, as he turned the prisoners over to the citizens to be fed.[436]

Other accounts declared that some members of the 22nd Virginia Infantry spent the night in the town with their families before the battle.

Private Joseph Sutton, 2nd (West) Virginia Cavalry, declared that "nearly all of the townspeople were '"cheering [the Confederates] ... on and shouting 'Drive the Yankees to the Ohio River.'"'[437]

Flag of Truce

On the evening of May 24th, Captain Stockton Heth, brother of General Heth, arrived at Lewisburg under a flag of truce. The purpose of his visit was to retrieve the bodies of some of the dead, and to inquire about the wounded Confederates. After attending to what was left undone by the Northern men, he departed for his camp on the morning of May 25th.[438]

Private William G. Felton, 44th Ohio, noted: "It was not long till the rebble [sic] Sergents & a detail of soldiers came to town with a flag of truce to take care of there [sic] dead & wounded."[439]

Captain E. H. Harman, 45th Virginia, noted "We heard from Lewisburg by flag of truce that we had 39 killed and ninety wounded and taken prisoner. The Yanks admit their loss was greater than ours, in fact, they reported to the bearer of the flag of truce that they lost as many killed as we did in total."[440]

In another letter, Harman related that they just learned "we killed some women & children who lived in Lewisburg with our shells. It is horrible to think of it. My God, to think that the enemy would shelter themselves in houses and force us to kill innocent women and children. The curse of Heaven be upon the invaders of our country."[441] This, however, appears to be only rumor.

At least one case of Brother against Brother is reported to have occurred at Lewisburg. Private Lewis G. Pyne (Pine), a native of Monroe County, took part in

---

435 *Home News*, Marietta, Ohio, June 13, 1862

436 Schmitt, p. 90

437 Ohio Civil War Genealogy Journal, Volume XIII, 2009, p. 5

438 *Public Ledger*, Philadelphia, Pa., June 5, 1862; OR, vol. 12, pt. 3, p. 242

439 Felton

440 Harman, VT

441 Harman, VT

the battle as a member of Company E, 8th Virginia Cavalry. On the opposing side, was a brother, and they had a friendly talk under flag of truce after the battle. The records show three men named Pine were in the ranks of the 2nd (West) Virginia Cavalry; one in Company B, and two in Company K. The one in Company B, 24-year old James Pine, is the one mentioned above. The two (James M., age 45, and William, age 19) in Company K were not at Lewisburg.[442]

Praise & Promotions

The soldiers of the two Ohio Regiments received much praise from their commanding officers, for their conduct on the battlefield at Lewisburg. Promotions for those in command would come in the following months.

Major E. B. Andrews, 36th Ohio, in a letter to the governor of Ohio, wrote: "I regard the result of our battle as mainly due to faithful & rigid discipline to which these regiments have been subjected."[443]

Although under fire for the first time, the men of the two regiments behaved well by all accounts. It was noted that only two men of the 36th Ohio flinched in battle, which earned them "a heavy slap with [the] sword" of Lieutenant Colonel Clarke.

Captain Israel Stough, commanding Company F, 44th Ohio, proclaimed that "well did my boys do their whole duty, with not a single exception."[444] Captain Stough, like many others, referred to the soldiers under their command as "boys", when more accurately, they should have been called men.

Perhaps some of the highest praise came from the lips of the Confederate prisoners after the battle. Private J. M. Clark, 36th Ohio, recorded that "One of the captured officers says if they Yankees had fought like men they would have easily whipped them, but, said he, they fought like Devils." Private Oliver Parker agreed, noting that "The Sessessh [sic] Colonel prisoner we got said we did not fight like men we fought like devils."[445]

Colonel Gilbert expressed his gratitude to the men of his regiment in an order: "Soldiers of the 44th Regiment, I congratulate you upon the soldier-like manner in which you have this day performed your duty. It is the reward of the labor you have been at in attaining that good state of discipline which alone can secure that morale which renders you irresistible.

---

442 Oren F. Morton. A History of Monroe County, West Virginia. Staunton, Va.: The McClure Co., Inc., 1916, p, 384; Compiled Service Records, 2nd West Virginia Cavalry

443 Andrews

444 Stough

445 Gallipolis Journal, Gallipolis, Ohio, June 5, 1862; Parker

I am assured by your conduct this day that whilst our country has such men for its defenders, our mothers, wives, and children need not fear its destruction at the hands of the base scoundrels who are in arms against us.

Soldiers, I am proud of your success and ask no higher glory than to lead you on to new victories."[446]

Colonel Crook likewise expressed his praises by issuing an order, dated Lewisburg, May 25, 1862: "It affords the undersigned great pleasure in congratulating the troops of his command on their brilliant success of the 23d inst. We were attacked by a greatly superior force, who not only had the choice of position, but had the moral of the attack. The 36th and 44th regiments formed line of battle under fire, a movement that veteran troops find very difficult to make. They then advanced in good order driving the enemy before them, dealing death and destruction as they went, until the enemy fled in great confusion, leaving over 100 of their killed and wounded on the field. We captured 4 pieces of artillery, 300 stand of arms and 100 prisoners. The 44th captured their battery and the 36th advancing under their heaviest infantry fire. The result fully justifies the high standard these regiments were expected to maintain.

To make particular mention would be invidious, since they behaved so nobly. The artillery by a misunderstanding was not brought into action.

The 2d Va. Cavalry being held in reserve, had the most difficult part to perform, that of being exposed to the enemy's fire without being able to participate. The Medical and Quartermaster's departments deserve great credit for their energy and zeal in carrying the wounded and dead from the field.

The Surgeons and Assistant Surgeons deserve particular mention for their skill and untiring attention to the wounded."[447]

Colonel George Crook received a promotion in September 1862 to the rank of Brigadier General for his gallant service on the field of Lewisburg, Virginia.

In December 1862, General Crook noted in a letter of recommendation for Gilbert, to Secretary of War E. M. Stanton: "At the battle of Lewisburg all credit is due to him [Gilbert] for the capture of all of the enemies artillery."[448] The following August, Crook noted Gilbert's conduct at Lewisburg: "At the battle of Lewisburg, Va. (23d of May 1862) his bravery, skill and coolness added materially to this, one of the most decisive and complete victories of the war."[449]

Despite recommendations by Crook and many others, Colonel Samuel A. Gilbert was passed over for promotion. During much of the time between the summer of 1862 and the spring of 1864, Gilbert commanded a brigade. In

---

446 *Springfield Republic*, Springfield, Ohio, *June* 4, 1862
447 *The Home News*, Marietta, Ohio, June 6, 1862
448 Letters Received By [the] Commission Branch, RG-94, National Archives, Washington, D. C. (hereafter cited as Commission Branch)
449 Commission Branch

April 1864, his regiment now organized as the 8th Ohio Cavalry, Gilbert resigned because of poor health. After the war, on November 22, 1866, President Andrew Johnson appointed Gilbert to the rank of Brevet Brigadier General, to rank from March 13, 1865. Gilbert died on June 9, 1868.

Writing an account of his service on November 23, 1865, Gilbert noted about Lewisburg: [punctuation added] "The only fair opportunity I ever had was at Lewisburg, Va., where the orders for battle were verbal, about as follows. [The] Enemy deploying into line on [the] opposite side of valley in plain sight, about three fourths of a mile distant, displaying more than double our numbers. The space between our forces and the enemy [was] occupied by the long straggling town. Col Crook and myself riding from the town to where our men were bivouacked [sic]. I asked "What are you going to do?" He answered, "Fight them." "How will we do it?" "You take the right and I'll take the left of the town and we'll go for them." "All right." The enemy opened upon us as we were forming with shell, killing one and wounding two of my men as they commenced moving towards us. We met about half-way in an open field, neither party having any cover. We reserved our fire until within about a hundred yards and then charged their battery which consisted of one twelve pdr. field howitzer, two three-inch rifled cannon, and one twelve pdr smooth bore, all of which we captured except two gun limbers. Their infantry ran away leaving forty or fifty killed, and about eighty wounded and over one hundred prisoners in our hands. Leaving a guard over these we pushed forward in pursuit until [checked] by the [burning of the] bridge over Greenbriar [sic] River. This is one of the few instances where the rebel journals of the day admitted a square defeat."[450]

---

450 NOAA

CROOK FALLS BACK TO MEADOW BLUFF

May 29 to June 30, 1862

In the days following the battle at Lewisburg, many of the Union troops started to feel uneasy about their position. Lieutenant Evans, the faithful correspondent of the *Springfield Republic* which signed himself "Zouave," noted: "Our position is interesting, if not critical. Four different roads center in this place, from three of which, we may be attacked at any moment. The negroes who predicted the fight of the 23d, are again predicting that we will be attacked in a few days by a large force."[451]

Various reasons are given for Crook's decision to fall back to Meadow Bluff, about 15 miles west of Lewisburg. Among those given were the lack of transportation and the scarcity of water. Colonel Crook, in a dispatch to General Cox, gave his reason as "General Banks' defeat renders my position very unsafe. Consequently I fell back to Meadow Bluffs to-day..."[452]

Despite their withdrawal from Lewisburg, the Federals continued to claim possession of the town. A squad of Federal cavalry visited Lewisburg on a daily basis, and after remaining several hours, would leave.[453]

When Crook withdrew from Lewisburg, he left between 25 and 30 wounded Confederate prisoners behind, they being too bad to be moved. These, it is

---

451 *Springfield Republic*, Springfield, Ohio, June 6, 1862

452 OR, Series I, Vol 12, part 3, p. 289; Confederate General Thomas J. "Stonewall" Jackson defeated General Nathanial Banks' forces at both Front Royal (May 23), and Winchester (May 25), driving them out of the Shenandoah Valley.

453 Edgar, p. 117

reported, were paroled by Crook, on the "condition of their joining me here [Meadow Bluff] as soon as their health would permit."[454] A number of these prisoners were later removed by force from Lewisburg by Confederate cavalry.

Reports of the welfare of the wounded prisoners in the hands of Crook's forces, reached the Confederates in late May. Captain Sheffey, 8th Virginia Cavalry, noted that the enemy "shamefully neglected our wounded men there. One of our surgeons will, I think, go over tomorrow to attend to the latter."[455]

After falling back to Meadow Bluff, Crook sent another group of rebel prisoners to Gauley Bridge on May 30th, a distance of 47 miles, again under the guard of a portion of the 2nd (West) Virginia Cavalry. That same day, Company B, 2nd (West) Virginia Cavalry was sent to Lewisburg with a wagon train. Along the way, they encountered a body of Confederates, and after a brief skirmish, got away with the loss of one man taken prisoner. The purpose of their journey is not known, but likely had to do with the wounded rebel prisoners.

Captain E. H. Harman, 45th Virginia Infantry, noted on June 2nd, that a force of Confederate cavalry had visited Lewisburg on the 31st, and discovered that the Yankees had left 32 Southern wounded there. The cavalry collected 22 of them, along with 65 who had not been wounded.[456]

The report of the rescue of sixty-five un-injured Confederate prisoners is likely in error. All of the un-injured prisoners had been removed from Lewisburg the day following the battle, leaving only a number of wounded prisoners there. According to Crook, these numbered "some 25."[457]

Several days after the battle, in late May or early June, Sergeant S. W. N. Feamster (Greenbrier Cavalry) was sent to Lewisburg with three other men, to ascertain who was killed, captured and wounded.[458] In the town, Feamster observed a large number of civilians gathered in front of the hotel where the wounded prisoners were being kept. The Confederates suddenly found themselves confronting a squad of Yankees, with wagons, come to remove the wounded prisoners. Feamster does not mention any skirmishing with the enemy, but it is likely there was, based on the foregoing information.[459]

Feamster later noted that a few nights later, the cavalry returned to Lewisburg and removed some of the wounded prisoners, among which was Major George M. Edgar. Captain Alfred M. Edgar provides some additional details concerning the removal of his cousin. Rumors persisted throughout the rebel camps that the

---

454 *Richmond Whig*, Richmond, Va., June 11, 1862; Col. Crook wrote Capt. Bascom from Meadow Bluff, May 30, (RG-393); OR, Series 2, Vol. 4, p. 859

455 Sheffey, p. 110

456 Harman, VT

457 OR, Series I, Vol. 12, pt. 3, p. 320

458 Feamster names them as C. T. Smith, Captain Johnston and John Miller (A Civil War Event, p.24).

459 A Civil War Event, p. 24 - 25

Federals would soon abandon Meadow Bluff, and it was feared that Major Edgar would be removed and sent to a prison. His friends feared that such a movement would prove fatal to the major, so arrangements were quickly made to bring him out to safety. The cavalrymen called upon David Creigh at Edgar's Mill, they borrowed his double buggy to comfortable removed the major. Creigh accompanied the troop of cavalry to Lewisburg. About an hour after dark, Major Edgar was removed from Lewisburg and taken to a point inside the Confederate lines. Although Captain Edgar does not mention it, it is very likely that other wounded Confederates were removed at the same time.[460]

By June 9, 1862, there remained at least a dozen wounded prisoners in Lewisburg. A detachment of the 2nd (West) Virginia Cavalry paroled twelve wounded prisoners on that date. Second Lieutenant W. M. Fortescue, Company F, 2nd (West) Virginia Cavalry, reported on June 10th: "On the morning of the 9th instant, with 33 men of Company C and 20 men of Company F, Second Virginia Cavalry, I started for Lewisburg, which place we reached about 1 o'clock p.m., and found the town unoccupied by any force. I proceeded to the hospital, and found 12 wounded prisoners, 2 having recovered sufficiently to leave since our

COLONEL GEORGE M. EDGAR
Greenbrier County Historical Society

last visit, on the 1st instant. Two of those that remained have been previously paroled. Two others were in such a critical condition that I thought it unnecessary to parole them, as they were then in a dying state. Those have died since our last visit. The remaining 8 I procured their signatures to the parole, all being anxious to give it. All the wounded are suffering for proper surgical attendance. From the last information there is no enemy encamped within 8 miles of Lewisburg, ... After remaining in town three hours we left for camp...."[461]

Two days later, the Northern cavalry started back to Lewisburg with several of the surgeons, to attend to the wounded rebels. Along the way "They met about 500 cavalry with two companies of infantry. They immediately sent word to camp when our regiment was ordered to be ready to march in one hour. We started after them thinking it was the advance guard of a large army and intending to hold them in check until the rest of the force would be ready to resist an attack or retreat in case the force was too large for us.

---

460 A Civil War Event, p. 26; Edgar, p. 117 - 18
461 OR, Series I, Vol. 12, part 3, p. 368-9

We marched about 7 miles when we found it was only a foraging party sent to a mill to get flour. We bivouacked there for the night and returned to camp this morning [13th]."[462]

Another account of the encounter was published in Wilmington, Ohio *The Watchman*, on June 26, 1862: "On Thursday of last week news reached our camp from Lewisburg that the wounded that were left after the battle, were dying for the want of medical attention. The assistant surgeon of the 47th, Dr. Hoeltze with two others started to their relief, with a small body guard of cavalry. When they were within two miles of the place they were greeted by the shouts of some six hundred secesh cavary, who fired on our men, but doing no damage; the fire was returned with like results. The enemy outnumbering us twenty to one we thought best to return to a more healthy climate, which was done in the best of order, concluding that the secesh might take care of their own wounds. The rebel cavalry consisted of Jenkins' and Clarkson's, and what was left of the Greenbriar [sic] cavalry."[463]

On June 27, 1862, an escort from Company I, 2nd (West) Virginia Cavalry, along with several ambulances, were sent to Lewisburg to remove the last of the wounded rebel prisoners. The records, however, do not state the number of wounded moved back to Meadow Bluff.

---

462 McKee, p. 36
463 *The Watchman*, Wilmington, Ohio, June 26, 1862

CHAPTER FOURTEEN

LEWISBURG MISCELLANY

Watching the Battle

A number of local citizens observed the fighting at Lewisburg on the morning of May 23, 1862. Among that number, were the guests of the Star Hotel, located in the main section of town, and in the heart of the battle.

Several residents of Edgar's Mill (now Ronceverte), learned from Confederate scouts on May 22nd that a battle would take place the next morning at Lewisburg. Wishing to see the battle, members of the Edgar Family, and neighbors Mrs. William Vogelsong, Randolph Morgan, and David L. Creigh, decided to go to the outskirts of Lewisburg on the morning of the 23rd. A Mr. James Fisk, a resident of Washington, D. C., who was boarding with David Creigh, accompanied them. The group went to Wagner's Hill, a high point, which they thought would be safe. This was also where the Confederate artillery was positioned.[464]

What they thought of the battle, and how close they came to the fighting is not known.

There were observers in the Union camp as well. "Those left to guard prisoners, baggage, &c., state that the whole affair was a splendid sight. A dense cloud of smoke hovered over our line, apparently advancing with it; sometimes hiding it entirely, and at others exposing it to their view. They could see the Rebels running back out of the smoke which they had made and hear us cheer as we advanced."[465]

---

464 Edgar, p. 113
465 *Home News*, Marietta, Ohio, June 6, 1862

Incidents of Battle

There are a number of incidents recorded as having taken place during the fighting at Lewisburg on the morning of May 23, 1862.

Private H. R. Hodson, a member of Edgar's Battalion, related the following years later: "On the march to Lewisburg, a comrade, in a spirit of mischief, loaded Hodson's gun. Enroute, about Organ Cave, Hodson forgot that his gun was loaded and rammed down another full charge. The battalion was stationed behind a rail fence, running from the colored Methodist Church east. Mr. Hodson stuck the muzzle of his gun through the fence where [it] commanded a view of Main Street at the M. E. Church South (Lee and Washington) and awaited the appearance of a column of Federal troops which had been observed to leave the western part of town from about the Masonic Hall (now the County Library and Museum). Mr. Hodson aimed his gun, intending to fire as soon as the head of the column emerged from behind the house now occupied by Mrs. Ellen McClung. He had not long to wait. The column emerged and Mr. Hodson pulled the trigger.

When Hodson came to, his comrades had withdrawn. The recoil had knocked him unconscious. He tried to get away up the hill, but about where the water tank now stands, in the new Garden Heights addition, he was captured. Hodson was imprisoned in D. J. Ford's old stone store on Main Street.

The next morning a Federal officer came in to look at the prisoners, and jocularly remarked [to Hodson]: "What kind of powder do you fellow[s] use now?"

"Why do you ask that question?", he was asked.

"Because yesterday ... just as we reached the church ... one shot was fired and I can swear that there was but one shot, and it killed two men and wounded a third."

Hodson added, to himself, "I could have told him that it nearly killed a fourth, but I thought it best to keep my mouth shut."[466]

Speaking of keeping one's mouth shut, Private Joseph V. Rollins, Company A, 22nd Virginia Infantry, would likely have been killed had he kept his mouth shut. Rollins noted that "while posted behind a fence waiting for the battle to open a comrade lowered his pants for a bowel movement. While so engaged the enemy broke through the line and the Rebels fled. The surprised soldier took off running with his pants yet around his ankles and Rollins paused to look at him and laugh. The laughter caused Rollin's mouth to open and a bullet passed through one jaw and out the other, and he later grew a beard to hide the scar. Had

---

466 "Gray Forces Defeated in Battle of Lewisburg", by J. W. Benjamin. West Virginia History, Vol. XX, No. 1 (October 1958), p. 34 – 35.

he not opened his mouth to laugh the wound could have been deadly, or at least knocked his teeth out."[467]

Private John A. McKee, 44th Ohio, related: "A little circumstance happened in the thickest of the fight which caused a great deal of laughter. One of the enemy wishing to desert the Rebel army slipped away from his company and came running toward us with a white pocket handkerchief on the end of his gun hollering, "Don't shoot me. I was forced into it." We sent him to the rear as a prisoner."[468]

Captain Hiram F. Devol, Company A, 36th Ohio, recorded a close call of one of his men. "The life of one of my men was saved by a Testament in his blouse pocket, just over his heart. The ball went through the book and his clothing, but stopped at his skin. He fell, but did not know what hit him till night, when he found the flattened ball."[469]

In another account which may relate to the same soldier, George Barker noted that William Barnhart, of Company A, was "struck by a ball which passed through his breast pocket, through two plugs of tobacco, a small blank book, glanced through one corner of his testament, striking him in the breast, and knocked him down."[470]

Private Isaac Overall, noted that "James Overall was in that Battle … he was shot through the cape [cap] on the lope [top] of his head and tore the cape all to pecies [sic]. He was a lodeing [sic] when the ball struck his cape and nock [sic] it a bout teen [ten] feet. He pick it upe [sic] and went a head."[471]

Private John E. Harrison, recorded in his dairy: "I here saw one fellow which had the side of his neck & face scratched with a ball; & a ball had also struck his gun at the lower band & cut the stock about half off."[472]

Another soldier remarked in a letter to a newspaper: "It is astonishing to see the number of bullet holes through the blouses, caps, pants and boots of our boys."[473]

An account of events in the Union camp tells a humorous observation: "… these men were compelled to laugh occasionally at the antics of the darkey cooks left behind. Whenever a shell would come squalling and cursing through the air at them, a general stampede would take place and such dodging, such scrambling

---

467 Terry D. Lowry. 22nd Virginia Infantry, Lynchburg, Va., H. E. Howard, Inc., 1988, p. 32

468 McKee, p. 37

469 Devol, p. 31

470 *The Intelligencer*, Marietta, Ohio, June 5, 1862

471 Overall Family Civil War Letters, June 2, 1862. https://goverall.wordpress.com/overall-family-civil-war-letters/the-letters/5/, last visited April 2016.

472 Harrison Diary

473 *The Spirit of Democracy*, Woodsfield, Ohio, June 11, 1862

among the rocks for shelter, and such an amazing amount of white shown in their eyes was enough to upset the gravity of any man."[474]

Towards the end of the fighting, the 2nd (West) Virginia Cavalry were ordered forward after the fleeing Confederates, either in an effort to capture as many as possible, or to hasten their retreat, or both. As the charging cavalry passed along Hardscrabble Hill (Washington Street), one horseman got too close to the edge of the road, and his horse slipped on a flagstone. Down went both horse and rider; the rider being rolled into the front yard of a nearby residence. The only injury was to the horseman's ego. The soldier quickly recovered his mount and rejoined the chase.[475]

Length of the battle

The reported length of the battle varies, ranging from 20 minutes to 2 ½ hours. Probably the true length of the battle is about an hour and a half, from 5:00 AM to 6:30 AM. The estimate of twenty minutes likely refers to the time the 36th and 44th became engaged until the Confederate line broke apart.

Requisition for New Artillery Pieces

After the battle of Lewisburg, when the men of Heth's command were regrouping and resupplying, Captain Thomas A. Bryan, is said to have submitted a requisition for several artillery pieces to replace those lost at Lewisburg. The commander of Bryan's Battery was still angry about being ordered to advance the artillery into what proved to be a disastrous position. His requisition called for "six pieces of artillery with bayonets affixed."[476]

General Heth was enraged by the disrespectful request, and in a fit of anger, sent an order to Bryan stating that the company was being split into two and assigned to the 26th Battalion of Infantry. Upon receiving Heth's order, Bryan gave his men the order to open fire. Other nearby batteries, taking the firing for a signal, also started firing their pieces.

Captain Bryan met with his men and informed them of Heth's order. The men were ready to fight, declaring they would "stand up before a thousand muskets and be shot" before joining the infantry. Finally, Heth agreed to allow Bryan to keep enough men to operate the two six-pounders that were left behind when

474 *Home News*, Marietta, Ohio, June 6, 1862

475 "Lewisburg Changed Sides Often During War Years: Residents Recalled Events During Battle." By J. W. Benjamin, undated newspaper clipping, Greenbrier Historical Society, Lewisburg, W. Va.

476 J. L. Scott. Lowry's, Bryan's, and Chapman's Batteries of Virginia Artillery. H. E. Howard, Inc., Lynchburg, Va., 1988, p. 35

they advanced to Lewisburg. The remainder of the men, about 80 in number, were temporarily assigned to the 26th Battalion until new artillery pieces could be obtained.[477]

The feud between Heth and Bryan continued until Heth was replaced by General William W. Loring. The replacement artillery did not arrive until October 1862.

---

477 Ibid.

BATTLE OF
LEWISBURG LOSSES

Confederate Casualties - May 23, 1862

G iven the lack of records for the Confederate troops engaged at Lewisburg, the casualty figures that appear here are only a best guess. They are, I believe, the most accurate compiled since the battle was fought in May 1862.

In reading over the wartime accounts of the battle, it becomes apparent that propaganda played a huge role in the reports by the Southerners. One of the most notable is a claim by Captain George G. Otey, that "We took some 75 prisoners, and lost none of our own except the wounded, who were left in the hands of the enemy, some of our surgeons who retired to visit our men, and possibly a few stragglers."[478]

An examination of the surviving prisoner of war records of the Confederate States Army, do not support the claim that 75 prisoners were taken at Lewisburg. The Northern military records are much more complete, and show only nine men taken prisoner on May 23, 1862 at (or near) Lewisburg. Northern prisoner of war records show a large number of Confederate prisoners taken on May 23, 1862, including a number of men who were not wounded.

A statement appended to Captain Otey's report, declared that on the day previous to the battle (May 22), the Confederates captured a scouting party of Yankee cavalry in Monroe County, near the Greenbrier River, numbering 42,

---

478 *Wilmington Journal*, Wilmington, N. C., June 5, 1862. The appended statement to Captain Otey's account, states that the 75 prisoners taken consisted of 40 cavalrymen and 35 infantry, including some of the pickets who where sleeping at their posts.

without firing a gun. The statement also noted that the Confederates took 80 prisoners and lost "none of our own."[479]

Once again, this seems to be a "feel good" statement, to soften the true facts surrounding the fight at Lewisburg, and is not supported by official records.

The official records, primarily Colonel George Crook's after action report, states "We have in our possession as prisoners Lieutenant-Colonel Finney, Major Edgar, and a number of minor officers and 93 privates; also 66 wounded prisoners and 38 dead…"[480]

A list of the wounded prisoners referred to by Colonel Crook is among the surviving records in the National Archives. Originally a part of the Union Army records, it is now filed with the Confederate States Army records in Record Group 109 as Confederate Manuscript number 3082. There is actually 67 entries on the list – the 67th one is for an unnamed soldier, who likely died of his wounds. The prisoner list names five officers as being wounded. A number of these men appear nowhere else in the surviving Confederate records.[481]

General Heth does not mention the number of casualties in his command for the Lewisburg battle, stating only "I cannot as yet ascertain our exact loss, but will furnish you [Loring] reports at my earliest convenience. By far the greater portion of the casualties were among the officers – a consequence of the panic."[482]

The records show that a total of nineteen Confederate officers were either killed, wounded, or captured at Lewisburg. The number of enlisted men and non-commissioned officers is far greater. If General Heth ever submitted a report of his casualties is not known; none has ever been found.

Existing records, however, show the Confederate loss at Lewisburg on May 23, 1862, as follows:

---

479 *Wilmington Journal*, Wilmington, N. C., June 5, 1862
480 OR, Series I, Vol. 12, part 1, p. 807
481 Manuscripts, No. 3082, War Department Collection of Confederate Records, RG-109, National Archives, Washington, D. C.
482 OR, Series I, Vol. 12, part 1, p. 813.

Unit	Killed	Wounded or Injured	POW	WD POW	WD POW DOD	WD POW DOW	WD DOW	MIA	POW DOD	TOTAL
22nd Virginia	13	15	44	22	1	9	1		1	106
Edgar's Battn.	13	9	33	19	1	14	2	1	1	93
45th Virginia	3	4	6				1			14
Bryan's Battery	1	2	1	1						5
Lowry's Battery		1								1
Otey's Battery							1			1
Chapman's Battery		1	1							2
8th Va. Cavalry		3	4	2						9
Heth's Staff		1								1
Unknown Units		1		6		2*				9
Total	30	36	89	50	2	25	5	1	2	240

* One individual, identified only as Rhodes, is mentioned in Union accounts as having been a guide for the 36th Ohio Infantry in the Cold Knob area, the previous March. Rhodes escaped from the Ohioans and was later found among the wounded prisoners at Lewisburg. John T. Booth recognized him, and noted that he died of his wounds on May 24th.[483]

The numbers reflected here are likely on the low side due to the scarcity of period records. For instance, an account of the battle appearing in the *Richmond*

---

483 Another Day, p. 269

Whig on May 28, 1862, noted that Bryan's Battery had five men killed and ten wounded.[484]

According to an account by Lieutenant William F. Bahlmann, the 22nd Virginia Infantry lost 149 out of 396 men engaged.[485]

Captain Edwin H. Harman, 45th Virginia Infantry estimated the loss to Heth's force as 300 killed, wounded and missing.[486] Harman's regiment sustained fewer casualties than the other infantry regiments in Heth's command, and feared that they would be blamed for not doing their duty because of it. Colonel Brown noted in his report: "There were few casualties in my regiment comparatively, owing to the fact that it was protected by the houses of the town."[487]

One Northern soldier, Sergeant Wallace Stanley, noted in his diary, the following numbers of rebel dead, wounded and captured:

Dead in our hands	60
Wounded in our hands	75
Wounded carried away	100
Prisoners	105
Died crossing the Greenbrier	3
Wounded crossing the Greenbrier	8
Cannon taken (2 10 pound parrot & rifle)	4
Small arms	300
Horses	24

Sergeant Stanley's account is the only one that mentions any Confederate loss while crossing the Greenbrier River. It is very likely that these casualties did occur, given the Confederates panic and desire to escape.[488]

Loss of Confederate Artillery

Colonel George Crook, in his official report, notes the capture of four artillery pieces at Lewisburg, two rifled and two smooth-bore. There may have been other artillery pieces captured or recovered during and after the Battle of Lewisburg.

484 *Richmond Whig*, Richmond, Va., May 28, 1862
485 Bahlmann, p. 60
486 Harman, VT
487 Harman, VT
488 Booth; Another Day, p. 244

Most Confederate accounts place the loss as four guns. A report in the *Richmond Whig*, May 28, 1862, states that "Bryant's [sic] Battery lost ... one six pounder, one twelve pounder and one six pounder rifle piece. Otey's Battery lost one six pounder rifle piece ..."[489]

Many accounts of the battle by Union soldiers indicate that more than four artillery pieces were taken at Lewisburg. Private Edwin Brown, 36th Ohio, reported that five cannon were captured.[490] Orderly Sergeant A. T. Ward, Company G, 36th Ohio, noted that the Confederates "took one cannon over the river, spiked it, and abandoned it by running it into the river. They also left two guns on the bridge, which fell into the river when it burned."[491]

An account appearing the *Troy Time*, noted that the 44th Ohio charged bayonet and took four guns. Later, at the [Greenbrier] bridge, two more pieces were taken, having been tumbled into the river.[492]

Samuel J. Harrison, 44th Ohio, noted that "We captured 4 pieces of artillery, two 10 pound, one 12 pound, & one 20 pound piece, besides one piece which they spiked & two other cannon which they spiked & throwed [sic] in the river."[493]

Lieutenant Shaw, 44th Ohio, stated that Heth brought 8 pieces of artillery to the field, four were taken, and three others were spiked and thrown into the river. He wrote: "...to show their panic, I will state that their artillery came to the bridge and only got one piece over before they broke it. The remaining fugitives plunged into the river, something over a hundred yards wide at this place."[494]

Major John J. Hoffman, 2nd (West) Virginia Cavalry, noted that the rebels had a 12-pound rifle piece on the opposite side of the Greenbrier River, which they "blew it up and destroyed it." The river, he noted, was too deep and swift to cross.[495]

Other accounts state that four rifled cannon were taken, while another says a rifled battery of six guns was taken.

Captain Otey, in his statement published in the Lynchburg newspapers, reported the cause of the capture of the latter was a misconception of the order to retreat." He does not elaborate further about the misconception.[496]

---

489 *Richmond Whig*, Richmond, Va., May 28, 1862

490 Edwin A. Brown Letter, Brown Family Collection, Robert E. & Jean R. Mahn Center for Archives and Special Collections, Vernon R. Alden Library, Ohio University, Athens, Ohio.

491 Another Day, p. 241

492 *Troy Times*, Troy, Ohio, June 5, 1862

493 S. Harrison letters

494 *Darke County Democrat*, Greenville, Ohio, June 11, 1862

495 *Jackson Standard*, Jackson, Ohio, June 5, 1862

496 Otey, *Wilmington Journal*, Wilmington, N. C., June 5, 1862

While most accounts report four cannon taken during the battle, an account by Captain Edwin H. Harman, 45th Virginia Infantry, acknowledges the loss of only three cannon. In speaking of the role of the artillery, Harman noted that none of the guns attached to the 45th Virginia were lost, and did good work. The regiment, he said, brought them off the field. Lieutenant Charles Fudge remained with his company, under Harman's command, trying to get out a cannon (one of Otey's) which had been run past our regiment into a garden, until all the horses were shot down. The Yankees were within fifty yards and the gun had to be abandoned. Harman again noted that the 45th was the last to leave the town.[497]

Trooper Jones, 2nd (West) Virginia Cavalry, noted that "When they thought we were retreating they run their canon [sic] so far down the hill & loosing part of their horses they failed to recover them."[498]

Trooper Jones also noted that the rebels "one after another took to their heals [sic] til the whole were routed leaving four pieces of canon [sic] upon the field unspiked and two others close to the Greenbrier bridge one of them a twenty-four pounder spiked with two foot of canister in it."[499]

It is likely that Colonel Crook only reported the capture of the four guns actually taken during battle, and did not mention the guns recovered at the bridge and from the river. It is also possible, that Crook did not report the capture of the "relic" gun, just those of any value.

It was said afterwards that Loring "advised Heath [sic] that when he next charged a Yankee force with artillery, not to neglect putting bayonets on his guns."[500] A similar account appearing in Captain Alfred M. Edgar's recollections, stated "It is said that some of the artillerists sent Gen. Heath [sic] word after the fight that they hoped he would provide bayonets for their guns before they were ordered into another battle."[501]

In addition to the number of small arms (more than 300) and artillery (at least four pieces), a number of horses (25), wagons, ammunition and baggage was taken by the victorious Northern army.

Union Casualties — May 23, 1862

The number of Northern casualties is much lower than those of the Confederates. According to the records, their loss is as follows:

---

497 Harman, VT
498 Jones Diary
499 Jones Letter
500 Abraham, p. 15
501 Edgar, p. 114

Unit	Killed	Wounded	Wd. DOW	Wd. DOD	POW	POW DOD	Total
36th Ohio Infantry	5	42	5	0	5	1	58
44th Ohio Infantry	6	24	1	1	0		32
2nd (West) Virginia Cavalry	--	--	--	0	3		3
Total	11	66	6	1	8	1	93

As stated before, the Union troops buried thirteen of their comrades near Lewisburg. Besides the eleven reported killed, two others died of their wounds by May 24th, when they were laid to rest. The others who died of their wounds or disease, succumbed elsewhere.

One company – Company G, 36th Ohio Infantry – which was engaged in the earliest skirmishing and during the main battle, did not have a man killed or wounded. They indeed lead a charmed life, as did four other companies who had no loss.

Company K of the 36th Ohio Infantry had the most casualties: 3 killed, 9 wounded, 1 wounded and died. Company D of the 44th Ohio Infantry suffered the greatest loss in that regiment: 1 killed, 8 wounded, 1 wounded and died.

Northern accounts claim that the Confederates carried off a number of their dead and wounded, to conceal the severity of their loss at Lewisburg. The same can be said of Southern accounts of the battle. An article in the *Richmond Whig* noted that the Federal loss was heavy, and "Among the number, fourteen officers, who are buried upon a hill west of town, their graves being railed in and marked; the privates were hauled off, and an attempt made to conceal their number."[502]

Blame for the Disaster

The Confederate disaster at Lewisburg naturally resulted in finger-pointing and the denunciation of leaders and regiments. From the evidence presented, it would appear that the fault lay in the hands of Brigadier General Henry Heth, who, it appears in his desire for a quick victory, totally mismanaged the entire affair at Lewisburg.

In his after-action report, General Heth concluded: "One of those causeless panics for which there is no accounting seized upon my command. Victory was

502 *Richmond Whig*, Richmond, Va., June 11, 1862

in my grasp, instead of which I have to admit a most disgraceful retreat. ... The only excuse that can be offered for the disgraceful behavior of three regiments and batteries is that they are filled with conscripts and newly officered under the election system. I do not wish to be understood as shifting the responsibility of what has occurred upon the soldiers of my troops for as a general is the recipient of honors gained, so he should bear his proportion of the result of the disaster."[503]

Several newspaper accounts spoke favorably of General Heth, stating that he "acted with signal bravery, being in the thickest of the fight at all times."[504] Another declared that General Heth attempted to rally the men, but failed. "In reviewing the battle, we see that great blame rests on some one. ... On fact is certain, we under estimated the force of the enemy. They could not have had less than five thousand men, while from every source of information we could obtain before the fight, we were continually told that there were only two regiments in the town."[505]

Captain Alfred M. Edgar in his recollections referred to Heth as being "incompetent to fill his position."[506] Soldiers of Heth's command harbored ill feelings against their commanding officer. Craig County soldier George Caldwell stated that "Our general is a mean man. ... If I get a chance I will split the old rascal wide open. He was drunk and like to got us kiled [sic] at Lewisburg."[507] Another Craig County soldier agreed in part, writing: "Heth ... was drinking and did not manage the army in the proper way,..."[508]

Sergeant S. W. N. Feamster, of the Greenbrier Cavalry, recalled: "It is said that Gen. Heath [sic] was drinking[.] Col. Finney was so disgusted with the way the fight was managed that he sat down on a rock at the side of the road & said he was going to sit there until he was captured & he did so. The Cavalry were ordered to rally the infantry but we were unable to do so I never saw a fight worse managed in my life: we could & should have whipped the Yankees without losing a 10th of the men we did lose"[509]

Rev. George Boardman Taylor, who participated in the battle, wrote to his brother soon afterward: "You have perhaps read some accounts in the papers of the battle of Lewisburg. I had the honor, or dishonor (as you please), of being engaged in that disastrous fight. It was one of the most complete, disastrous, 'bull

---

503 OR, Series I, Vol. 12, part 1, p. 813

504 *Richmond Daily Dispatch*, Richmond, Va., May 28, 1862

505 *Richmond Daily Dispatch*, Richmond, Va., June 3, 1862

506 Edgar, p. 114

507 Jane Echols Johnston & Brenda Lynn Williams, Comp. & Ed. Hard Times: 1861 – 1865: A Collection of Confederate Letters, Court Minutes, Soldiers' Records, and Local Lore from Craig County, Virginia, n.p., 1986, p. 66 (hereafter cited as Hard Times).

508 Hard Times, p. 291

509 A Civil War Event, p. 24

run' defeats of the war. I have been surprised and grieved beyond expression to think that we had such incompetent generals and cowardly soldiers in our army. The defeat was due in the first place to General Holt's [Heth's] ordering the troops in a position where the enemy had every advantage, and secondly to the cowardice of the men who would not stand till reinforcements could be sent to their aid."[510]

Captain John P. Sheffey, 8th Virginia Cavalry, wrote: "But Genl. Heth is pursuing a very mean and dastardly course in endeavoring to shirk the responsibility and throw it upon his men. But in that he will signally fail. He is responsible for the surprise and the consequent reaction. If he had used the proper precautions, his men would have continued the fight with the utmost enthusiasm and bravery. The victory would have been won notwithstanding the odds which I believe – and if I can trust the evidence of my own senses – know to have been against us."[511]

Fielding R. Cornett, 8th Virginia Cavalry, noted: "…we attacked an overwhelming force in Lewisburg, Greenbrier Co., who had the protection of houses and strong plank fences. After a tremendous fire of an hour we were compelled to fall back with a loss of 200 men. I do not know how many we killed of the Yankees. … We lost the victory by nothing in the world but bad generalship. I never want to see any set of people who threw bullets at me with both hands before. I do not think that I ever saw hail fall thicker and faster in my life than the bullets fell around me that day."[512]

Blame for the disaster was cast unjustly upon the 45th Virginia Infantry, who occupied the center of Heth's line. Captain, later lieutenant-colonel, Edwin H. Harman noted that "a great blunder" was committed in the plan of our action. "To think of throwing the artillery in rear of a battalion, none of which [were ever] under fire, and to keep them advanced when a better position for them was on a hill in our rear, the proper place for artillery."[513]

As previously mentioned, some members of the 22nd Virginia Infantry observed troops to their left in a panic, leaving the field. From their prospective, they believed it to be the 45th Virginia regiment, when in fact, it was Finney's and Edgar's men that broke first.

One of the correspondents in the Richmond newspapers stated that the blame lay with the 45th Virginia Infantry, who "for some unknown cause … became panic stricken and fled." [514]

---

510 G. Taylor, p. 70-1

511 Sheffey, p. 109

512 Fielding R. Cornett letter, Miscellaneous Virginia Papers, 1829 – 1905, Accession #8978-j, Special Collections Department, University of Virginia Library, Charlottesville, Va.

513 Harman, VT

514 *Richmond Dispatch*, Richmond, Va., May 31, 1862

Many rumors circulated blaming the 45th Virginia, some calling it the "running regiment," and others, the "panic strikers."

Captain Harman strongly defended his regiment in both letters and the newspapers. Harman, writing from Salt Sulphur Springs, Va., on June 2, commented: "Our regiment seemed to be destined to suffer the whole blame for our defeat, because on account of better management in the field there were fewer casualties. Better management I repeat, for I have it from reliable men who were in Lewisburg after the action that nearly all the killed and wounded were shot after the retreat was commenced. Who knows better than the cavalry regiment which was dismounted and kept in the rear as a reserve and saw the whole movement, and they are bold in saying to everybody that the 45th was the only regiment which came from the field in any order at all and that our regiment did retire in good order after the flanks had been turned, and that it reformed on the hill and was the only force which did so, and only left their post after orders from Gen. Heth. Instead of Browne [and] my self trying to get the men to stand and failed, Browne ordered our regiment to fall back to the hill. Our men stood, as Browne told Heth, as well as he wanted them to do. I say the same thing."[515]

In a letter to the *Lynchburg Daily Republican*, Harman wrote: "At that critical moment the infantry lost its support, and the battalion was compelled to fall back. I will not say it did so under order, but this I will say knowingly, the 45th stood fast, immovable and unshaken, even after the enemy had passed their line on the left, until commanded to fall back to a higher position on the hill, which it did in [good] formation, *the last from the field*"[516]

The captain cast the blame for the defeat exactly where it should have fallen – upon the officers, writing: "The battle was badly conducted on our side ... we had no skirmishers ahead [of us, and] the artillery never ought to have been all permitted to follow closely in line of battle."[517] Harman singled out one officer as the source of the defamation of the 45th Virginia, declaring that Captain Randolph H. Finney "is to blame for most of the mischief, to screen his brother."[518] Captain Finney was General Heth's Assistant Adjutant General, and a brother of Lieutenant Colonel William W. Finney.

Harman reserved some blame for the men of the battalion on the left of the line, stating: "Why is nothing said of the battalion ... it left the field in bad order and had let the Yankees pass our [45th Regiment] left nearly 200 yards before our regiment was ordered to fall back. "Shame, eternal shame."""[519]

---

515 Harman, VT

516 *Lynchburg Daily Republican,* Lynchburg, Va., June 10, 1862, letter signed as "A Soldier" concerning 45th Va. Inf., most likely written by Captain Edwin H. Harman.

517 Harman, VT

518 Harman, VT

519 Harman, VT

Private Joseph A. Brown recalled: "The crest-fallen soldiers indulged themselves in abusive comments against the blundering order which during the fight virtually turned things over to the Federals who had been advancing far beyond the battle line and into the town, by some inconceivable mistake. Vindictive expressions from the Confederates were often heard, threatening the lives of the officers who were responsible for the mistake and disgrace should they engage in another battle." [520]

Ultimately, the blame settled on the men of Edgar's battalion (26th Battalion Virginia Infantry). The hard feelings were so strong, that men of other regiments refused to go into battle with them, and often fought among themselves. This, however, changed a year later, at the battle of White Sulphur Springs. Edgar, with his battalion, repeatedly repulsed a Yankee force and saved the day, proving the fighting prowess of his men; all was forgiven. [521]

---

520 Brown, p. 21
521 22nd Virginia Infantry, p. 33

THE CONFEDERATE CASUALTIES

The names which appear on this list of Confederate casualties for the Battle of Lewisburg (including those taken by Crook's men earlier in May 1862), were compiled from a variety of sources. The Compiled Service Records for many of these men are very confusing, as they give erroneous regimental information, if any at all. Information concerning the arrest of the citizens of Alleghany and Greenbrier Counties can be found in the Union Provost Marshal Files or in the Miscellaneous records. The list presented below is arranged alphabetically. When looking for an individual, keep in mind that the spellings of names are often different.

The men who are listed as being exchanged on August 25, 1862, were actually sent on that day to Vicksburg, Mississippi, onboard the Steamer Jno. H. Done. They arrived at that place on September 11, 1862, and finally declared exchanged at Aiken's Landing, Virginia on November 10, 1862. Any exceptions are noted in the sketch of each soldier.

Adkins, Levi – Private, Company I, 22ⁿᵈ Virginia Infantry. **Captured**, and sent to the Atheneum Prison at Wheeling, then to Camp Chase Prison in Ohio, May 30, 1862. Described as being 21 years of age, 5 feet 11 ½ inches tall, having a light complexion, brown hair and blue eyes, and very light whiskers on his chin; a resident of Boone County. Exchanged August 25, 1862.

Alderman, Francis Marion – Private, Company F, 45ᵗʰ Virginia Infantry. **Captured**, and sent to the Atheneum Prison at Wheeling, then to Camp Chase Prison in Ohio, May 30, 1862. Described as being 21 years of age,

6 feet tall, having a fair complexion, black hair, and dark grey eyes, and starting to grow whiskers; a resident of Bland County. He was sent to the Johnson's Island Prison, Sandusky, Ohio on September 6, 1862, and sent to Vicksburg for exchange on November 22, 1862. He arrived at Vicksburg on December 8, 1862, on board the Steamer Charm.

Alexander, Henrie H. – Lieutenant. **Injured**. Mentions in a letter that his horse was killed, and that his arm was "put out of place." Most likely belonged to the 51st Virginia Infantry, but no records found. On June 10, 1862, he stated he was attached to the 22nd Virginia Infantry.

Allen, John – Citizen of Alleghany County. **Arrested** in Alleghany County, May 17, 1862. Sent to the Atheneum Prison at Wheeling, then to Camp Chase Prison in Ohio, May 30, 1862. Described as being 70 years of age, 6 feet tall, having a dark florid complexion, grey hair and blue eyes, and a grey beard, a resident of Alleghany County. Charged with aiding the Rebels. Allegedly tried to persuade Union men to enlist in the Confederate service. Dennis Cook, an Irish laborer on the Virginia Central Railroad testified that Allen was a violent secessionist, and that he had visited Cook's home on May 12, 1862, carrying a rifle and accoutrements, going to Camp Alleghany too meet the Yankees. James O'Connell, also an Irish laborer on the railroad, testified that Allen demanded that he join the Confederate army on May 5, 1862, and had on a former occasion said he would shoot him as quick as he would a damned Yankee. O'Connell stated that Allen said at anytime he could shoot 15 Yankees. Took the oath of allegiance and released December 26, 1862 and ordered to go to Columbus, Ohio by Governor Todd. Declared exchanged February 18, 1863.

Amos, Martin V. – Private, Company A, 22nd Virginia Infantry. **Killed**. Born in Putnam County.

Armistead, Thomas Jefferson – Private, Company E, 22nd Virginia Infantry. **Captured**. Compiled Service Record states that Armistead was "thought to be captured." No prisoner of war records found to support the claim.

Ankrum, William R. – Private, Company B, 22nd Virginia Infantry. **Captured**. Sent to the Atheneum Prison, at Wheeling, then to Camp Chase, Ohio, May 30, 1862. Described as being 18 years of age, 5 feet 8 ¾ inches tall, having a very dark complexion, black hair and greenish grey eyes, a resident of Jackson County. Exchanged August 25, 1862.

Asbury, Lorenzo D. – Private, Company D, 22nd Virginia Infantry. Also listed as Edgar's Battalion. **Captured**. Sent to the Atheneum Prison, at Wheeling, then to Camp Chase, Ohio, May 30, 1862. Described as being 20 years of age, 5 feet 9 ¾ inches tall, having a fair complexion, light hair, grey eyes, a scattering of whiskers; resident of Greenbrier County. Exchanged August 25, 1862.

Bahlmann, William F. – 1st Lieutenant, Company K, 22nd Virginia Infantry. **Wounded & Captured**, shot through right arm and in right hand. Fainted from blood loss. Harlow Huse tied up his wounds. Sent to a hospital in Charleston, then to Gallipolis, Ohio, June 11, 1862 for treatment of a gunshot wound. Released and sent to the Atheneum Prison at Wheeling, July 2, 1862, then to Camp Chase, Ohio, arriving there on July 8, 1862. Described as being 25 years of age, 5 feet 10 inches tall, having a fair complexion, brown hair and hazel eyes; resident of Fayette County, and a law student. Exchanged August 25, 1862.

Bailey, Allen – Private, Company I, 59th Virginia Infantry. Also as Edgar's Battalion. **Wounded & Captured**. No Compiled Service Record or prisoner of war records to support claim. Does appear on a list of wounded prisoners at Lewisburg compiled by order of Crook.

Baker, Lewis F. – Private, Company D, 22nd Virginia Infantry. **Captured** and sent to the Atheneum Prison, at Wheeling, then to Camp Chase, Ohio, May 30, 1862. Described as being 20 years of age, 5 feet 11 inches tall, having a dark complexion, black hair and hazel eyes, a resident of Nicholas County. Exchanged August 25, 1862.

Basham, Augustus – Private, Company C, 59th Virginia Infantry. Also as Edgar's Battalion. Name appears as Mashim on records. **Wounded & Captured** and sent to the Atheneum Prison, at Wheeling, then to Camp Chase, Ohio, May 30, 1862. Described as being 22 years of age, 6 feet 1 inch tall, having a fair complexion, light hair and blue eyes, sandy whiskers, a resident of Monroe County. **Died** of fever at Camp Chase, Ohio, October 31, 1862.

Bess, John Lee – Private, Company G, 22nd Virginia Infantry. **Wounded** in left arm (shoulder, ball not removed, too close to an artery). Described as being 25 years of age, 5 feet 7 inches tall, having a fair complexion, dark hair and blue eyes, a farmer residing in Alleghany County.

Black, John Dice – Private, Company I, 50ᵗʰ Virginia Infantry. **Captured** and sent to the Atheneum Prison, at Wheeling, then to Camp Chase, Ohio, May 30, 1862. Described as being 19 years of age, 6 feet 4 inches tall, having a fair complexion, black hair and dark eyes, light mustache; resident of Pulaski County. Exchanged August 25, 1862.

Blake, Major Claudius – 1ˢᵗ Sergeant, Company K, 22ⁿᵈ Virginia Infantry. **Wounded** shot through thigh. Treated at Montgomery White Sulphur Springs. Described as being 20 years of age, 5 feet 5 inches tall, having a fresh complexion, sandy hair and grey eyes, a resident of Fayette County.

Boggs (Boggess), John W. – Private, Company __, 22ⁿᵈ Virginia Infantry. **Wounded** pistol shot to neck, causing loss of right eye.

Bones (Bowers), Edward T. – Private, Company K, 22ⁿᵈ Virginia Infantry. **Captured** and sent to the Atheneum Prison, at Wheeling, then to Camp Chase, Ohio, May 30, 1862. Described as being 28 years of age, 5 feet 10 ½ inches tall, having a light complexion, dark hair and blue eyes, sandy whiskers, light, on chin and mustache; resident of Montgomery County. Exchanged August 25, 1862.

Boswell, William O. – Sergeant, Company E, Edgar's Battalion. **Killed.** Resident of Greenbrier County.

Braxton, Tomlin – Assistant Surgeon, Edgar's Battalion. **Captured** and sent to the Atheneum Prison, at Wheeling, then to Camp Chase, Ohio, May 30, 1862. Described as being 27 years of age, 5 feet 6 ½ inches tall, having a fair complexion, light hair and hazel eyes, a light brown beard; resident of King William County. Released unconditionally by order of Governor Todd, June 19, 1862.

Breedon, Hamilton V. – Private, Company A, 22ⁿᵈ Virginia Infantry. **Captured** and sent to the Atheneum Prison, at Wheeling, then to Camp Chase, Ohio, May 30, 1862. Described as being 25 years of age, 5 feet 8 inches tall, having a fair complexion, light hair and blue eyes, sandy whiskers; resident of Kanawha County. Exchanged August 25, 1862.

Brewer, Edward L. – Private, Vawter's Battery. Also as Edgar's Battalion. **Wounded.**

Brooks, Leonidas L. – Private, Company K, 45ᵗʰ Virginia Infantry. **Captured** and sent to the Atheneum Prison, at Wheeling, then to Camp Chase, Ohio,

May 30, 1862. Described as being 20 years of age, 5 feet 10 inches tall, having a florid complexion, dark brown hair and blue eyes; resident of Morgan County, Kentucky. Exchanged August 25, 1862.

Brown, Joseph Rufus – 1st Sergeant, Company B, 45th Virginia Infantry. **Wounded** in hand, slight.

Brown, John Steward – Private, Company B, 22nd Virginia Infantry. **Wounded & Captured**. Remained at Lewisburg, and was paroled at Lewisburg, June 8, 1862. Rescued by the 8th Virginia Cavalry.

Brown, William C. – Private, Company D, Edgar's Battalion. **Wounded & Captured**. Remained at Lewisburg, no prisoner of war records. Described as being 18 years of age, 5 feet 9 inches, having a light complexion, light hair and grey eyes, a farmer residing in Greenbrier County.

Brown, William M. – Citizen of Alleghany County. **Arrested** in Alleghany County, May 17, 1862. Claims to have done nothing wrong. Thought to be a Moccasin Ranger, a source of much trouble to Union men. On May 21, 1862, Geo. W. Wolf, a native of Philadelphia and an employee on the Covington & Ohio Railroad, testified that he frequently saw Brown in Alleghany Pass, going to the camp of the Moccasin Rangers; that the neighborhood considered him to be a bushwhacker. After the news of the Union army arrival at Lewisburg, Wolf heard Brown say that he would go into the bushes and shoot the Yankees as they passed. Sent to the Atheneum Prison, at Wheeling, then to Camp Chase, Ohio, May 30, 1862. Described as being 36 years of age, 6 feet tall, having a fair complexion, black hair and brownish grey eyes, a light mustache; resident of Alleghany County. No further record.

Bryant, Harrison – Private, Company D, 22nd Virginia Infantry. **Killed**. Resident of Nicholas County.

Burdett, George Washington – Private, Company A, 22nd Virginia Infantry. **Captured** and sent to the Atheneum Prison, at Wheeling, then to Camp Chase, Ohio, May 30, 1862. Described as being 22 years of age, 5 feet 11 inches tall, having a fair complexion, brown hair and grey eyes, sandy whiskers; resident of Monroe County. Exchanged August 25, 1862.

Buzzard, Andrew J. – Private, Company B, Edgar's Battalion. **Wounded & Captured; Died of Wounds** at Lewisburg, May 30, 1862. Resident of Greenbrier County.

Caldwell, Andrew F. – Private, Company C, Edgar's Battalion. **Captured** and sent to the Atheneum Prison, at Wheeling, then to Camp Chase, Ohio, May 30, 1862. Described as being 24 years of age, 5 feet 11 inches tall, having a dark complexion, black hair and dark eyes, black whiskeers; resident of Mercer County. Exchanged August 25, 1862.

Campbell, Andrew Nelson – Sergeant, Bryan's Battery. **Wounded** through right ankle, slight. His daughter, Nannie Campbell, recorded the following incident: After Andrew N. Campbell was wounded in the retreat, he was lying helpless on the ground. A large gray mare came along with the bridle reins dragging on the ground, and Campbell grabbed them. He pulled himself up onto his left foot and was attempting to mount the horse, when a large man of a Tazewell company came rapidly by. Without a word, he grabbed Campbell (a large man, weighing nearly 250 pounds) and threw him onto the horse. At the top of the hill, he overtook some of his company with a caisson. They took him off the horse and put him onto the caisson, until they could find an ambulance. At Union, two doctors removed the bullet from his ankle, and sent Campbell on to a hospital in Montgomery County.

Campbell, John F. – 2nd Lieutenant, Company D, 22nd Virginia Infantry. **Captured** and sent to the Atheneum Prison, at Wheeling, then to Camp Chase, Ohio, May 30, 1862. Described as being 5 feet 9 inches tall, having a dark complexion, dark hair and dark eyes; resident of Nicholas County. Sent to Johnson's Island, Sandusky, Ohio, July 3, 1862. Sent to Vicksburg, Mississippi, September 1, 1862 to be exchanged on the Steamer Jno. H. Done. Arrived at Vicksburg, September 20, 1862. Declared exchanged at Aiken's Landing, Virginia on November 10, 1862.

Campbell, John H. – Private, Company K, 22nd Virginia Infantry. **Captured** and sent to the Atheneum Prison, at Wheeling, then to Camp Chase, Ohio, May 30, 1862. Described as being 23 years of age, 5 feet 7 ½ inches tall, having a light complexion, sandy hair and blue eyes, sandy whiskers; resident of Monroe County. Exchanged August 25, 1862.

Carrico (Caraco), William A. – Private, Company C, 8th Virginia Cavalry. **Wounded & Captured** and sent to the Atheneum Prison, at Wheeling, then to Camp Chase, Ohio, May 30, 1862. Described as being 24 years of age, 5 feet 8 inches tall, having a fair complexion, dark hair and blue eyes, light whiskers; resident of Grayson County. Pension record states he was wounded in the right ankle while running from the Yankees at Lewisburg. Exchanged August 25, 1862.

Carson, Martin V. B. – Private, Company K, 22nd Virginia Infantry. **Captured** and sent to the Atheneum Prison, at Wheeling, then to Camp Chase, Ohio, May 30, 1862. Described as being 24 years of age, 6 feet 4 inches tall, having a light complexion, black hair and dark eyes, dark whiskers; resident of Monroe County. Exchanged August 25, 1862.

Casto, Isaac J. – Private, Company B, 22nd Virginia Infantry. **Wounded & Captured**. No prisoner of war records. Compiled Service Record and Union list of wounded prisoners as proof.

Cauley, George – Private, Company C, Edgar's Battalion. **Wounded, Captured, Died of Wounds** at Lewisburg, May 27, 1862. Resident of Monroe County.

Chambers, Robert – Private, Company I, 22nd Virginia Infantry. **Wounded, Captured, Died of Wounds** at Lewisburg, date unknown.

Chandler, William T. – Private, Company D, Edgar's Battalion. Also as Vawter's Battery. **Wounded & Captured**, sent to a hospital at Charleston, then to Gallipolis, Ohio, arriving there June 11, 1862 for treatment of a gunshot wound. Sent to the Atheneum Prison at Wheeling, July 2, 1862, then to Camp Chase, Ohio, arriving there July 8, 1862. Exchanged August 25, 1862.

Chase, Ben – Captain, Company B, 22nd Virginia Infantry. **Killed**, shot through the heart, fell on his face. Resident of Jackson County.

Chewning, Andrew J. "Jack" – Private, Company __, 22nd Virginia Infantry. **Arrested** in Alleghany County, May 18, 1862. Sent to the Atheneum Prison at Wheeling, then to Camp Chase, Ohio, May 30, 1862. Described as being 25 years of age, 6 feet ½ inch tall, having a dark complexion, dark hair, and brown eyes, sandy whiskers; resident of Braxton County. Sent to Wheeling on June 8, 1862 for trial, and returned to Camp Chase on June 25, 1862. Exchanged August 25, 1862.

Chewning, Charles L. – Private, Company H, 22nd Virginia Infantry. **Killed** by friendly artillery fire. Resident of Kanawha County.

Cock, S. D. – Corporal, Company I, 45th Virginia Infantry. **Killed**.

Conley, Joseph H. – Private, Company I, 50th Virginia Infantry. **Wounded & Captured**, thigh broken. No prisoner of war records found. Described as being 24 years of age, 5 feet 10 inches tall, having a dark complexion, dark hair and hazel eyes, a miller residing in Bland County.

Connelly, Russell F. – Private, Company __, 8th Virginia Cavalry. **Captured** and sent to the Atheneum Prison, at Wheeling, then to Camp Chase, Ohio, May 30, 1862. Described as being 42 years of age, 5 feet 11 inches tall, having a dark complexion, grey hair, and blue eyes, grey whiskers; resident of Pulaski County. Exchanged August 25, 1862.

Cook, Samuel H. – Private, Company D, 22nd Virginia Infantry. **Wounded & Captured**, no prisoner of war records. Appears on list of wounded prisoners compiled at Lewisburg.

Copenhaver, Thomas – Private, Company A, 8th Virginia Cavalry. **Wounded**.

Cox, George Lafayette – Private, Company I, 45th Virginia Infantry. **Captured** and sent to the Atheneum Prison, at Wheeling, then to Camp Chase, Ohio, May 30, 1862. Described as being 21 years of age, 5 feet 7 inches tall, having a fair complexion, red hair and grey eyes; resident of Carroll County. Exchanged August 25, 1862.

Crawford, Samuel Owen – Citizen of Alleghany County. **Arrested** in Alleghany County, May 19, 1862, charged with aiding the Rebels. Sent to the Atheneum Prison, at Wheeling, then to Camp Chase, Ohio, May 30, 1862. Described as being 16 years of age, 5 feet 9 ½ inches tall, having a fair complexion, brown hair and brown eyes; resident of Alleghany County. Released on oath of allegiance, August 25, 1862. Brother to William T. Crawford.

Crawford, William T. – Citizen of Alleghany County. **Arrested** in Alleghany County, May 19, 1862, says he has done nothing wrong. Sent to the Atheneum Prison, at Wheeling, then to Camp Chase, Ohio, May 30, 1862. Described as being 22 years of age, 5 feet 10 ¾ inches tall, having a fair complexion, black hair and blue eyes; resident of Alleghany

County. Released on oath of allegiance, August 25, 1862, by order of the Commissary General of Prisoners. Brother to Samuel Owen Crawford.

Creager, Calvin R. – Private, Company I, 45th Virginia Infantry. **Captured** and sent to the Atheneum Prison, at Wheeling, then to Camp Chase, Ohio, May 30, 1862. Described as being 25 years of age, 6 feet 1 inch tall, having a dark complexion, black hair and grey eyes, light brown whiskers on his chin; resident of Wythe County. Exchanged August 25, 1862.

Daugherty, Edward A. – Private, Company G, 22nd Virginia Infantry. **Wounded**. Described as being 19 years of age. Sent to Montgomery White Sulphur Springs for treatment.

Davis, John M. – Private, Company B, Edgar's Battalion. **Captured** and sent to the Atheneum Prison, at Wheeling, then to Camp Chase, Ohio, May 30, 1862. Resident of Greenbrier County. Exchanged August 25, 1862.

Dehart, John – Private, Bryan's Battery. **Wounded** in arm, just above wrist of left hand. Described as being 25 years of age, 5 feet 9 inches tall, having a dark complexion, dark hair and blue eyes, a farmer residing in Monroe County.

Dillworth, Joseph W. – Private, Company B, 22nd Virginia Infantry. **Captured** and sent to the Atheneum Prison, at Wheeling, then to Camp Chase, Ohio, May 30, 1862. Described as being 21 years of age, 5 feet 8 inches tall, having a light complexion, brown hair and hazel eyes, a light beard; resident of Jackson County. Exchanged August 25, 1862.

Dillworth, Josiah S. – Private, Company B, 22nd Virginia Infantry. **Captured** and sent to the Atheneum Prison, at Wheeling, then to Camp Chase, Ohio, May 30, 1862. Described as being a resident of Jackson County. Exchanged August 25, 1862.

Dodd, Lorenzo R. – 1st Lieutenant, Company I, 22nd Virginia Infantry. **Captured** and sent to the Atheneum Prison, at Wheeling, then to Camp Chase, Ohio, May 30, 1862. Described as being 29 years of age, 5 feet 11 inches tall, having a fair complexion, black hair and dark eyes, black whiskers; resident of Craig County. Exchanged August 25, 1862.

Dyche, Elijah – Private, Company A, 22nd Virginia Infantry. **Captured** and sent to the Atheneum Prison, at Wheeling, then to Camp Chase, Ohio, May

30, 1862. Described as being 36 years of age, 5 feet 9 inches tall, having a fair complexion, dark brown hair and black eyes, sandy whiskers, dark on the chin; resident of Greenbrier County. Exchanged August 25, 1862.

Eagle, William J. – Private, Company B, 59th Virginia Infantry. Also as Edgar's Battalion. **Captured** and sent to the Atheneum Prison, at Wheeling, then to Camp Chase, Ohio, May 30, 1862. Described as being 33 years of age, 6 feet 1 inch tall, having a dark complexion, black hair and grey eyes, dark whiskers; resident of Greenbrier County. Exchanged August 25, 1862.

East, Charles W. – Private, Company C, 59th Virginia Infantry. Also as Edgar's Battalion. **Killed**. Resident of Pittsylvania County.

Edgar, George M. – Major, Edgar's Battalion. **Wounded & Captured**, shot in the chest (breast), severe. The *Richmond Whig* reports that after Edgar was wounded that four or five Yankees rushed him and would have bayoneted him had not their captain drawn his revolver and kept them off. "This shows what savages we are fighting." Taken to the home of a relative, John Withrow, and cared for. This house is now a part of the General Lewis Inn. Rescued by Confederate Cavalry in June 1862. No prisoner of war records, other than appearing on the list of wounded prisoners.

Elkins, Joseph – Private, Company I, 50th Virginia Infantry. **Wounded**.

Elkins, Ralph (Rafe, Rufus) – Private, Company I, 50th Virginia Infantry. **Wounded & Captured**, sent to a hospital in Charleston, then to Gallipolis, Ohio, arriving there June 11 1862, for treatment of a gunshot wound. Released and sent to the Atheneum Prison, at Wheeling, July 14, 1862, and then to Camp Chase, Ohio, arriving there on July 22, 1862. Described as being 28 years of age, having a fair complexion, light hair and blue eyes; resident of Pulaski County. Exchanged August 25, 1862.

Ellison, Lewis A. – Private, Company C, 59th Virginia Infantry. Also as Edgar's Battalion. **Captured** and sent to the Atheneum Prison, at Wheeling, then to Camp Chase, Ohio, May 30, 1862. Described as being 22 years of age, 6 feet 4 ½ inches tall, having a dark complexion, black hair and grayish hazel eyes, a light mustache and black whiskers; resident of Monroe County. Exchanged August 25, 1862.

Engles (Ingalls), Lewis – Private, Unit Unknown. **Wounded, Captured, Died of Wounds** at Lewisburg, May 23, 1862. Described as being age 34.

Evans, Moab – Private, Company F, 50th Virginia Infantry. **Captured** and sent to the Atheneum Prison, at Wheeling, then to Camp Chase, Ohio, May 30, 1862. Described as being a resident of Augusta County. Exchanged August 25, 1862.

Fall, B. F. – Private, Company B, 22nd Virginia Infantry. **Wounded & Captured.** No prisoner of war records. Probably died of his wounds.

Farmer, Alexander – Private, Company F, 50th Virginia Infantry. **Killed.** Resident of Bedford County.

Finney, Randolph H. – Captain, Assistant Adjutant General, Heth's Staff. **Wounded** in the side, not dangerously. Brother of William W. Finney.

Finney, William Wood – Lieutenant Colonel, 50th Virginia Infantry, commanding Edgar's Battalion. **Captured** and sent to the Atheneum Prison, at Wheeling, then to Camp Chase, Ohio, May 30, 1862. Described as being 33 years of age, 5 feet 9 inches tall, having a fair complexion, black hair and dark grey eyes, black whiskers; resident of Powhatan County. Sent to Johnson's Island Prison, Sandusky, Ohio, July 3, 1862. Sent to Vicksburg, Mississippi for exchange, September 1, 1862. Finney, an 1848 graduate of the Virginia Military Institute, was one of the co-founders of the Pony Express.

Firestone, William L. – Private, Company I, 22nd Virginia Infantry. **Captured** and sent to the Atheneum Prison, at Wheeling, then to Camp Chase, Ohio, May 30, 1862. Described as being 18 years of age, 5 feet 8 inches tall, having a light complexion, dark brown hair and light eyes; resident of Botetourt County. Exchanged August 25, 1862.

Flack, Samuel Jr. – Private, Company D, Edgar's Battalion. **Wounded, Captured & Died of Wounds** at Lewisburg, May 23, 1862.

Flint, James Joseph – Private, Company C, Edgar's Battalion. **Captured** and sent to the Atheneum Prison, at Wheeling, then to Camp Chase, Ohio, May 30, 1862. Described as being 25 years of age, 5 feet 10 inches tall, having a light complexion, brown hair and grey eyes, dark whiskers on the chin; resident of Greenbrier County. **Died of Disease** at Camp Chase Prison, September 16, 1862.

Flint, Samuel D. – Private, Company C, Edgar's Battalion. **Captured** and sent to the Atheneum Prison, at Wheeling, then to Camp Chase, Ohio, May 30, 1862. Described as being 27 years of age, 5 feet 11 inches tall, having a light complexion, dark hair and grey eyes, sandy whiskers; resident of Greenbrier County. Exchanged August 25, 1862.

Fowler, Allen – Private, Lowry's Battery. **Wounded**, badly.

Gillaspie, George P. – Private, Company B, 22nd Virginia Infantry. **Captured** and sent to the Atheneum Prison, at Wheeling, then to Camp Chase, Ohio, May 30, 1862. Described as being 23 years of age, 5 feet 7 ½ inches tall, having a dark complexion, dark hair and blue eyes, dark whiskers; resident of Jackson County. Sent to Johnson's Island Prison, Sandusky, Ohio, September 6, 1862. Sent to Vicksburg, Mississippi for exchange, November 22, 1862 on board the Steamer Charm. Arrived at Vicksburg, December 8, 1862.

Given, Samuel – Private, Company K, 22nd Virginia Infantry. **Captured** and sent to the Atheneum Prison, at Wheeling, then to Camp Chase, Ohio, May 30, 1862. Described as being 21 years of age, 5 feet 11 inches tall, having a dark complexion, black hair and light blue eyes, dark whiskers; resident of Alleghany County. **Died of Disease** at Camp Chase Prison, July 26, 1862.

Gooch, Benjamin Porter – Private, Company I, 59th Virginia Infantry. Also as Edgar's Battalion. **Wounded** in the face. Resident of Summers County.

Goodman, John E. – Private, Company B, 45th Virginia Infantry. **Wounded**, in the right shoulder, sent home to Wythe County to recover.

Graham, Lanty J. – Private, Company A, 22nd Virginia Infantry. **Captured** and sent to the Atheneum Prison, at Wheeling, then to Camp Chase, Ohio, May 30, 1862. Described as being 20 years of age, 5 feet 10 inches tall, having a fair complexion, mouse color hair, and dark grey eyes, light mustache; resident of Monroe County. Exchanged August 25, 1862.

Gray, Osborn W. – Private, Company B, 59th Virginia Infantry. Also as Edgar's Battalion. **Captured** and sent to the Atheneum Prison, at Wheeling, then to Camp Chase, Ohio, May 30, 1862. Described as being 28 years of age, 5 feet 7 inches tall, having a dark complexion, black hair and greenish grey eyes, dark whiskers; resident of Floyd County. Exchanged August 25, 1862.

Gray, William T. – Private, Company C, Edgar's Battalion. **Captured** and sent to the Atheneum Prison, at Wheeling, then to Camp Chase, Ohio, May 30, 1862. Described as being 33 years of age, 5 feet 11 ½ inches tall, having a fair complexion, black hair and grey eyes, sandy whiskers; resident of Monroe County. Exchanged August 25, 1862.

Griffith, Isaac – Private, Company I, 8th Virginia Cavalry. Also as 50th Virginia Infantry. **Captured** and sent to the Atheneum Prison, at Wheeling, then to Camp Chase, Ohio, May 30, 1862. Described as being 36 years of age, 5 feet 11 inches tall, having a light complexion, dark hair and light eyes, sandy whiskers; resident of Pulaski County. No additional details.

Grubb, John A. – Private, Company C, 45th Virginia Infantry. **Wounded & Died of Wounds** at Pearisburg, June 15, 1862.

Gunn, William – Private, Company I, 50th Virginia Infantry. **Captured** and sent to the Atheneum Prison, at Wheeling, then to Camp Chase, Ohio, May 30, 1862. Described as being 20 years of age, 5 feet 4 ½ inches tall, having a light complexion, dark hair, and grey eyes; resident of Pulaski County. Exchanged August 25, 1862.

Hall, Henry L. – Private, Company G, 22nd Virginia Infantry. **Captured** in Alleghany County, May 17, 1862. Sent to the Atheneum Prison, at Wheeling, the to Camp Chase, Ohio, May 30, 1862. Described as being 48 years of age, 5 feet 10 inches tall, having a fair complexion, grey hair and brown eyes, grey whiskers; resident of Nicholas County. Exchanged August 25, 1862.

Hall, John W. – Private, Unit Unknown. **Wounded & Captured**. No prisoner of war records, but does appear on a list of wounded prisoners at Lewisburg. Probably died.

Hamilton, Samuel D. – Private, Company A, 22nd Virginia Infantry. **Captured** and sent to the Atheneum Prison, at Wheeling, then to Camp Chase, Ohio, May 30, 1862. Described as being 18 years of age, 5 feet 11 inches tall, having a dark complexion, mouse color hair and hazel eyes; resident of Alleghany County, Maryland. Exchanged August 25, 1862.

Hanger, John Henry – Private, Company B, Edgar's Battalion. **Wounded, Captured & Died of Wounds**. Shot in the hip and died of wounds at Lewisburg, June 13, 1862.

Hansbarger, William T. – Private, Company D, Edgar's Battalion. **Wounded & Captured**, sent to a hospital in Charleston, then to Gallipolis, Ohio, arriving there June 11, 1862 for treatment of a gunshot wound. Sent to Wheeling, July 2, 1862, then to Camp Chase Prison, where he arrived on July 8, 1862. Described as being 18 years of age, 5 feet 7 inches tall, having a fair complexion, dark brown hair and brown eyes; resident of Roanoke County. Exchanged August 25, 1862.

Harlow, Benjamin F. – Private, Greenbrier Cavalry. **Captured** at Lewisburg, May 12, 1862, and sent the guard house at Charleston; there on May 15, 1862; then was sent to the Atheneum Prison, at Wheeling, then to Camp Chase, Ohio, May 30, 1862. Described as being 27 years of age, 5 feet 9 ¼ inches tall, having a light complexion, light hair and grey eyes, light whiskers; resident of Greenbrier County. No addition details.

Harman, Edwin H. – Captain, Company H, 45th Virginia Infantry. **Wounded** in right breast, grazed by a bullet on left leg, at top of his boot, and bruised on the right arm.

Harris, William A. – Private, Company A, 22nd Virginia Infantry. **Captured** and sent to the Atheneum Prison, at Wheeling, then to Camp Chase, Ohio, May 30, 1862. Described as being a resident of Monroe County. Exchanged August 25, 1862.

Harrison, John – Private, Unit Unknown. **Wounded & Captured**, no prisoner of war records, but does appear on a list of wounded prisoners at Lewisburg.

Hebsel, Philip M. – Private, Company E, Edgar's Battalion. **Killed**. Described as being 21 years of age, 5 feet 11 inches tall, having a fair complexion, fair hair and blue eyes, a farmer residing in Pocahontas County.

Hefner, Franklin "Frank" – Private, Company E, Edgar's Battalion. **Killed**.

Hefner, James F. – Private, Company E, Edgar's Battalion. **Wounded** in shoulder. Described as being 20 years of age, 6 feet 2 inches tall, having a dark complexion, dark hair and brown eyes; a farmer residing in Pocahontas County.

Hefner, William D. – Captain, Company E, Edgar's Battalion. **Wounded, Captured, Died of Wounds**, shot in the thigh, crushing the bone; died at Lewisburg, June 1, 1862.

Hendrickson, John – Private, Company C, 22nd Virginia Infantry. **Captured** and sent to the Atheneum Prison, at Wheeling, then to Camp Chase, Ohio, May 30, 1862. Described as being 27 years of age, 6 feet tall, having a dark complexion, dark hair and grey eyes, dark whiskers; resident of Nicholas County. Exchanged August 25, 1862.

Hereford, James – Private, Company E, 8th Virginia Cavalry. **Wounded**, right eye shot out, though to be mortal, but survived.

Hickman, George R. – Private, Company D, 22nd Virginia Infantry. **Captured** and sent to the Atheneum Prison, at Wheeling, then to Camp Chase, Ohio, May 30, 1862. Described as being 22 years of age, 5 feet 4 inches tall, having a fair complexion, black hair and grey eyes, light mustache; resident of Nicholas County. Exchanged August 25, 1862.

Hicks (Hix), Andrew J. – Private, Company B, 22nd Virginia Infantry. Also as Edgar's Battalion. **Wounded & Captured**, wounded severely. Sent to a hospital at Charleston, then to Gallipolis, Ohio, arriving there June 11, 1862 for treatment of a gunshot wound. Sent to Camp Chase Prison, September 18, 1862. Described as being 19 years of age, 5 feet 7 inches tall, having a dark complexion, dark hair and hazel eyes; resident of Greenbrier County. No further details.

Hill, John J. – Private, Company __, Edgar's Battalion. **Captured** and sent to the Atheneum Prison, at Wheeling, then to Camp Chase, Ohio, May 30, 1862. Described as being 20 years of age, 5 feet 6 inches tall, having a dark complexion, dark hair, and black eyes; light whiskers; resident of Monroe County. Exchanged August 25, 1862.

Hodson (Hudson), Henry R. – Private, Company D, 59th Virginia Infantry. Also as Edgar's Battalion. **Captured** and sent to the Atheneum Prison, at Wheeling, then to Camp Chase, Ohio, May 30, 1862. Described as being 25 years of age, 5 feet 10 inches tall, having a light complexion, dark hair, and grey eyes, a dark beard; resident of Greenbrier County. Exchanged August 25, 1862.

Holderby, George W. – 1st Lieutenant, Company E, 8th Virginia Cavalry. **Wounded** at the Greenbrier River bridge on the morning of May 23, 1862.

Holliday, Charles Turner – Private, Company D, Edgar's Battalion. **Captured** and sent to the Atheneum Prison, at Wheeling, then to Camp Chase, Ohio,

May 30, 1862. Described as being 23 years of age, 5 feet 8 inches tall, having a light complexion, brown hair and blue eyes; a farmer residing in Greenbrier County. Exchanged August 25, 1862.

Honiker, Peter Augustus C. – Private, Company I, 50th Virginia Infantry. **Captured** and sent to the Atheneum Prison, at Wheeling, then to Camp Chase, Ohio, May 30, 1862. Described as being a resident of Pulaski County. Possibly wounded. Exchanged August 25, 1862.

Huddle, Eli – Private, Company B, 45th Virginia Infantry. **Wounded** in the right thigh. Resident of Wythe County.

Hume, William H. H. – Private, Greenbrier Cavalry. **Captured** at Lewisburg, May 12, 1862. Confined in the guard house at Charleston, May 15, 1862. Sent to the Atheneum Prison, at Wheeling, then to Camp Chase, Ohio, May 30, 1862. Described as being 21 years of age, 6 feet 2 ½ inches tall, having a dark complexion, dark hair and blue eyes; resident of Greenbrier County. Exchanged August 25, 1862.

Humphreys, Matthew N. – Private, Company D, Edgar's Battalion. **Captured** and sent to the Atheneum Prison, at Wheeling, then to Camp Chase, Ohio, May 30, 1862. Described as being 18 years of age, 5 feet 4 inches tall, having a fair complexion, dark hair and blue eyes, few and light whiskers; resident of Greenbrier County. Remained behind to care for his twin brother, Robert Humphreys who had been wounded. Exchanged August 25, 1862.

Humphreys, Milton W. – Lieutenant, Bryan's Battery. **Arrested** near White Sulphur Springs, May 16, 1862. Humphreys was very sick at the time, and Colonel George Crook paroled him, as it was considered too dangerous to move him.

Humphreys, Robert – Private, Company D, Edgar's Battalion. **Wounded, Captured, & Died of Wounds** at Lewisburg, May 24, 1862. Age 18 years, 6 months. Twin brother of Matthew N. Humphreys.

Hurst, Zacariah – Private, Company I, 50th Virginia Infantry. **Killed.**

Huse, Harlow – Private, Company K, 22nd Virginia Infantry. **Captured** and sent to the Atheneum Prison, at Wheeling, then to Camp Chase, Ohio, May 30, 1862. Described as being 28 years of age, 5 feet 8 ½ inches tall, having a dark complexion, dark hair with grey mixture, hazel eyes, a thin, dark beard; resident of Fayette County. Exchanged August 25, 1862.

Ingalls – See Engles

Jackson, William – Private, Unit Unknown. **Wounded & Captured**. No prisoner of war records, but does appear on a list of wounded prisoners at Lewisburg.

Jesse, Joseph B. – Private, Company B, 22nd Virginia Infantry. **Wounded & Captured**. Shot in the ankle. No prisoner of war records found; Compiled Service Record states he was wounded, captured, and later discharged. Described as being 21 years of age, 5 feet 8 inches tall, having a fair complexion, light hair and black eyes; a student, born in Caroline County.

Johns, James C. – 1st Lieutenant, Company B, 22nd Virginia Infantry. **Captured** and sent to the Atheneum Prison, at Wheeling, then to Camp Chase, Ohio, May 30, 1862. Described as being 26 years of age, 5 feet 11 ½ inches tall, having a dark complexion, dark hair and greyish blue eyes, dark whiskers; resident of Jackson County. Sent to Johnson's Island Prison, Sandusky, Ohio, July 3, 1862. Sent to Vicksburg, Mississippi for exchange September 1, 1862 on board the Steamer Jno. H. Done. Arrived at Vicksburg September 20, 1862, and declared exchanged at Aiken's Landing, Virginia, November 10, 1862.

Johnson, Collins J. – Private, Company F, 22nd Virginia Infantry. **Captured** and sent to the Atheneum Prison, at Wheeling, then to Camp Chase, Ohio, May 30, 1862. Described as being a resident of Louisa County. Exchanged August 25, 1862.

Johnson, Henry J. – Private Company F, 22nd Virginia Infantry. **Wounded & Captured** and sent to the Atheneum Prison, at Wheeling, then to Camp Chase, Ohio, May 30, 1862. Described as being 30 years of age, 5 feet 11 inches tall, having a fair complexion, light hair and grey eyes; a resident of Louisa County. Exchanged August 25, 1862.

Johnson, John M. – Private, Unit Unknown. **Wounded & Captured**, no prisoner of war records, but does appear on a list of wounded prisoners at Lewisburg.

Johnson, Mathew A. – Private, Greenbrier Cavalry. **Captured** at Lewisburg, May 12, 1862. Confined at the guard house in Charleston, May 15, 1862. Sent to the Atheneum Prison, at Wheeling, then to Camp Chase, Ohio, May 30, 1862. Described as being 20 years of age, 5 feet 8 ½ inches tall, having a light complexion, light hair and grey eys; a resident of Greenbrier County. Exchanged August 25, 1862.

Johnson, Miles A. – Private, Company __, 22nd Virginia Infantry. **Killed**, shot through the temple.

Jones, Joseph Warren – Sergeant, Company K, 22nd Virginia Infantry. **Killed**. There is a poem about him in the Richmond Dispatch, June 13,1862, page 2.

Keyser, Andrew S. – Private, Company G, 22nd Virginia Infantry. **Captured** and sent to the Atheneum Prison, at Wheeling, then to Camp Chase, Ohio, May 30, 1862. Described as being 29 years of age, 6 feet 1 inch tall, having a dark complexion, dark hair and blue eyes, sandy whiskers; a resident of Alleghany County. Exchanged August 25, 1862.

Kidd, John M. – Private, Company F, 8th Virginia Cavalry. **Captured** and sent to the Atheneum Prison, at Wheeling, then to Camp Chase, Ohio, May 30, 1862. Described as being 32 years of age, 5 feet 9 inches tall, having a florid complexion, light hair and grey eyes, red whiskers; resident of Bland County. No other details.

Kimbleton (Kembleton), John Henry – Private, Vawter's Battery. Also as Edgar's Battalion. **Killed**.

Kinder (Neider), John G. – Private, Company B, 45th Virginia Infantry. **Captured** and sent to the Atheneum Prison, at Wheeling, then to Camp Chase, Ohio, May 30, 1862. Described as being 21 years of age, 5 feet 9 inches tall, having a light complexion, dark hair and blue eyes, dark whiskers; resident of Bland County. Exchanged August 25, 1862.

King, Chapman – Private, Company I, 50th Virginia Infantry. Also as 8th Virginia Cavalry. **Captured** and sent to the Atheneum Prison, at Wheeling, then to Camp Chase, Ohio, May 30, 1862. Described as being 20 years of age, 5 feet 10 inches tall, having a dark complexion, dark hair and hazel eyes; resident of Pulaski County. Exchanged August 25, 1862.

Laidley, Richard S. – Captain, Company H, 22ⁿᵈ Virginia Infantry. **Wounded** in arm.

Lawson, Peter – Private, Company I, 50ᵗʰ Virginia Infantry. **Wounded, Captured & Died of Wounds**, probably at Lewisburg, date unknown. No prisoner of war records found, but does appear on a list of wounded prisoners at Lewisburg.

Leach, Joshua – Private, Bryan's Battery. **Killed**.

Lindsey, James S. – Private, Company I, 50ᵗʰ Virginia Infantry. **Missing in Action**, no prisoner of war records, presumed killed.

Linthicum, Daniel A. – Private, Company D, 59ᵗʰ Virginia Infantry. Also as Edgar's Battalion. **Captured** and sent to the Atheneum Prison, at Wheeling, then to Camp Chase, Ohio, May 30, 1862. Described as being 30 years of age, 5 feet 3 ½ inches tall, having a dark complexion, black hair and black eyes, black whiskers; resident of Greenbrier County. Released August 25, 1862 on oath of allegiance by order of the Commissary General of Prisoners.

Lipps, Joseph H. – Private, Company B, 22ⁿᵈ Virginia Infantry. **Wounded**.

Lollis, William E. – Private, Company B, 22ⁿᵈ Virginia Infanatry. **Captured** and sent to the Atheneum Prison, at Wheeling, then to Camp Chase, Ohio, May 30, 1862. Described as being 32 years of age, 5 feet 10 ½ inches tall, having a dark complexion, dark hair and light blue eyes, brown whiskers; resident of Botetourt County. Exchanged August 25, 1862. Possibly wounded slightly.

Looney, Alexander C. – Private, Company K, 22ⁿᵈ Virginia Infantry. **Wounded** in right shoulder. Resident of Craig County.

Lowdermilk (Lowderbach), James – Private, Company F, 22ⁿᵈ Virginia Infantry. **Captured** and sent to the Atheneum Prison, at Wheeling, then to Camp Chase, Ohio, May 30, 1862. Described as being a resident of Greenbrier County. Exchanged August 25, 1862.

Lowry, Samuel B. – Private, Company E, 59ᵗʰ Virginia Infantry. Also as Edgar's Battalion. **Captured** and sent to the Atheneum Prison, at Wheeling, then to Camp Chase, Ohio, May 30, 1862. Described as being 18 years of age,

5 feet 6 ½ inches tall, having a light complexion, dark hair and grey eyes; resident of Greenbrier County. Exchanged August 25, 1862.

Lugar, John A. – Private, Company C, 22nd Virginia Infantry. **Wounded** in left hip. Resident of Craig County.

Lykens (Likens), James E. – Private, Company C, 22nd Virginia Infantry. **Captured** and sent to the Atheneum Prison, at Wheeling, then to Camp Chase, Ohio, May 30, 1862. Described as being 32 years of age, 5 feet 8 ¾ inches tall, having a dark complexion, black hair and hazel eyes, black whiskers; resident of Fayette County. Exchanged August 25, 1862.

Lyons (Lynn), W. Harrison H. – Private, Company A, 59th Virginia Infantry. Also as Edgar's Battalion. **Captured** and sent to the Atheneum Prison, at Wheeling, then to Camp Chase, Ohio, May 30, 1862. Described as being 35 years of age, 5 feet 5 inches tall, having a fair complexion, black hair and grey eyes, sandy whiskers; resident of Carroll County. Exchanged August 25, 1862.

Maddy, Elisha V. – Private, Company C, Edgar's Battalion. **Wounded, Captured, Died of Wounds** at Lewisburg, May 26, 1862. Resident of Monroe County.

Magan, Darias M. – Private, Chapman's Battery. **Captured** and sent to the Atheneum Prison, at Wheeling, then to Camp Chase, Ohio, May 30, 1862. Described as being 30 years of age, 6 feet ½ inch tall, having a dark complexion, mouse color hair and light blue eyes, dark whiskers; resident of Monroe County. Exchanged August 25, 1862.

Mahoney, John C. – Private, Company B, 22nd Virginia Infantry. **Captured** and sent to the Atheneum Prison, at Wheeling, then to Camp Chase, Ohio, May 30, 1862. Described as being a resident of Greenbrier County. Exchanged August 25, 1862.

Mann, John A. – Private, Chapman's Battery. **Wounded**. Resident of Monroe County.

Marshall, Alvin (Alvis) S. – Private, Company I, 50th Virginia Infantry. **Wounded & Captured**, shot in left thigh and both ankles. Sent to a hospital in Charleston, then to Gallipolis, Ohio, arriving there June 11, 1862 for treatment of a gunshot wound. Sent to the Atheneum Prison, at Wheeling, arriving there November 10, 1862. Transferred to Camp Chase, Ohio, arriving on November 13, 1862. Described as being 20 years of age, 5 feet 7 ½ inches tall, having a fair complexion, black hair and dark eyes, sandy whiskers; resident of Carroll County. Sent to Cairo, Illinois November 20, 1862 to be exchanged. Received at Vicksburg, Mississippi onboard the Steamer Charm, December 8, 1862. Pension record show wounds to the right ankle joint, left ankle and the left leg.

Marshall, Calvin – Private, Company I, 50th Virginia Infantry. **Wounded, Captured & Died of Wounds**.

Marshall, Joseph Nathan – Private, Company I, 50th Virginia Infantry. **Wounded & Captured**, shot in the left side of his face. Was sent to a hospital in Charleston, then to Gallipolis, Ohio, arriving there on June 11, 1862 for treatment of a gunshot wound. Described as being 26 years of age, 5 feet 7 inches tall, having a dark complexion, dark hair and dark eyes; resident of Carroll County. Sent to the Atheneum Prison, at Wheeling, arriving there November 10, 1862. Transferred to Camp Chase, Ohio, arriving there November 13, 1862. Sent to Cairo, Illinois November 20, 1862 to be exchanged. Arrived at Vicksburg, Mississippi onboard the Steamer Charm, December 8, 1862.

Martin, Thomas – Private, Company B, 22nd Virginia Infantry. **Wounded**.

Mason, Thomas L. – 1st Lieutenant, Company A, 22nd Virginia Infantry. **Wounded, Captured & Died of Wounds** most likely at Lewisburg, date not known. Name appears on a list of wounded prisoners at Lewisburg.

Mays, Jesse D. – Private, Company D, 22nd Virginia Infantry. **Wounded, Captured & Died of Wounds**, most likely at Lewisburg, June 8, 1862.

Meadows, Granville C. – Private, Company I, 59th Virginia Infantry. Also as Edgar's Battalion. **Captured** and sent to the Atheneum Prison, at Wheeling, then to Camp Chase, Ohio, May 30, 1862. Described as being 23 years of age, 5 feet 8 inches tall, having a light complexion, dark brown hair and blue eyes, black whiskers; resident of Monroe County. Exchanged August 25, 1862.

Miller, George W. – Private, Company I, 59th Virginia Infantry. Also as Edgar's Battalion. **Captured** and sent to the Atheneum Prison, at Wheeling, then to Camp Chase, Ohio, May 30, 1862. Described as being 19 years of age,

5 feet 8 inches tall, having a light complexion, light hair and grey eyes; resident of Mercer County. Exchanged August 25, 1862.

Mills, William F. – Private, Company B, 59th Virginia Infantry. Also as Edgar's Battalion. **Captured** and sent to the Atheneum Prison, at Wheeling, then to Camp Chase, Ohio, May 30, 1862. Described as being 30 years of age, 5 feet 10 inches tall, having a dark complexion, black hair and hazel eyes, dark whiskers; resident of Monroe County. Exchanged August 25, 1862.

Mitchell, John Wesley – Private, Company I, 50th Virginia Infantry. **Wounded & Captured**. Sent to a hospital at Charleston, then to Gallipolis, Ohio, arriving there June 11, 1862 for treatment of a gunshot wound. Sent to the Atheneum Prison, at Wheeling, July 14, 1862, and then to Camp Chase, Ohio, arriving there July 22, 1862. Exchanged August 25, 1862.

Mitchell, Stephen W. – Private, Company I, 8th Virginia Cavalry. Also as 50th Virginia Infantry. **Wounded & Captured**, shot in side of head, not badly. Sent to the Atheneum Prison, at Wheeling, then to Camp Chase, Ohio, May 30, 1862. Described as being 24 years of age, 5 feet 11 inches tall, having a fair complexion, black hair and blue eyes, light and scattering whiskers; resident of Carroll County.

Montgomery, Abner – Private, Company C, 59th Virginia Infantry. Also as Edgar's Battalion. **Wounded, Captured & Died of Wounds** at Lewisburg, May 25, 1862. Resident of Carroll County.

Morgan, Enoch H. – Private, Company B, Edgar's Battalion. Also listed as Virginia Artillery. **Captured** and sent to the Atheneum Prison, at Wheeling, then to Camp Chase, Ohio, May 30, 1862. Described as being a resident of Greenbrier County. Exchanged August 25, 1862.

Morris (Morse), Augustus – Private, Company E, Edgar's Battalion. Also as Atkin's Battalion. **Wounded & Captured**, sent to a hospital in Charleston, then to Gallipolis, Ohio, arriving there June 11, 1862 for treatment of a gunshot wound. Sent to the Atheneum Prison, at Wheeling, July 14, 1862, and then to Camp Chase, Ohio, arriving there July 22, 1862. Described as being 21 ½ years of age, having a fair complexion, dark hair and grey eyes, dark whiskers; resident of Monroe County. Exchanged August 25, 1862.

Morrison, Fountain – Citizen of Alleghany County. **Arrested** in Alleghany County, May 18, 1862, charged with being a bushwhacker. Colonel

George Crook testified that Morrison was found on the road with gun in hand, waylaying the road. Sent to Camp Chase, Ohio, May 30, 1862. Described as being 62 years of age, 5 feet 6 inches tall, having a dark complexion, black hair, turning grey, and greenish grey eyes, a mustache and black whiskers on his chin; resident of Alleghany County. Released on oath of allegiance November 19, 1862, by order of the Secretary of War.

Muncy, Van B. – Private, Company D, 22nd Virginia Infantry. **Wounded, Captured & Died of Wounds**, probably at Lewisburg, on October 5, 1862.

Murray, Patrick (Park) – Private, Company K, 22nd Virginia Infantry. **Wounded & Captured**, shot through the thigh. Sent to a hospital at Charleston, then to Gallipolis, Ohio, arriving there June 11, 1862 for treatment of a gunshot wound. Sent to Camp Chase, July 14, 1862, arrived there on July 22, 1862. Described as being 22 years of age, having a fair complexion, black hair and dark brown eyes; a resident of Fayette County. Exchanged August 25, 1862.

McAlexander, John – Company D, 51st Virginia Infantry. **Wounded & Captured**, shot in the right hip, destroying the right testicle. No prisoner of war records; Compiled Service Record states wounded and captured. Resident of Patrick County.

McCutcheon, George – Private, Company C, 22nd Virginia Infantry. **Captured**, no prisoner of war records found; Compiled Service Record states he was taken at Lewisburg.

McCutcheon, William T. – Private, Company D, 22nd Virginia Infantry. **Wounded & Captured**. No prisoner of war records, but does appear on a list of wounded prisoners.

McDermott, Charles – Private, Company D, 22nd Virginia Infantry. **Killed**.

McKinney, James H. – Private, Company G, 22nd Virginia Infantry. **Wounded & Captured**, shot in the thigh. Sen to a hospital at Charleston, then to Gallipolis, Ohio, arriving there June 11, 1862 for treatment of a gunshot wound. **Died of Wounds** at Gallipolis, Ohio, June 19, 1862, and is buried in the Pine Street Cemetery in Gallipolis; one of four Confederates buried there.

McKinney, James M. – Private, Company D, 22nd Virginia Infantry. Also as Edgar's Battalion and Virginia Artillery. **Captured** and sent to the Atheneum Prison, at Wheeling, then to Camp Chase, Ohio, May 30, 1862. Described as being 23 years of age, 5 foot 8 ¾ inches tall, having a dark complexion, black hair and hazel eyes; resident of Greenbrier County. Exchanged August 25, 1862.

McKnight, George – Private, Company G, 22nd Virginia Infantry. **Wounded, Captured & Died of Disease**. Shot in both thighs and sent to a hospital at Charleston, then to Gallipolis, Ohio, arriving there June 11, 1862 for treatment of a gunshot wound. Died at Gallipolis, Ohio of consumption, date not known.

Neighbors, Wilson – Private, Company K, 22nd Virginia Infantry. Name sometimes appears as Wilson Abers. **Wounded & Captured**, sent to a hospital at Charleston, then to Gallipolis, Ohio, arriving there on June 11, 1862. Described as being 47 years of age, 5 feet 7 ½ inches tall, having a fair complexion, sandy hair and blue eyes, sandy whiskers; resident of Monroe County. Sent to the Atheneum Prison, at Wheeling, July 2, 1862, and then to Camp Chase, Ohio, where he arrived on July 22, 1862. Exchanged August 25, 1862, and later admitted to the Montgomery White Sulphur Springs hospital.

Neil, James M. – Private, Company D, Edgar's Battalion. Also as Edgar's Virginia Artillery. **Captured** and sent to the Atheneum Prison, at Wheeling, then to Camp Chase, Ohio, May 30, 1862. Described as being 33 years of age, 5 feet 10 inches tall, having a dark complexion, brown hair and blue eyes, sandy whiskers; resident of Monroe County. Exchanged August 25, 1862.

Neil, William H. H. – Private, Company D, 22nd Virginia Infantry. **Captured** and sent to the Atheneum Prison, at Wheeling, then to Camp Chase, Ohio, May 30, 1862. Described as being 21 years of age, 5 feet 9 ½ inches tall, having a dark complexion, black hair and blue eyes, dark whiskers; resident of Nicholas County. Exchanged August 25, 1862.

Nichols, Jesse – Private, Company I, 50th Virginia Infantry. **Wounded & Captured**, shot in the right shoulder joint. Sent to a hospital at Charleston, then to Gallipolis, Ohio, arriving there on June 11, 1862. Described as being 22 years of age, 5 feet 7 inches tall, having a fair complexion, dark hair and blue eyes; a farmer living in Carroll County. Sent to the Atheneum

Prison, at Wheeling, and then to Camp Chase, Ohio, where he arrived November 13, 1862. Transferred to Cairo, Illinois November 20, 1862 to be exchanged.

Oiler, John A. – Private, Company D, 59th Virginia Infantry. Also as Edgar's Battalion. **Captured** and sent to the Atheneum Prison, at Wheeling, then to Camp Chase, Ohio, May 30, 1862. Described as being 19 years of age, 5 feet 9 ¼ inches tall, having a fair complexion, dark brown hair and dark grey eyes; resident of Greenbrier County. Exchanged August 25, 1862.

Old, Thomas J. – Private, Company B, 22nd Virginia Infantry. **Wounded & Captured**, shot in the left arm. Described as being 32 years of age, 6 feet 1 inches tall, having a fair complexion, dark hair and blue eyes; a farmer living in Botetourt County. No prisoner of war records found, but his name does appear on a list of wounded prisoners at Lewisburg. Pension records states that escaped from the enemy at Lewisburg.

Orr, John S. – Private, Unit Unknown. **Wounded & Captured**, no prisoner of war records found, but his name appears on a list of wounded prisoners at Lewisburg. Name could be Ott or Opp.

Otey, George Gaston – Captain, Otey's Battery. **Wounded**, shot in the shoulder. **Died of Wounds** at Lynchburg, October 21, 1862.

Ott, Addison – Private, Company A, 22nd Virginia Infantry. **Killed**.

Ott, Jewit – Private, Company A, 22nd Virginia Infantry. **Wounded, Captured & Died of Wounds**, at Lewisburg, August 20, 1862.

CAPTAIN GEORGE G. OTEY
Virginia Military Institute Archives

Oyler (Oiler), Miles P. – Private, Company D, 59th Virginia Infantry. Also as Edgar's Battalion. **Captured** and sent to the Atheneum Prison, at Wheeling, then to Camp Chase, Ohio, May 30, 1862. Described as being 17 years of age,

5 feet 7 ½ inches tall, having a florid complexion, dark brown hair and blue eyes; resident of Greenbrier County. Exchanged August 25, 1862.

Parker, Samuel – Private, Company __, 22nd Virginia Infantry. **Wounded, Captured & Died of Wounds**, at Lewisburg, May 23, 1862. Age 19.

Perkins, Joseph R. – Private, Company E, 59th Virginia Infantry. Also as Edgar's Battalion. **Captured** and sent to the Atheneum Prison, at Wheeling, then to Camp Chase, Ohio, May 30, 1862. Described as being 19 years of age, 5 feet 7 inches tall, having a light complexion, light hair and grey eyes; resident of Greenbrier County. Exchanged August 25, 1862.

Perry, Henry E. – Private, Company B, 59th Virginia Infantry. Also as Edgar's Battalion. **Captured** and sent to the Atheneum Prison, at Wheeling, then to Camp Chase, Ohio, May 30, 1862. Described as being 23 years of age, 6 feet 1 inch tall, having a light complexion, light hair and hazel eyes; resident of Greenbrier County. Exchanged August 25, 1862.

Powell, Washington A. J. – Private, Company D, 22nd Virginia Infantry. **Killed**.

Rader, Adam S. – Private, Company B, 22nd Virginia Infantry. **Wounded, Captured & Died of Wounds**, shot in the thigh. Was sent to a hospital at Charleston, then to Gallipolis, Ohio, arriving there June 11, 1862, admitted under the name of Baden. Died of consumption at Gallipolis, Ohio, July 16, 1862, and buried in the Pine Street Cemetery there. The following letter was sent to his family in Botetourt County, Virginia: "Aug. 19, 1862. [died] of an affection of the lungs. He was wounded and taken prisoner at Battle of Lewisburg but wound had healed. He would have fully recovered if lungs had been sound. He was well cared for in every respect and died happy. His dying message to you all was that he hoped to meet you all in heaven. He is decently buried in this place. I have seen him many times in the hospital and speak advisedly when I say that he wanted for nothing to make him comfortable. I enclose you a lock of his hair. Respectfully, Mrs. M. M. Cushing."[522]

Radford, Henry – Private, Company H, 22nd Virginia Infantry. **Killed** early in the battle.

Rand, Noyes – Lieutenant, Adjutant, 22nd Virginia Infantry. **Captured** and sent to the Atheneum Prison, at Wheeling, then to Camp Chase, Ohio, May

---

522 The Gallia County Glade, Vol. 33, No. 4, Winter 2008

30, 1862. Described as being 22 years of age, 5 feet 6 ¼ inches tall, having a dark complexion, black hair and dark eyes, dark whiskers on his chin; resident of Charleston, Kanawha County. Parents (Mr. & Mrs. W. J. Rand) visited their son at Camp Chase and commented that he was being well treated. Appealed to Brig. Gen. J. D. Cox on June 27, 1862 for Noyes' release to them. Request denied. Sent to Johnson's Island Prison, Sandusky, Ohio, July 3, 1862. Sent to Vicksburg, Mississippi September 1, 1862, to be exchanged. Arrived at Vicksburg onboard the Steamer Jno. H. Done, September 20, 1862. Declared exchanged at Aiken's Landing, Virginia, November 10, 1862.

Ratliff (Radcliffe), Owen – Private, Company D, 22nd Virginia Infantry. **Wounded & Captured**, shot in the leg. Sent to the Atheneum Prison, at Wheeling, arriving there July 10, 1862. Dr. Frissell extracted the ball from Ratliff's leg on July 15, 1862, using chloroform. Sent to Camp Chase, August 29, 1862. Described as being 18 years of age, 5 feet 7 inches tall, having a fair complexion, light hair and grey eyes; resident of Nicholas County. Sent to Johnson's Island Prison, Sandusky, Ohio, September 6, 1862, to be exchanged. Sent to Vicksburg, Mississippi, November 22, 1862, onboard the Steamer Charm. Arrived at Vicksburg, December 8, 1862.

Remley, Mason – Private, Company D, 22nd Virginia Infantry. **Captured** and sent to the Atheneum Prison, at Wheeling, then to Camp Chase, Ohio, May 30, 1862. Described as being 21 years of age, 5 feet 10 inches tall, having a dark complexion, dark hair and dark eyes; resident of Nicholas County. Exchanged August 25, 1862.

Repass, James Walter – Private, Company B, 45th Virginia Infantry. **Killed**.

Rhodes, [first name unknown] – Private, Unit Unknown. **Wounded, Captured & Died of Wounds**. Private John T. Booth, 36th Ohio Infantry, related that after the battle of Lewisburg, he and several others visited the Confederate wounded in the hospital. He observed one man who made an effort to hide his face, and discovered that the man was named Rhodes. This man had been a guide for the Union army in March 1862, and had abandoned them and carried information to Confederate forces. Booth noted that Rhodes died soon after from the effects of his wounds.

Rhodes, Christopher – Private, Company D, 22nd Virginia Infantry. **Wounded & Captured**. Sent to a hospital at Charleston, then to Gallipolis, Ohio, arriving there June 11, 1862, for treatment of a gunshot wound. Described as being 20 years of age, 5 feet 11 inches tall, having a fair complexion, dark hair and dark eyes; a farmer living in Greenbrier County. Sent to the Atheneum Prison, at Wheeling, arriving there July 5, 1862, then to Camp Chase Prison, arriving there July 8, 1862. Exchanged August 25, 1862.

Rollins, Joseph – Private, Company A, 22nd Virginia Infantry. **Wounded**, shot through the face (both cheeks).

Rouk, George Washington – Private, Company E, Edgar's Battalion. **Wounded, Captured & Died of Wounds** at Lewisburg, June 16, 1862. No prisoner of war records, but name appears on a list of wounded prisoners at Lewisburg.

Sandridge, William H. "Bud" – Private, Company K, 22nd Virginia Infantry. **Killed**.

Saunders, William – Private, Company A, 22nd Virginia Infantry. **Killed**.

Showver, William C. – Private, Company C, 22nd Virginia Infantry. **Captured** and sent to the Atheneum Prison, at Wheeling, then to Camp Chase, Ohio, May 30, 1862. Described as being 29 years of age, 5 feet 10 inches tall, having a florid complexion, sandy hair and blue eyes, sandy whiskers; resident of Greenbrier County. Exchanged August 25, 1862.

Shumate, James H. – Private, Company F, 22nd Virginia Infantry. **Wounded**, shot in the knee joint.

Simmons, William R. – 2nd Corporal, Company K, 22nd Virginia Infantry. **Wounded**, sent to Montgomery White Sulphur Springs to recover.

Simpson, Andrew J. – Citizen of Alleghany County. **Arrested** in Alleghany County, May 18, 1862, charged with aiding the Rebels. Colonel George Crook testified that Simpson was found running bullets for a body of bushwhackers. Sent to the Atheneum Prison, at Wheeling, then to Camp Chase, Ohio, May 30, 1862. Described as being 33 years of age, 5 feet 10 inches tall, having a fair complexion, dark hair and brown eyes, black whiskers; resident of Alleghany County. Took the oath of allegiance and was released December 27, 1862, by order of the Secretary of War.

Singleton, Albert R. – Private, Company B, 22nd Virginia Infantry. **Captured** and sent to the Atheneum Prison, at Wheeling, then to Camp Chase, Ohio,

May 30, 1862. Described as being 19 years of age, 5 feet 11 ½ inches tall, having a dark complexion, black hair and hazel eyes, black whiskers; a resident of Campbell County, Kentucky. Exchanged August 25, 1862.

Smith, Ballard Jr. – Citizen of Greenbrier County. **Arrested** at Lewisburg, May 12, 1862. James F. Byers, 2nd West Virginia Cavalry testified that he captured Smith "in arms against the government of the United States, as he was passing along a fence with rifle in hand and an abundant supply of ammunition on his person." Another man, James Nichols, testified that Smith "fired his gun once and reloaded to us it against the Federal troops." Sent to the Atheneum Prison, at Wheeling, then to Camp Chase, Ohio, May 30, 1862. Described as being 40 years of age, 5 feet 8 ½ inches tall, having a dark complexion, dark hair and blue eyes; resident of Greenbrier County. Released on oath of allegiance, December 29, 1862.

Smith, Isaac – Private, Company I, 50th Virginia Infantry. **Wounded**, in the leg. Resident of Carroll County.

Smith, James Calvin – Private, Company I, 50th Virginia Infantry. **Wounded & Captured**, shot in the leg. Sent to a hospital at Charleston, then to Gallipolis, Ohio, arriving there June 11, 1862, for treatment of a gunshot wound. Described as being 27 years of age, having a fair complexion, black hair and grey eyes, black whiskers; resident of Carroll County. Sent to the Atheneum Prison, at Wheeling, July 14, 1862, then to Camp Chase, Ohio, arriving there July 22, 1862. Exchanged August 25, 1862.

Smith, John O. – Private, Company A, 22nd Virginia Infantry. **Wounded & Captured**. Sent to a hospital at Charleston, then to Gallipolis, Ohio, arriving there June 11, 1862, for treatment of a gunshot wound. Described as being 34 years of age, 5 feet 8 inches tall, having a dark complexion, dark hair and blue eyes; a farmer living in Putnam County. Sent to the Atheneum Prison, at Wheeling, July 2, 1862, then to Camp Chase, Ohio, arriving there on July 8, 1862. Exchanged August 25, 1862.

Smith, Richard – Private, Company K, 8th Virginia Cavalry. **Captured** and sent to the Atheneum Prison, at Wheeling, then to Camp Chase, Ohio, May 30, 1862. Described as being 20 years of age, 6 feet 1 inch tall, having a light complexion, light hair and blue eyes; resident of Wayne County. Exchanged August 25, 1862.

Smith, Westley (Wesley) – Private, Company I, 50th Virginia Infantry. **Wounded & Captured**, shot in the shoulder. Sent to the Atheneum Prison, at Wheeling, then to Camp Chase, Ohio, May 30, 1862. Described as being a resident of Carroll County. Exchanged August 25, 1862.

Smith, William Leander – Private, Company I, 50th Virginia Infantry. **Wounded & Captured**, shot in the right leg. Sent to a hospital at Charleston, then to Gallipolis, Ohio, arriving there June 11, 1862, for treatment of a gunshot wound. Described as being 19 ½ years of age, 5 feet 10 ¼ inches tall, having a dark complexion, brown hair and grey eyes; resident of Carroll County. Sent to the Atheneum Prison, at Wheeling, July 2, 1862, then to Camp Chase, Ohio, arriving there July 8, 1862. Exchanged August 25, 1862.

Snow, Preston H. – Private, Company I, 50th Virginia Infantry. **Wounded & Captured**, shot through the right shoulder. Sent to a hospital at Charleston, then to Gallipolis, Ohio, arriving there June 11, 1862, for treatment of a gunshot wound. Described as being 18 ½ years of age, 5 feet 3 ½ inches tall, having a fair complexion, brown hair and hazel eyes; a farmer living in Carroll County. Sent to the Atheneum Prison, at Wheeling, July 2, 1862, then to Camp Chase, Ohio, arriving there July 8, 1862. Exchanged August 25, 1862.

Sprigg (Spriggs), John S. – Captain, Company B, Virginia Rangers. **Captured** in Alleghany County on May 16, 1862. Sent to the Atheneum Prison, at Wheeling, then to Camp Chase, Ohio, May 30, 1862. Described as being 29 years of age, 5 feet 11 inches tall, having a light complexion, light hair and grey eyes, a red beard; resident of Braxton County. Was sent to Johnson's Island Prison, Sandusky, Ohio, July 3, 1862. Sent to Vicksburg, Mississippi, November 20, 1862 to be exchanged. Arrived at Vicksburg onboard the Steamer Charm, December 8, 1862.

Sprowl, William B. – Citizen of Greenbrier County. **Arrested** near White Sulphur Springs, May 19, 1862. Sprowl was the superintendent of the turnpike company, and claimed to have done nothing wrong. George W. Wolf, a brick mason working on the Virginia Central Railroad testified on May 21, 1862, that on May 16th, Sprowl informed two scouts of the Moccasin Rangers that the Union men were coming, giving the number and route of the cavalry and infantry. Sprowl also threatened Union men, saying those who voted for the Union, he would tar and feather. Sent to the

Atheneum Prison, at Wheeling, then to Camp Chase, Ohio, May 30, 1862. Described as being 47 years of age, 5 feet 7 ½ inches tall, having a dark complexion, dark grey hair and dark eyes, short dark grey beard; a resident of Greenbrier County. On July 7, 1862, a petition signed by 51 citizens of Greenbrier County was presented to Colonel Crook, asking for Sprowl's release, stating that Sprowl is an honest man of integrity. Crook wrote that he knew some of the men who signed the petition, and believes them to be loyal men. On November 23, 1862, Crook wrote the Provost Marshal General, Major Joseph Darr, Jr., regarding the petition, and stating that the evidence against Sprowl is false; that he is a loyal man. After taking the oath of allegiance on December 5, 1862, Sprowl was released.

Stevenson, William – Private, Company I, 50th Virginia Infantry. **Killed**.

Stone, Thomas Ingram – Private, Company E, Edgar's Battalion. **Wounded, Captured & Died of Wounds**, at Lewisburg, May 27, 1862. Wounded in the back by a bayonet. Stone was taking cover in a fence corner during the battle, shooting through the rails at Union troops. A Union soldier sneaked up behind him and stabbed Stone with his bayonet. Stone's son, Allen, tried to shoot the soldier, but his gun would not fire. Stone was taken to the Old Stone Church, which was being used as a hospital.

Stull, George L. – Private, Company A, 22nd Virginia Infantry. **Wounded & Captured**. Sent to a hospital at Charleston, then to Gallipolis, Ohio, arriving there June 11, 1862, for treatment of a gunshot wound. Described as being 23 years of age, 5 feet 7 ½ inches tall, having a fair complexion, dark hair and hazel eyes; resident of Alleghany County. Sent to the Atheneum Prison, at Wheeling, July 2, 1862, and then to Camp Chase, Ohio, arriving there July 8, 1862. Exchanged August 25, 1862.

Suter, Mortimer W. – Private, Company B, 22nd Virginia Infantry. **Captured** and sent to the Atheneum Prison, at Wheeling, then to Camp Chase, Ohio, May 30, 1862. Described as being 26 years of age, 5 feet 5 inches tall, having a light complexion, black hair and blue eyes, brown whiskers; resident of Brooke County. Exchanged August 25, 1862.

Sutphin, Elijah – Private, Company I, 50th Virginia Infantry. **Captured** and sent to the Atheneum Prison, at Wheeling, then to Camp Chase, Ohio, May 30, 1862. Described as being 32 years of age, 5 feet 10 inches tall, having a light complexion, sandy hair and blue eyes, sandy whiskers; resident of Carroll County. Exchanged August 25, 1862.

Sutphin, Henson (Henderson) – Private, Vawter's Battery. Also as 22nd Virginia Infantry. **Killed**. Resident of Monroe County.

Sutton, William – Private, Company I, 50th Virginia Infantry. **Wounded**.

Taylor, James W. – Private, Company F, 50th Virginia Infantry. **Killed**. Born in Amherst County.

Taylor, John J. – Private, Company A, 22nd Virginia Infantry. **Wounded & Captured**. Sent to the Atheneum Prison, at Wheeling, where he arrived July 10, 1862. Described as being 23 years of age, 5 feet 10 inches tall, having a fair complexion, black hair and grey eyes; a farmer and resident of Putnam County. Sent to Camp Chase, Ohio, arriving there on July 14, 1862. Exchanged August 25, 1862.

Taylor, John W. – Sergeant, Company F, 22nd Virginia Infantry. **Wounded & Died of Wounds**. Died May 31, 1862, place unknown.

Taylor, William J. "Bill" – Private, Company K, 22nd Virginia Infantry. **Wounded & Captured**, shot through thigh. Sent to a hospital at Charleston, then to Gallipolis, Ohio, arriving there June 11, 1862, for treatment of a gunshot wound. Described as being 20 years of age, 5 feet 9 ¾ inches tall, having a fair complexion, brown hair and hazel eyes; resident of Greenbrier County. Sent to the Atheneum Prison, at Wheeling, July 2, 1862, then to Camp Chase, Ohio, arriving there on July 8, 1862. Exchanged August 25, 1862.

Taylor, William T. – Private, Company D, 22nd Virginia Infantry. **Killed**.

Thomas, Joseph B. – Private, Company I, 22nd Virginia Infantry. **Captured** and sent to the Atheneum Prison, at Wheeling, then to Camp Chase, Ohio, May 30, 1862. Described as being 33 years of age, 5 feet 7 inches tall, having a dark complexion, black hair and hazel eyes, black beard; resident of Alleghany County. No additional records.

Thompson, John Koontz – Captain, Company A, 22nd Virginia Infantry. **Wounded & Captured**, had right eye shot out. Sent to a hospital at Charleston, where he was paroled and released on June 3, 1862. His father was a Union man, and applied for his parole and release.

Thompson, Nelson – Private, Company I, 50th Virginia Infantry. **Killed**.

Thompson, Thomas W. – Captain, Company C, Edgar's Battalion. **Wounded**, right knee and left thigh, badly.

Thrasher, Robert James – Private, Company I, 22nd Virginia Infantry. **Wounded, Captured & Died of Wounds**, shot in the thigh. Sent to a hospital at Charleston, then to Gallipolis, Ohio, arriving there June 11, 1862, for treatment of a gunshot wound. Described as being 29 years 10 months of age, 5 feet 10 inches tall, having a dark complexion, black hair and dark eyes, a farmer living in Botetourt County. Died at Gallipolis, Ohio, October 1, 1862. Buried in the Pine Street Cemetery, Gallipolis, Ohio, one of four Confederates buried there.

PRIVATE ROBERT J. THRASHER
Howard R. Hammond

Tincher, Christopher L. – Private, Company A, 22nd Virginia Infantry. **Wounded & Captured**, no prisoner of war records. Name appears on a list of wounded prisoners at Lewisburg.

Triplett, Marshall – Captain, Virginia Rangers. **Captured** in Alleghany County, May 17, 1862, while on recruiting service. Sent to the Atheneum Prison, at Wheeling, then to Camp Chase, Ohio, May 30, 1862. Described as being 46 years of age, 6 feet ½ inch tall, having a dark complexion, brown hair and blue eyes, grey beard; resident of Clay County. Sent to Johnson's Island Prison, Sandusky, Ohio, July 3, 1862. Sent to Vicksburg, Mississippi November 22, 1862 to be exchanged. Arrived at Vicksburg, December 8, 1862, onboard the Steamer Charm.

Tucker, John – Private, Company K, 22nd Virginia Infantry. **Wounded & Captured**, no prisoner of war records. Name appears on a list of wounded prisoners at Lewisburg.

Vance, Adam C. – Private, Bryan's Battery. **Wounded & Captured**, no prisoner of war records. Name appears on a list of wounded prisoners at Lewisburg.

Vass, Anderson C. – Private, Company C, Edgar's Battalion. **Wounded**, shot in the left let.

Vaught, Stephen R. – Company B, 45th Virginia Infantry. **Killed**.

Warren, Burruss – Private, Company F, 50th Virginia Infantry. **Wounded & Captured**, no prisoner of war records. Name appears on a list of wounded prisoners at Lewisburg.

Warren, Larkin – Private, Company F, 50th Virginia Infantry. **Killed**.

Watson, Joseph – Private, Company E, 59th Virginia Infantry. Also as Edgar's Battalion. **Captured** and sent to the Atheneum Prison, at Wheeling, then to Camp Chase, Ohio, May 30, 1862. Described as being 35 years of age, 5 feet 7 ½ inches tall, having a dark complexion, dark hair and blue eyes, black whiskers; resident of Greenbrier County. Exchanged August 25, 1862.

Wethered, Pere (Perry) B. – Citizen of Greenbrier County. **Arrested** at Lewisburg, May 12, 1862, charged with bushwhacking for being armed. Sent to the Atheneum Prison, at Wheeling, then to Camp Chase, Ohio, May 30, 1862. Described as being 70 years of age, 5 feet 9 inches tall, having a fair complexion, grey hair and grey eyes, grey beard; a resident of Greenbrier County. Released on oath of allegiance, November 4, 1862, by order of the Secretary of War, and directed to report to Governor Pierpont at Wheeling.

Wetzel, George W. – Bugler, Bryan's Battery. **Captured** and sent to the Atheneum Prison, at Wheeling, then to Camp Chase, Ohio, May 30, 1862. Described as being a resident of Greenbrier County. Exchanged August 25, 1862.

White, John T. – Private, Company E, Edgar's Battalion. **Wounded & Captured**. Sent to a hospital at Charleston, then to Gallipolis, Ohio, arriving there June 11, 1862 for treatment of a gunshot wound. Described as being 19 years of age, 5 feet 11 inches tall, having a dark complexion, brown hair and blue eyes, a farmer living in Greenbrier County. Sent to the Atheneum Prison, at Wheeling, July 2, 1862, then to Camp Chase, Ohio, arriving there, July 8, 1862. Exchanged August 25, 1862.

Wickle, George C. – Private, Vawter's Battery. Also as Edgar's Battalion. **Captured** and sent to the Atheneum Prison, at Wheeling, then to Camp Chase, Ohio, May 30, 1862. Described as being a resident of Monroe County. Exchanged August 25, 1862.

Wickline, M. R. – Private, Company __, 22nd Virginia Infantry. **Wounded**, shot through the foot, amputated.

Wickline, William F. – Private, Company __, 50th Virginia Infantry. **Wounded, Captured & Died of Wounds**, shot in the forehead. Sent to a hospital at Charleston, then to Gallipolis, Ohio, arriving there June 11, 1862 for treatment of a gunshot wound. Died at Gallipolis, Ohio, of wounds, June 15, 1862. Buried in the Pine Street Cemetery as W. Z. Wickline; one of four Confederates buried there.

Williams, David Franklin – Private, Company B, 22nd Virginia Infantry. **Captured** and sent to the Atheneum Prison, at Wheeling, then to Camp Chase, Ohio, May 30, 1862. Described as being 25 years of age, 5 feet 8 inches tall, having a fair complexion, light hair and blue eyes, sandy whiskers; resident of Greenbrier County. Released after taking the oath of allegiance, August 14, 1862.

Williams, E. C. – Private, Unit Unknown. **Wounded & Captured**, no prisoner of war records. Name appears on a list of wounded Confederates at Lewisburg.

Williams, J. W. – Private, Company B, 22nd Virginia Infantry. **Captured** at Lewisburg, May 12, 1862. Sent to the Atheneum Prison, at Wheeling, then to Camp Chase, Ohio, May 30, 1862. No additional details.

Williams, James H. – Private, Company E, 22nd Virginia Infantry. **Captured** and sent to the Atheneum Prison, at Wheeling, then to Camp Chase, Ohio, May 30, 1862. Described as being 18 years of age, 5 feet 6 inches tall, having a fair complexion, light hair and grey eyes; resident of Greenbrier County. Exchanged August 25, 1862.

Wilson, Samuel J. – Private, Company K, 22nd Virginia Infantry. **Captured** and sent to the Atheneum Prison, at Wheeling, then to Camp Chase, Ohio, May 30, 1862. Described as being 34 years of age, 5 feet 8 inches tall, having a dark complexion, black hair and hazel eyes, black whiskers: resident of Fayette County. Exchanged August 25, 1862.

Withrow, A. W. – Private, Company A, 22nd Virginia Infantry. **Wounded & Captured**. No prisoner of war records. Name appears on a list of wounded prisoners at Lewisburg.

Withrow, Nathaniel W. – Private, Company A, 22nd Virginia Infantry. **Wounded**.

Workman, Claiborne – Private, Company __, 22nd Virginia Infantry. **Wounded**. Resident of Monroe County.

Workman, John A. – Private, Company H, 45th Virginia Infantry. **Captured** and sent to the Atheneum Prison, at Wheeling, then to Camp Chase, Ohio, May 30, 1862. Described as being 21 years of age, 5 feet 5 ¾ inches tall, having a dark complexion, light hair and grey eyes; resident of Tazewell County. Exchanged August 25, 1862.

Workman, Slaven – Private, Company __, Edgar's Battalion. **Killed**.

Workman, William C. – Private, Company D, 59th Virginia Infantry. Also as Edgar's Battalion. **Wounded & Died of Wounds**, at Lewisburg, May 23, 1862.

Wright (Right), James N. – Private, Company A, 59th Virginia Infantry. Also as Edgar's Battalion. **Wounded, Captured & Died of Wounds**, died at Lewisburg, May 27, 1862. Resident of Monroe County.

Wyatt, William H. – Private, Company A, 22nd Virginia Infantry. **Captured** and sent to the Atheneum Prison, at Wheeling, then to Camp Chase, Ohio, May 30, 1862. Described as being 22 years of age, 5 feet 7 inches tall, having a fair complexion, light hair and grey eyes, sandy whiskers; resident of Greenbrier County. Sent to Johnson's Island Prison, Sandusky, Ohio, September 6, 1862. Sent to Vicksburg, Mississippi, November 22, 1862 to be exchanged. Arrived at Vicksburg, December 8, 1862, onboard the Steamer Charm.

Unidentified Solder – Letter of Lt. Henrie H. Alexander mentions a soldier at Salt Sulphur Springs that was wounded. Most likely a member of Co. H, 51st Virginia Infantry.

THE UNION
CASUALTIES

Records for the casualties in the Union Army, naturally, are more complete. Despite that fact, some names are omitted from the "official" record, usually for soldiers whose wounds were not severe enough to make the lists. The descriptions of the wounds are mostly taken from the records prepared by the surgeons, and now preserved at the National Archives.

Albaugh, Patrick – See William Allspaugh

Alkire, Jacob C. – Corporal, Company H, 36th Ohio Infantry. **Captured** at the Greenbrier River bridge while on picket duty on the morning of May 23, 1862. Confined at Richmond, May 30, 1862. Released and sent to Salisbury, North Carolina, June 3, 1862.

Allen, Levi – Private, Company D, 36th Ohio Infantry. **Wounded & Died of Wounds**. Shot in the neck. When other wounded were sent to the rear, Allen remained. He was "suffering from a loathsome disease before he was wounded, which naturally complicates his case, and renders his recovery doubtful." Died of wounds at Charleston, June 1, 1862.

Allen, William – Private, Company K, 36th Ohio Infantry. Name also as William Alton. **Wounded**, shot in scalp (top of head), slightly.

Allspaugh, William – Private, Company B, 44th Ohio Infantry. **Killed**, shot in the forehead and died on the battlefield. Buried at Lewisburg, then later moved to the Staunton National Cemetery.

Alt, Adam S. – Private, Company F, 44th Ohio Infantry. **Killed**. Probably the first member of the 44th Ohio to be killed. Captain Israel Stough wrote to Adam's father: "It becomes my sad duty to inform you of the death of your son Adam, who fell pierced by a ten pound shell, through his body. **** But let it be your pride, that he died, yes, nobly died in defence [sic] of our much loved country and rest assured that he has been fully avenged, for as soon as I came in range of the battery, I directed the fire of my company immediately upon it, and charged, and I rejoice that Company F succeeded in carrying one splendid gun, caisson,

THE ALT BROTHERS,
44TH OHIO INFANTRY

Daniel, Adam, and James – Credit: Janie Martin Whitty, Eustis, Florida (deceased)

ammunition, and ten horses, from the grasp of their owners, and they now stand in pride before our quarters. Our regiment lost but six killed – two of which were from my company – your son Adam, and Francis M. Runyon, of Pleasant township, and three wounded. **** I have had Adam nicely washed and dressed, and he, with the rest of our glorious dead will be buried by the regiment, in one hour from this, and his grave properly marked, so that his remains may be found hereafter without difficulty."[523] Cannon ball passed through his abdomen. He lived for nearly an hour, fully conscious. Buried near Lewisburg, and later removed to the Staunton National Cemetery.

Anderson, John J. – Private, Company K, 36th Ohio Infantry. **Wounded**, shot in the arm and hand, slightly.

Ault, Andrew G. – Corporal, Company E, 36th Ohio Infantry. **Captured** at the Greenbrier River bridge while on picket duty on the morning of May

---

523   *Springfield Republic*, Springfield, Ohio, June 4, 1862

23, 1862. Confined at Richmond, May 30, 1862. Paroled and sent to Salisbury, North Carolina, June 3, 1862.

Baker, Michael – Private, Company D, 44th Ohio Infantry. **Wounded**, struck in the head by a piece of shell, bad wound, but will recover.

Barker, James – Private, Company E, 36th Ohio Infantry. **Wounded**, shot in right thumb, amputated. One account says "right thumb shot off."

Bennett, Gordon – Private, Company F, 36th Ohio Infantry. **Wounded**, slightly.

Berington, Samuel – Private, Company B, 44th Ohio Infantry. **Wounded**, shot through flesh behind right knee, slight. Treated with cold water and anodynes (a pain killer).

Brown, Edwin A. – Private, Company C, 36th Ohio Infantry. **Wounded**, forefinger of right hand shot off, but wanted to continue to fight. Sent to the general hospital at Gauley.

Brown, Edward A. – Private, Company E, 36th Ohio Infantry. **Wounded** shot in the right side, severely.

Cashon, Patrick – Private, Company D, 44th Ohio Infantry. **Wounded**, musket ball through muscles of right arm, penetrating the right breast, splintering the sixth rib slightly, exiting four inches in front, severe. Treated with Antipyretics (to reduce fever) and anodynes (pain killer).

Cassidy, Edward – Private, Company D, 44th Ohio Infantry. **Killed**, shot through sternum, died on the battlefield. Buried at Lewisburg, and later removed to the Staunton National Cemetery.

Cole, Thomas McD. – Private, Company K, 36th Ohio Infantry. **Killed**, shot in the heart, and died on the battlefield. Buried at Lewisburg, and later removed to the Staunton National Cemetery.

Conley, Hugh – Private, Company F, 36th Ohio Infantry. **Wounded**, shot in the leg, below the knee, fracturing the bones, severe.

Crook, George – Colonel, 36th Ohio Infantry. Commanding brigade at Lewisburg. **Wounded**, shot in left foot by a nearly spent ball.

Culver, James Alonzo – Private, Company C, 36th Ohio Infantry. **Killed**, shot in the heart, died on the battlefield. Wounded early in the battle. One account states that he was taken to the hospital and died there. Buried at Lewisburg, then later moved to the Staunton National Cemetery.

Daniels, John – Private, Company B, 2nd West Virginia Cavalry. **Captured** at Lewisburg on the morning of May 23, 1862, while on picket duty. Confined at Richmond, May 30, 1862. Released and sent to Salisbury, North Carolina, June 3, 1862.

Davis, Andrew – Private, Company A, 36th Ohio Infantry. **Wounded**, shot in the left arm, slightly.

Dotze, Augustus – Lieutenant, Company H, 44th Ohio Infantry. **Wounded**, shot in the finger.

Downey, Ashael – Private, Company K, 36th Ohio Infantry. **Wounded & Died of Wounds**, shot in the right breast, very sever, clavicle fractured. Sent to a hospital at Charleston, and died there of his wounds, June 10, 1862.

Dyer, Joseph – Corporal, Company A, 36th Ohio Infantry. **Wounded**, shot in the right thigh. Sent to the general hospital at Charleston. Is said to have told a lieutenant "don't stop for me Lieutenant, but give them fits."

Farrar, Asa – Corporal, Company K, 36th Ohio Infantry. **Wounded**, shot in the hand, slightly.

Faulkner, John T. – Private, Company B, 44th Ohio Infantry. **Wounded**, slightly.

Fields, Charles – Private, Company D, 44th Ohio Infantry. **Wounded & Died of Disease**, shot in the right knee joint, but did not injure the bones. The ball could not be found so it could be extracted. Sent to a hospital at Gauley Bridge on May 24, 1862, and died there of inflammation of the bowels on May 30, 1862.

Galliher, William – Corporal, Company E, 36th Ohio Infantry. **Wounded**, shot in the leg, slightly.

Gillmore, W. W. – Corporal, Company F, 36th Ohio Infantry. **Captured** at the Greenbrier River bridge while on picket duty on the morning of May 23, 1862. Confined at Richmond, May 30, 1862. Released and sent to Salisbury, North Carolina, June 3, 1862.

Glidden, James – Private, Company A, 36th Ohio Infantry. **Killed**, shot in the bowels, taken to the hospital and died there on May 23, 1862. Buried at Lewisburg, then later moved to the Staunton National Cemetery.

Goff, J. L. – Private, Company F, 44th Ohio Infantry. **Wounded**, slightly.

Goff, Sylvanus – Private, Company K, 36th Ohio Infantry. **Killed**, shot in the heart and died on the battlefield. Buried at Lewisburg, then later moved to the Staunton National Cemetery.

Grisso, Joseph – Private, Company F, 44th Ohio Infantry. **Wounded**, slightly.

Groves, Henry – Private, Company F, 36th Ohio Infantry. **Wounded & Died of Wounds**, shot in the breast, taken to the hospital, and died there on May 24, 1862. Buried at Lewisburg, then later moved to the Staunton National Cemetery.

Hale, Oscar – Private, Company D, 44th Ohio Infantry. **Wounded**, slight scratch on the leg, above the knee.

Hampton, John N. – Private, Company C, 36th Ohio Infantry. **Captured** at the Greenbrier River bridge while on picket duty on the morning of May 23, 1862. Confined at Richmond, May 30, 1862. Released and sent to Salisbury, North Carolina, June 30, 1862.

Harring, Eli – Private, Company C, 36th Ohio Infantry. **Captured** at the Greenbrier River bridge while on picket duty on the morning of May 23, 1862. **Died of Disease**, at Salisbury, North Carolina, July 4, 1862. Name as Hanning.

Harvey, Samuel W. – Sergeant, Company F, 36th Ohio Infantry. **Wounded**, shot in the right breast by a spent ball. Confined at Richmond, May 30, 1862, listed as Eli Hanning. Released and sent to Salisbury, North Carolina, June 30, 1862.

Hensley, John T. – Private, Company B, 44th Ohio Infantry. **Wounded**, slightly.

Houston, George W. – Private, Company C, 36th Ohio Infantry. **Wounded**, shot in the leg, slightly. Struck on the shin bone by a spent ball, not much injured.

Howell, S. C. – 2nd Lieutenant, Company D, 44th Ohio Infantry. **Wounded**, shot just above and on the inside of the left knee, ball passing upwards and toward the back, touching the femur. The ball lodged in his trousers. Treated with anodynes (pain killer).

Hupp, Elijah – Private, Company E, 36th Ohio Infantry. **Wounded**, both legs, slightly.

Jackson, Thomas P. – Private, Company A, 36th Ohio Infantry. **Wounded**, shot in the right thigh, not severe. Was the first to be wounded in the company, and after being wounded, he continued to load and shoot.

Kelly, John S. – Corporal, Company K, 36th Ohio Infantry. **Wounded**, shot in the finger, slightly.

Kiser, Amos N. – Private, Company E, 44th Ohio Infantry. **Wounded**, slightly.

Kline, Jacob – Private, Company C, 44th Ohio Infantry. **Wounded**, shot in the left thigh, flesh wound, not serious.

Laird, John – Private, Company K, 36th Ohio Infantry. **Wounded**, shot in the foot, slightly.

Langston, J. C. – Captain, Company B, 44th Ohio Infantry. **Wounded**, shot through the calf of the leg, not considered dangerous. Treated with cold water dressing and anodynes (pain killer).

Litteral, Samuel – Private, Company E, 44th Ohio Infantry. **Killed**, shot in the left breast, and died instantly on the battlefield. Buried at Lewisburg, then later moved to the Staunton National Cemetery.

Livingston, Samuel – Private, Company B, 44th Ohio Infantry. **Wounded**, slightly.

Long, George – Private, Company A, 36th Ohio Infantry. **Wounded**, left arm, severely. Sent to a hospital at Charleston.

Louthan, Oliver Perry – Private, Company F, 36th Ohio Infantry. **Wounded**, shot in the foot, slightly.

Love, Charles W. – Private, Company F, 36th Ohio Infantry. **Captured** at the Greenbrier River bridge while on picket duty on the morning of May

23, 1862. Confined at Richmond, May 30, 1862. Released and sent to Salisbury, North Carolina, June 23, 1862.

Louderback, Andrew – Private, Company D, 36th Ohio Infantry. **Wounded**, shot in the leg and right hand; one finger amputated. Severe.

Marsh, Amos – Private, Company D, 36th Ohio Infantry. **Wounded**, shot in the breast.

Martin, Charles – Sergeant, Company D, 36th Ohio Infantry. **Wounded**, shot in the left arm and hand, severely.

McClintock (McClintick), John O. – Private, Company D, 44th Ohio Infantry. **Wounded**, slightly.

McClung, William – Private, Company C, 36th Ohio Infantry. **Wounded**.

McClure, Dyer B. – Private, Company A, 36th Ohio Infantry. **Wounded & Died of Wounds**, shot in the left knee, badly. Sent to his home in Washington County, Ohio, and died there on June 18 or 19, 1862.

McDonald, Peter – Private, Company D, 36th Ohio Infantry. **Wounded**, shot in the right forearm, fracture, severe.

McVay, William – Private, Company C, 36th Ohio Infantry. **Wounded**, shot through the calf of the leg, not serious.

Musselman, Martin – Private, Company D, 44th Ohio Infantry. **Wounded**, shot in the arm, inside of left elbow. Arm elevated while in the act of shooting, and passed upwards, fracturing the humorous and lodging. Ball not removed. Treated with cold water and splints.

Nave, Jacob – Private, Company F, 44th Ohio Infantry. **Wounded**, slightly.

O'Conner, James – Private, Company K, 36th Ohio Infantry. **Wounded**, shot in the thigh, severe.

Pegg, Charles – Private, Company E, 44th Ohio Infantry. **Wounded**, shot through the calf of the leg, slight. Treated with cold water dressings.

Phillips, Milton – Private, Company D, 36th Ohio Infantry. **Wounded**, shot in the right breast, dangerous wound, broke two ribs. Ball lodged against the skin in front. When shot, he remained on the field. Said to have been shot through the body with a squirrel rifle, in the hands of a citizen. Was shot early in the battle, and walked a mile to camp. Thought to be a mortal wound, but he recovered, and lived until 1914.

Price, Elias – Private, Company I, 36th Ohio Infantry. **Wounded**, shot in the ankle, badly.

Raher, Michael – Private, Company D, 44th Ohio Infantry. **Wounded & Died of Wounds**, shot in the head, scalp wound, considered severe. Treated with cold water dressings. Admitted to a hospital in Cincinnati, June 16, 1862, and died June 21, 1862.

Reck, John T. – Private, Company B, 44th Ohio Infantry. **Killed**, shot in the left breast, died on the battlefield. Buried at Lewisburg, then later moved to the Staunton National Cemetery.

Reece, John W. – Private, Company F, 36th Ohio Infantry. **Wounded**, shot in the left leg, below the knee.

Richendollen, Henry – Private, Company I, 36th Ohio Infantry. **Wounded**, shot in the arm, severe.

Roberts, Ezekiel – Private, Company A, 36th Ohio Infantry – **Wounded**, shot in the left forearm, slight. Sent to a hospital at Charleston.

Rose, William – Private, Company I, 36th Ohio Infantry. **Wounded**, shot in the forehead, slight.

Rose, William H. H. – Private, Company K, 36th Ohio Infantry. **Wounded**, shot in the hand, slight.

Runyon, Francis M. "Frank" – Private, Company F, 44th Ohio Infantry. **Killed**, shot through the left breast, died on the battlefield. Captain Israel Stough wrote: "In my charge upon the gun I lost a fine boy, Little Frankie, as we called him. He had fired his piece three times & had the fourth cart[ridge], half home when he was struck in the breast by two balls causing almost instant death." His last words were "I die happy, tell my parents I will meet them in Heaven." Buried at Lewisburg, then later moved to the Staunton National Cemetery.

Sanders, Oscar W. – Private, Company B, 2nd West Virginia Cavalry. **Captured** at Lewisburg while on picket duty. Confined at Richmond, May 30, 1862. Released and sent to Salisbury, North Carolina, June 3, 1862.

Scarff, W. H. H. – Private, Company C, 44th Ohio Infantry. **Wounded**, slightly.

Shaffer, John – Private, Company A, 36th Ohio Infantry. **Wounded**, shot in both thighs, not severe. Sent to a hospital at Charleston. Gave his musket to a lieutenant, who fired it three times.

Sherer, George – Private, Company D, 36th Ohio Infantry. **Killed**. Was first wounded in the hand, severely, and died on the battlefield, being shot in the heart from a house while going from the field to the hospital. Buried at Lewisburg, then moved later to the Staunton National Cemetery.

Sherrer, William – Corporal, Company D, 44th Ohio Infantry. **Wounded**, slightly.

Simmons, Samuel T. – Private, Company K, 36th Ohio Infantry. **Killed**, shot in the heart and throat, died on the battlefield. Buried at Lewisburg, then later moved to the Staunton National Cemetery.

Slack, John – Private, Company B, 2nd West Virginia Cavalry. **Captured** at Lewisburg, while on picket duty. Confined at Richmond, May 30, 1862. Released and sent to Salisbury, North Carolina, June 3, 1862.

Stratton, George W. - Corporal, Company C, 44th Ohio Infantry. **Wounded**, shot in the left hand, slightly. Name appears as "Shotton."

Tulleys, Lysander W. – Captain, Company D, 44th Ohio Infantry. **Wounded**, slightly. "Never allowed it to interfere with his duties."

Venters, George – Private, Company D, 36th Ohio Infantry. **Wounded**, shot in the right arm, slightly.

Wallace, Fred S. – Sergeant, Company K, 36th Ohio Infantry. **Wounded**, shot in the right side of the face (cheek), not dangerous.

Ward, Isaac – Private, Company D, 36th Ohio Infantry. **Wounded**, shot in the leg, slightly.

Wharton, Charles – Private, Company K, 36th Ohio Infantry. **Wounded**, shot in the hand.

Wilson, James – Private, Company A, 36th Ohio Infantry. **Wounded**, shot in the abdomen, slightly. Name also as Amos Wilson.

Wilson, Sanford – Private, Company D, 44th Ohio Infantry. **Wounded**, shot in the calf of the leg, slight. Treated with a cold water dressing.

Wright, John – Private, Company I, 36th Ohio Infantry. **Wounded**, shot in the leg, slightly.

Yeager, James H. – Private, Company D, 36th Ohio Infantry. **Wounded**, shot in the right arm, fracture, severe.

Young, Peter – Corporal, Company E, 44th Ohio Infantry. **Wounded**, shot in the head, above the right eye, cutting a severe gash along the side of his head, above the ear. Not considered dangerous, and Young refused to go to the hospital. Treated with a cold water dressing.

False Claims

These men claimed to have been wounded at Lewisburg, May 23, 1862, but after investigation, they were wounded elsewhere.

Brown, William Wilson – Private, Company E, 44th Ohio Infantry. Applied for a pension, stating he had been wounded in the foot at "Louisburg", which shattered the bones and resulted in a lengthy hospitalization. The Adjutant General's Office ruled that there was "no record of g.s.w. [gun shot wound] or results therefrom at the battle of Louisburg, West, Va., May 22, 1862, as alleged."

Rockwell, James – Private, Company K, 36th Ohio Infantry. Applied for a pension January 22, 1863, alleging disability due to the loss of the index finger of the right hand, received at the battle of Lewisburg, Va., May 23, 1862. In 1871, he stated a different circumstance of his injury. At Meadow Bluff, while asleep in a tent, a comrade threw down a musket, which discharged and struck Rockwell. Claim rejected, there being no proof or witness to support his claim.

CHAPTER EIGHTEEN

REUNION

May 23, 1904

In late April 1904, Jewett Palmer, former Major of the 36th Ohio Infantry, announced that the regiment would hold its annual reunion at Lewisburg on May 23, 1904 – 42 years after the battle. Palmer extended the invitation to members of the 44th Ohio, Bolles' Battalion (2nd West Virginia Cavalry), and the detachment from the 47th Ohio. Palmer also extended the invitation to the surviving Confederate soldiers, asking to meet them again at Lewisburg, in the spirit of friendship.[524]

Notices of the upcoming reunion appeared in the columns of the *Greenbrier Independent*, stating that "The annual reunion of the 36th Ohio Infantry will be held at Lewisburg, W. Va., on May 23, 1904, the forty-second anniversary of that battle. All survivors of the battle – Union or Confederate – are invited."[525]

On the day of the reunion, Lewisburg Mayor John W. Arbuckle gave the welcome address to the old soldiers. General H. F. Devol and Major Jewitt Palmer responded on behalf of the visiting Union soldiers. Local attorney and commander of the Camp Creigh chapter of the United Confederate Veterans, Thomas H. Dennis, responded to the mayor's address on behalf of the Southern soldiers assembled there. Following the speeches, a "feast" was held on the grounds of the Old Stone Church, served by the ladies of Lewisburg.

The *Monroe Watchman* reported that about 25 survivors of the 36th Ohio participated in the event, along with a number of other Union soldiers. An

---

524 Circular dated April 26, 1904 from Jewett Palmer, Noyes Rand Papers, Civil War Collection, MS79-18, West Virginia Department of Archives and History, Charleston, W. Va. (hereafter cited as Rand Papers)

525 Greenbrier Independent, May 12, 1904

estimated 200 Confederate Veterans attended the reunion.[526] Noyes Rand, formerly the adjutant of the 22nd Virginia Infantry, noted that the reunion was a "unique" one.[527]

The West Virginia News, published in nearby Ronceverte, West Virginia, reported the names of the 25 veterans of the 36th Ohio which attended the reunion:

Brig. Gen. H. F. Devol	Major Jewett Palmer	Capt. J. T. Barker
Capt. M. A. Stacy	Lieutenant Amos Clark	Joseph Dyer
Sam'l. Skipton	James Zeering	Wm. Lancaster
M. McMillin	John Steed	George Hechler
Jas. N. Bobo	John Zeering	A. R. Cooper
A. P. Beach	John Arr	H. F. Nibert
James Wikle	George Martin	John King
O. J. Owen	P. W. Clements	Jno. D. Groves
Wm. Bush[528]		

526 Monroe Watchman, May 26, 1904
527 Rand Papers
528 The West Virginia News , Ronceverte, W. Va., May 28, 1904

Reunion of Greenbrier Confederate Veterans and
36th Ohio Infantry, at Lewisburg, May 23, 1904
History of Greenbrier County, W. Va. (Cole)

APPENDIX A

Devol Map

This map or plan, is titled "Plan of Lewisburg, Va., By Capt. H. F. Devol. Sketched the day After the Battle." It was originally published in *Biographical Sketch, Bvt. Brig.-Gen. H. F. Devol, 36th Ohio Veteran Volunteer*, published in 1903.

Captain Devol drew the map on May 24, 1862, the day after the battle. The map is not drawn to scale. It is rather unique in that it shows the location of the dead from both sides, and contains many notations. The notations are sometimes difficult to read, so a transcription is included with an accompanying location number. The map has been enlarged in five sections so that the details can be more easily viewed. A digital version of the map is available on the publisher's web site at www.35thstar.com.

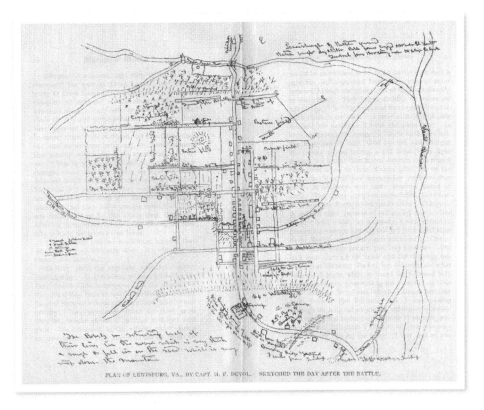

PLAN OF LEWISBURG, VA., BY CAPT. H. F. DEVOL. SKETCHED THE DAY AFTER THE BATTLE.

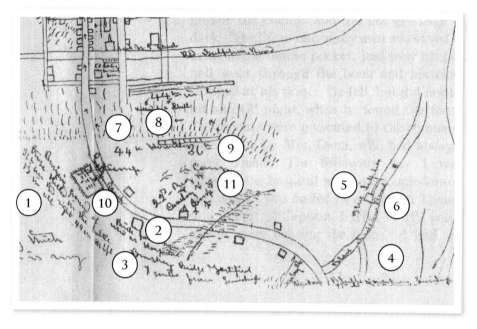

Map Section I

1. Burying ground of those killed in the battle. 36th on the right, 44th on the left. 13 in all.

2. Brick farm house used as hospital

3. Brushey Ridge fortified 7 miles from Lewisburg

4. Meadow Bluff __ miles from Lewisburg. 47th (Ohio) [Road name just to the left of this notation is not known.]

5. Blue Sulphur

6. Blue Sulphur Road

7. 44th Camp

8. Howitzers

9. 36th Camp

10. Gauley Road

11. 22d Reg. Cavalry Camp (should be 2d Reg.)

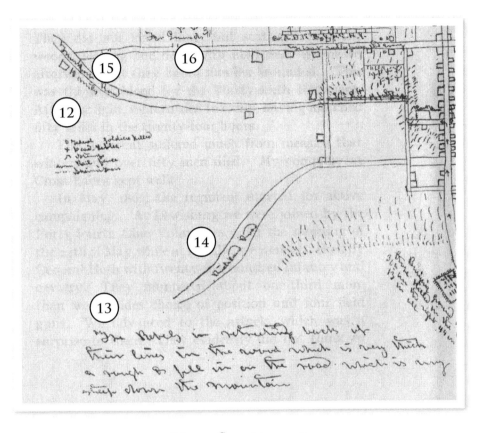

Map Section 2

12. Federal Soldiers killed. Dead Rebles [sic]. Stumps. Rail Fence. Skirmishers.

13. The Rebels in retreating back of their lines in the wood which is very thick & rough & fell in on the road which is very steep down the mountain

14. Richland Road

15. Frankford Road, 10 miles

16. Fair Grounds

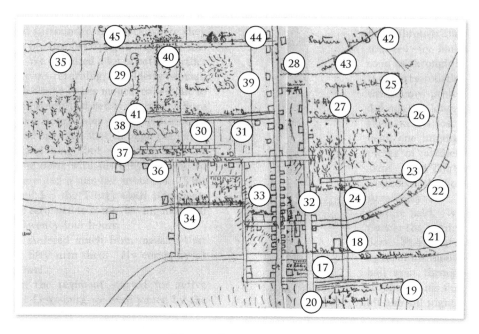

Map Section 3

17. 50 Rebles [sic] buried here

18. [unknown] W. S. Church

19. 44th in line

20. Killed by a shell [Adam S. Alt]

21. Red Sulphur Road

22. Edgar Ferry Road

23. 44th in line

24. North M. E. Church

25. Wheat field

26. Enemy in line

27. [Note two artillery pieces in position]

28. Cannon

29. Pasture Field

30. 22d Inf

31. 45th Infy

32. Hospital

33. Court House

34. 36th [unknown]

35. One Co. Sharpshooters

36. Great (giant) volley from the enemy

37. [36th Ohio] Co. A, B, K, __, __, E, H, G

38. Plowed field

39. Pasture field

40. Plowed field

41. 22d [unknown]

42. Pasture field

43. North

44. [Unknown] stacks

45. Rebel pile

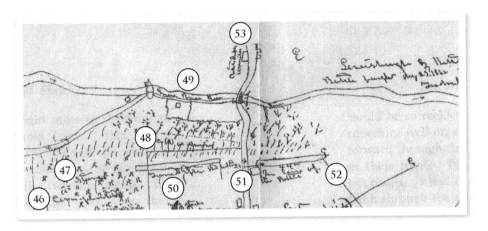

Map Section 4

46. Corn planted

47. Stumps

48. Co. (A) as skirmishers

49. Green Briar River

50. Formed after the battle

51. 24 pounder

52. 44th the line of battle

53. Reble [sic] Infy [unknown]

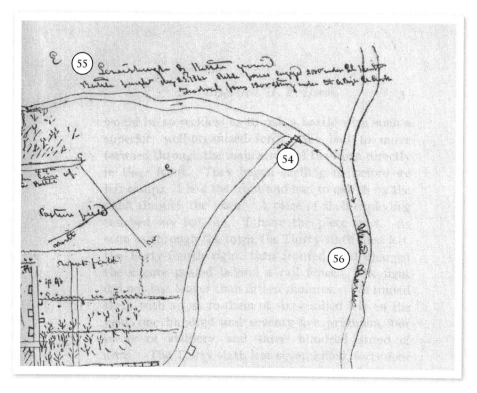

Map Section 5

54. Ferry

55. Lewisburgh [sic] Battle ground. Battle fought May 23, 1862. Rebel forces engaged 2500 under Genl. Heth, Federal force 1200 strong under [unknown] Col. Crook.

56. [unknown] River

APPENDIX B

Poetry

The Fight at Lewisburg.

"Caught on a hook,"
Was Colonel Crook,
So the Rebel "Gen. Heath" concluded,
A "very nice trap,'"
Without any mishap,
Which the Colonel wily eluded.

The armies met,
Most deadly set,
Did the Rebels make to conquer;
But Colonel Crook,
"At the end of a hook,"
Soon proved the Yankees were stronger.

The traitors run,
Every son of a gun,
Leaving their dead the soil to pollute;
They burn the bridge,
And over the ridge,
Like scared Kangaroos take the "shute."

'Tis said two men
Of the South; ten
Yankees can thrash accordin'
But Harry Heath,
Half scared to death,
Found a "debbil of a hard way over Jordin"

Inversed was the rule,
Taught in Crook's school,
One Yankee to three seceshers;
With two to carry,
Like the lord Harry,

Away skedaddle all the bushwhackers.

To shoot in the street,
The wounded and weak,
Did the *ladies* of Lewisburg strive;
We know not why,
In the wink of an eye,
Crook didn't "wipe out" the Rebel hive.

Ben. Butler's creed,
For so bloody a deed,
Would surely not prove too cruel;
To let them all pass,
As part of that class,
Who to the passions of men furnish fuel.

The time has "arriv','"
When Rebels should live
Down below, where they all might revel
In treason and lies,
That blast their eyes,
Jeff. Davis would kick out the devil.

Rip. Saw.

Gallipolis Journal, Gallipolis, Ohio, June 5, 1862

Battle Of Lewisburg.

Down in Lewisburg section, we had a little action.
Old Heath thought the Yankee's wouldn't fight him:
But old Gen. Crook got them on a hook,
And jerked them to the Happy Land of Canaan.
Chorus –
Ho, boys, Ho! We all for the Union go,
And we'll give the Kanawha riflemen a training.
With a minute to repeat, and a piece of Yankee hemp.
We'll send them to the Happy Land of Canaan!

On the 23d of May, about the break of day,
For Lewisburg old Heath was aiming.
And Gen. Heath did swear that he'd eat his breakfast there –
That he'd send us to the Happy Land of Canaan!
Chorus – Ho, boys, Ho! &c.
When the drums began to rattle, we formed our line of battle,
Co. D was sent out to entertain them:
When within one hundred yards, the Rebels made a charge,
For to send us to the Happy Land of Canaan!
Chorus –
But our Captain was too quick, he showed them a Yankee trick:
He told us to lie down and do good aiming.
And every ball that flew cut a Rebel half in two,
And sent him to the Happy Land of Canaan!
Chorus –
For half an hour we fought, the battle became hot.
Although the battle they were sure of gaining.
When our brigade came out, and made them right about –
They started for the Happy Land of Canaan!
Chorus –
Oh, to us it was fun to see the Rebels run,
As fast the tested ground we were gaining:

But they scampered down the ridge and burnt the river bridge,
    And started for the Happy Land of Canaan!
    Chorus –
When they thought it time to run, they threw away their guns,
    And they left us twenty horses and four cannon,
Three hundred stand of arms and ammunition all unharmed.
    Which we took to the Happy Land of Canaan!
    Chorus –
Now if old Gen. Heath ain't satisfied with this defeat,
    If he'll come to Meadow Bluff where we're staying,
For a very moderate bill, we'll give him a Yankee pill,
    That will send him to the Happy Land of Canaan!
    Chorus –
Now it is just a little walk, and there is no need to talk,
    Come right along, Gen., and don't be complaining,
The 44th and 36th can very soon have you fixed
    For a trip to the Happy Land of Canaan!
    Chorus –

This song was published at Lewisburg, W. Va.
The Jackson Standard, Jackson, O., September 9, 1886

Appendix C

The Cemeteries

The Confederate Cemetery

The Confederate Cemetery in Lewisburg shelters the remains of nearly a hundred soldiers, and perhaps many more. The vast majority of these soldiers are unknown; the identities of only three of the soldiers are recorded.

The mass grave, in the form of a cross, contain the remains of the Confederate soldiers who were killed or died of wounds received in the Battle of Lewisburg, fought on May 23, 1862. Others who lie here died of disease during the war, while others died at Lewisburg from wounds received in the November 1863 battle at Droop Mountain, in nearby Pocahontas County. The wounded soldiers were left there by their comrades as the Confederate forces retreated through the town of Lewisburg.

Two of the identified graves belong to soldiers who died after the war, and one who died of wounds received in the Battle of Dry Creek, near White Sulphur Springs in 1863.

The Confederate dead from the Battle of Lewisburg were first interred by the Union troops after the battle. The victorious Union troops refused to allow the patriotic Southern citizens in Lewisburg to care for the dead. It is said that permission was denied because of the firing on wounded Union soldiers in the

CONFEDERATE CEMETERY, LEWISBURG
Steve Cunningham

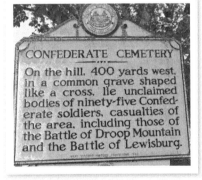

Steve Cunningham

town during the battle. A number of the Confederate dead were claimed by their family or friends, and buried elsewhere.

A long trench, fifty feet long and several feet deep, was dug by the Union men on the south side of the Old Stone Church. Into this trench the bodies of the dead Confederates were laid. If a hat or cap was available, it was laid over their faces before being covered over with dirt.

Two years after the War Between the States ended, the Confederate dead were disinterred and moved to their present location, and laid to rest in a cross shaped grave. The upright portion of the cross is approximately 80 feet in length, and the cross arm is about 40 feet in length. The width of the cross is nearly ten feet. The cemetery is marked by a bronze plaque, which reads: "Here rests the remains of approximately 95 unknown Confederate soldiers killed or died of disease and wounds in the Battle of Lewisburg."[529]

In the ensuing years since the war, many errors have crept into the accounts of the Battle of Lewisburg and the story of the Confederate Cemetery. One of those, published in 1956, stated that the cemetery "contains the remains of 59 Confederates and 26 Union soldiers."[530] This claim is not true.

In late March 1867, a brief notice in the *Greenbrier Independent* noted that "Col. B. H. Jones has been selected … to superintend the removal of the Confederate dead, from the churchyard, to the lot on the hill. Due notice of the exact time will be given through the papers, and by hand bills; and it will be desired and expected, that all the surviving Confederate soldiers in the county – as well as those elsewhere – who may feel willing to assist, will attend, provided with shovels, spades, and other utensils, necessary to complete the work."[531]

On June 13, 1867, the *Greenbrier Independent* reported: "The removal of the remains of the Confederate dead, buried in the Presbyterian Graveyard, in this place, mentioned in our last issue, has been completed. Capt. [J. W.] Branham, under whose supervision the work was conducted, informs us that 269 bodies have been removed to the soldiers Cemetery, near town, and that the following States are represented: Georgia, Mississippi, Tennessee, Kentucky and Virginia. The work was conducted under the auspices of the Ladies' Memorial Association, of this place."[532]

Based on Captain Branham's statement, there are far more than 95 soldiers buried in the Confederate Cemetery at Lewisburg.

---

529 *Register and Post-Herald*, Beckley, W. Va., December 8, 1956

530 *Register and Post-Herald*, Beckley, W. Va., December 8, 1956; this appears to be a falsehood, no evidence of Union soldiers being interred with the Confederates has been found, other than this article.

531 *Greenbrier Independent*, Lewisburg, W. Va., March 21, 1867

532 *Greenbrier Independent*, Lewisburg, W. Va., June 13, 1867

The Union Cemetery

The Union dead were buried about three-quarters of a mile west of Lewisburg, along present day Route 60, on a farm now owned by Mrs. Jack Wallace.[533] A memorial plaque near the road marks the site, and indentations where fifteen bodies lay can still be seen.

It is interesting that the indentations show that fifteen soldiers were interred there, when only thirteen died at Lewisburg. Records of the National Cemetery at Staunton, Virginia and the Burial Registers kept by the U. S. Army, records the name of a soldier removed from Lewisburg, who is not listed among those who were killed or died of wounds. The name of Norad Cameron cannot be found in the records of the Ohio soldiers who died there. The only possible explanation is that sometime during the war, Cameron was buried with the other Northern troops. This still leaves one burial unaccounted for.

According to one account, after the Union troops left Lewisburg, "vandals" tore down the fence about the graveyard and desecrated the graves of the Northern dead.[534]

The removal of the Union dead from Lewisburg is noted in the Burial Registers kept by the U. S. Army. Unfortunately, the registers do not note the date of removal, only a brief description of the location removed from, names (when known), and where re-buried. The records indicate that the dead were removed from "J. E. Bells Farm, ½ mile west [of] Lewisburg, 200 yards of [the] pike, 50 yards east of [a] fence, under a large oak tree."[535]

On November 20, 1866, the *Staunton Spectator* reported the presence of about seventy Federal soldiers in the vicinity of Staunton, for the purpose of establishing a cemetery for the Federal dead from the surrounding area. The notice indicated that the remains of Union soldiers

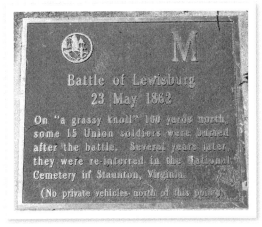

MARKER INDICATING LOCATION OF ORIGINAL GRAVES
OF UNION DEAD OF LEWISBURG

Steve Cunningham

---

533 The original cemetery is located on private land, and permission is needed to go upon it.

534 Booth

535 Burial Registers of Military Posts and National Cemeteries, 1862 – 1960. Records of the Office of the Quartermaster General, 1774 – 1985, RG-92, National Archives, Washington, D. C.

killed at Port Republic, Piedmont, and McDowell, "and such others as have been buried in other places within the space around Staunton described by a radius forty miles in length."[536] Lewisburg, however, lies (in a straight line) 80 miles from the Staunton National Cemetery.

When the initial work was completed, the cemetery became the resting place for at least 753 Federal soldiers, 232 of whom are identified. A newspaper article published in 2014 concerning the National Cemetery, noted "In several instances two or even three unknown soldiers were buried together in one plot."[537] Therefore, the cemetery initially held more than the 753 remains mentioned.

An article in the *Ohio Civil War Genealogy Journal*, noted that the Union dead were buried on the farms of Johnston Ewing Bell and J. G. Bell. Between November 1866 and December 1867, the bodies were removed to the National Cemetery at Staunton, Virginia.[538]

---

536 *Staunton Spectator*, Staunton, Va., November 20, 1866
537 *The News Leader*, Staunton, Va., March 14, 2014
538 Ohio Civil War Genealogy Journal, Volume XIII, 2009, p. 6

APPENDIX D

General Heth's Artillery

One of the least understood aspects of Brigadier General Henry Heth's command, is the composition of his artillery arm. In his official report, Heth states that he brought "3 batteries" to Lewisburg.

One must now ask "what constitutes a battery?" The accepted definition places the number of guns or pieces in a battery at six, divided into sections of two guns each. According to the 1862 "The [Confederate] Field Manual for the Use of the Officers on Ordnance Duty," a battery of artillery consisted of six pieces (4 guns, 2 howitzers).[539] Taking Heth's statement of "3 batteries", it can be assumed that he had at least twelve and possibly eighteen pieces of artillery before Lewisburg.

Each battery (ideally), consisted of six artillery pieces, six caissons, one travelling forge, and one battery wagon. A battery of 6-pounders required a total of 91 horses: 84 to pull the pieces, caissons, forge, and wagon, with 7 spare animals. Six horses were assigned to each piece, caisson, forge and wagon.

One possible source to help determine the number of artillery pieces in each company or battery, is the number horses required by each. These numbers appear on the requisition for forage documents found in the Compiled Service Records of the battery officers, and are fragmentary at best. An analysis of the existing numbers reveals the following **suggested** configuration of the batteries before and after the battle.

Battery	Date	Horses	Possible Configuration
Lowry's	August 1861	13	1 piece, 1 caisson, 1 spare
Lowry's	April 1862	39	2 pieces, 2 caissons, 2 wagons, 3 spare
Lowry's	Early June 1862	38	2 pieces, 2 caissons, 2 wagons, 2 spare
Bryan's	Early May 1862	60	4 pieces, 4 caissons, 2 wagons, 0 spare
Bryan's	June 14, 1862	53	3 pieces, 3 caissons, 2 wagons, 5 spare
Chapman's	April 30, 1862	64	5 pieces, 5 caissons, 0 wagons, 4 spare

---

539 Batteries were identified as a "12-pounder" or "6-pounder" battery, both totaling six pieces each. No mention of the requirements of "mixed" batteries (those containing different sizes of artillery pieces). Several of Heth's companies contained a mixture of sizes.

Chapman's (detachment)	June 1862	32	4 pieces, 4 caissons, 0 wagon, 2 spare
Chapman's (Monroe Co.)	June 1862	21	1 piece, 1 caisson, 1 wagon, 3 spare
Otey's	June 1862	26	2 pieces, 2 caissons, 0 wagons, 2 spare
Vawter's	May 1862	70	4 pieces, 4 caissons, 2 wagons, 10 spare

A great many of the accounts of the battle of Lewisburg indicate Heth brought six pieces of artillery with him, and left four of them in the hands of the victorious Federals. A careful study of the available records and accounts reveal that Heth brought between eight to ten pieces of artillery to the battlefield at Lewisburg. One newspaper account states that the Confederates brought 16 pieces of artillery to the field, while a letter written by one of the artillerists states they had 11 pieces. Not all of the artillery pieces, however, were brought into action.

Besides the four pieces captured on the battlefield by Crook's men, an additional three or four pieces of artillery were spiked and abandoned at or near the Greenbrier River Bridge, at present-day Caldwell. Heth's demoralized men salvaged only two pieces – Captain George G. Otey saved one, and Captain George B. Chapman saved his 24-pounder.

One of the few Confederate newspaper accounts of the battle named the units which left the Narrows of the New River after dark on May 19th. The writer, identified only as "Dane," noted that Otey's Battery brought two guns, Bryan's Battery brought four, and Lowry's Battery brought three, for a total of nine pieces of artillery.[540] The account does not mention Chapman's Battery and Vawter's Western Artillery.

Records for Captain Lewis A. Vawter's Battery, known as the Western Artillery, are very scarce. It is known that the battery was armed with at least two mountain howitzer's before the battle of Lewisburg, and following the battle, they had none. If they were not lost at Lewisburg, what happened to them? Since they were a relatively new company, having been organized in March 1862, it was likely combined with Bryan's or Lowry's commands during the battle. In the summer of 1862, Vawter's company became a part of the 30th Battalion Virginia Sharpshooters. Had the decision to relinquish the big guns for small arms been made prior to Lewisburg? Was Vawter's artillery broken up by General Heth in the May 15, 1862 reorganization of his command? It is known that Vawter's command was actively engaged in the fighting at Lewisburg as two of his men

---

540 *Richmond Daily Dispatch*, Richmond, Va., June 3, 1862

were killed, and at least one wounded. In late May 1862, Vawter was commanding a company in Edgar's Battalion.

A total of five companies of artillery were assigned to Heth's command prior to the Lewisburg battle. A letter dated May 8, 1862, was signed by four artillery captains: Bryan, Lowry, Chapman, and Vawter.[541] Although Captain George G. Otey's company was assigned to Heth's command, his name does not appear on the letter.

The following table shows the configuration of the artillery companies in May 1862, as far as can be determined from the existing records and accounts.

Company	Guns Assigned	Iron 6-pounder (smooth-bore)	6-pounder rifled	12-pounder (smooth-bore)	12-poundeer Howitzer	12-pounder Mtn. Howitzer	24-pounder	Unknown size	On Detached Service	Guns at Lewisburg	Saved	Captured	Spiked & Abandoned
Captain Lowry	2	1		1						2		2	
Captain Bryan	5	3	1	1					2	3		1	2
Captain Chapman	5	2			2		1		4	1	1		
Captain Otey	4		1	1				2	2	2	1	1	
Captain Vawter*	2					2				2			2
Total	18	6	2	3	2	2	1	2	8	10	2	4	4
Alternate Total	16	6	2	3	2	0	1	2	8	8	2	4	2

* Captain Vawter's "Western Artillery" may have been broken up by General Heth in the May 15, 1862 reorganization of his command. Should this be the case, the totals shown should be reduced by 2 guns (see Alternate Total line).

To fully understand the above table, and how the numbers were arrived at, we need to take a look at the early history of each battery.

541 Staff file, John Floyd King

Lowry's Battery

This battery of light artillery was organized by Captain William M. Lowry in early 1861, mustered into service on July 2, 1861, and became Company C of the Wise Legion Artillery. In December, Lowry, along with the two other companies of the Wise Legion Artillery were ordered to Richmond, and soon thereafter to Norfolk. According to Colonel Charles F. Henningsen (59th Virginia Infantry), commander of the Wise Legion Artillery, the three companies arrived at Norfolk about noon on January 28, 1862, with "five pieces, and five caissons."[542]

That same day, General Wise directed Lieutenant James H. Pearce, his ordnance officer, to see General Benjamin Huger and obtain from him a gun, carriage and limber (either a 12-pounder or 9-pounder). Lieutenant Pearce was further directed by Wise to call upon Flag Officer French Forrest at the Navy Yard, and ask for a brass howitzer. Wise also directed Pearce to make application at the Navy Yard for two iron 12-pounders, with their carriages and caissions.[543]

It appears that Lieutenant Pearce was only somewhat successful in his quest for artillery; a single piece of artillery – an iron 6-pounder – was added to the Wise Legion Artillery. This is shown in Colonel Henningsen's report. On January 30, the colonel recorded that "There were now unexpectedly six guns (a sixth iron 6-pounder without caissons having been received at Norfolk),"[544] General Wise, in a later document, confirms this, stating "Five of the pieces of my artillery were brought with my artillery corps from western Virginia; one of the pieces only was obtained at Norfolk."[545]

Captain Lowry's company returned to western Virginia in the early spring of 1862, and was by the latter part of April at Jackson River Depot, in Alleghany County. The company joined General Heth's command, and was reorganized on May 15, 1862. When Lowry joined Heth, he is known to have had a 12-pounder, and it would appear an iron 6-pounder obtained at Norfolk. Both of these guns went into action at Lewisburg on the morning of May 23, 1862.

Bryan's Battery

This battery of light artillery was organized March 27, 1862, by Captain Thomas A. Bryan, and formed a part of Brigadier General Heth's artillery arm. Soon after

---

542 OR, Series I, Vol. IX, p. 143

543 OR, Series I, Vol. IX, p. 142

544 OR, Series I, Vol. IX, p. 143

545 Staff File, Brigadier General Henry A. Wise, letter dated Feb. 22, 1862. A letter the following week, on March 1, 1862, Wise makes a comment that Captain Lowry did not have any artillery pieces in his company. Yet, by the time he returned to western Virginia, Lowry had two guns.

organization, the battery received three iron 6-pounders. On May 6, 1862, the company received two additional pieces at Jackson River Depot, one of which was a 6-pounder rifled gun.

In the middle part of May, as preparations were being made to move against Crook at Lewisburg, Bryan divided his company, leaving two of the iron 6-pounders behind. Captain Bryan considered them to be of little use.

Three pieces of artillery made the trip to Lewisburg: one iron 6-pounder, and the two new pieces. After reaching the Greenbrier River before Lewisburg, Captain Bryan further divided his company, leaving two of his three pieces near the bridge as a rear guard. Most of the accounts of the battle state that Bryan lost a total of three pieces at Lewisburg.

Chapman's Battery

This battery was organized April 25, 1862 by Captain George B. Chapman, and received a full compliment of five guns at Jackson River Depot soon after. He received sixty horses and three two-horse wagons there on April 30th. The sizes of his artillery pieces were: one 24-pounder, two 12-pounder howitzers, and two 6-pounders.

After the fighting at Princeton, Va., on May 15 – 17, 1862, Chapman divided his company, leaving a detachment of four pieces at the New River. Captain Chapman, with the 24-pounder, accompanied Heth to Lewisburg, and took an active part in the fighting there. Except for Johnston's history of Chapman's Battery, none of the accounts of the battle mention any artillery on the Confederate right flank, so the exact role of Chapman's gun is unknown.

Otey's Battery

This battery of light artillery was organized at Richmond, Va., on March 14, 1862, and was assigned to duty with General Heth's command on March 21st. Captain George Gaston Otey, still without artillery pieces, was ordered to report to Heth, who had guns waiting for him at Lewisburg. Sometime prior to the movement against Lewisburg, Otey detached two guns at Rocky Gap, and took the other two into battle: a 6-pound rifled piece, and a 12-pounder. Captain Otey was wounded while bringing the 12-pounder off the field, leaving the rifled piece to fall into the enemy's hands.

Vawter's Western Artillery

This company was organized on March 26, 1862, by Captain Lewis A. Vawter, and is the fifth battery of Heth's command. The company went without artillery pieces until early May 1862, when two 12-pounder mountain howitzer's were assigned to the company. Two light 6-pounders have also been associated with Vawter's company, and it may be possible that he received a total of four artillery pieces. This is further strengthened by a requisition for forage dated May 5, 1862 at Dublin, Va., for a total of 70 horses (May 5 – 14). This was the only requisition for forage found for Vawter, giving more strength of the possibility of the company being broken up during the reorganization.

General Heth reorganized his command on or about May 15, 1862. What effect this may have had upon Vawter's company is unknown. As mentioned before, perhaps Vawter's men decided to become an infantry company (as they later did), and relinquished their field pieces. As it is known that Vawter's men were actively engaged in the battle of Lewisburg, perhaps they had already taken up small arms and acted as infantry on the Confederate left, with Edgar and Finney. Documents dated two days after the battle, show Vawter's men as part of Edgar's Battalion. In August 1862, the company became part of the 30th Battalion Virginia Sharpshooters.

At least one Confederate account reports the number of guns at Lewisburg at 11. This report is seconded by a Union account, which also reports 11 pieces of artillery. Private Oliver Parker, 36th Ohio Infantry, noted that they "took 4 peaces [sic] and 2 afterwards.", a total of six guns.[546]

Thomas Thomson Taylor, a member of the 47th Ohio Infantry, writing from Meadow Bluff the day after the battle, noted that the Confederates had seven pieces of artillery, four of which were taken by Crook's men. Later on, Taylor, notes that Crook captured six guns, and recovered one that had been spiked and thrown into the river.[547] This would total 7 guns.

Points to Ponder

Colonel Crook's official report indicates only four cannon were taken: two smooth-bore, and two rifled. The following questions now arise about the report and the conflicting reports:

    A. Did Crook report **only** those guns captured during the actual fighting?

    B. Did Crook fail to report a fifth cannon because it was considered a relic?

---

546 Parker

547 Taylor

C. Did Crook consider the cannon spiked and abandoned not worthy of mention in his official report because they were not taken in "battle"?

D. Did the Union Army even make an attempt to recover the abandoned guns (from the river), or just leave them?

The answers to these questions will likely never be known. The number of Confederate artillery pieces at Lewisburg will continue to be debated long after the publication of this volume.

APPENDIX E

The Relic Gun

The Lewisburg Cannon

The Clark County Heritage Center in Springfield, Ohio, has a wonderful trophy from the Civil War – a beautiful artillery piece, captured by the 44th Ohio Volunteer Infantry at the Battle of Lewisburg, [W.] Va., on the morning of May 23, 1862.

The artillery piece has a long history, and was considered a relic when it was captured more than 150 years ago. It has since been "on duty" in Springfield, Ohio. Exactly when the old cannon arrived in Springfield cannot be determined, but it is known to have been in the city by January 1864, when the 44th Regiment converted to the 8th Ohio Cavalry.

Civil War era cannon are not uncommon, however, in this Ohio city. Eighteen years after the close of the war (1882), the United States War Department ordered that four condemned cast iron cannon (20-pounders) be sent to Springfield for decoration in Ferncliff Cemetery. In addition, four cannon balls were sent along with the big guns.

Wartime accounts concerning the artillery piece and its capture agree for the most part, with the exception of the age of the gun, and what size or caliber it is. The gun has been called a relic of the Revolutionary War, having been surrendered by the British at Yorktown. The size is reported as a 6-pounder, 10 pounder, or 12-pounder.

ARTILLERY PIECE CAPTURED BY THE
44TH OHIO INFANTRY AT THE BATTLE
OF LEWISBURG, LOCATED AT THE
CLARK COUNTY HERITAGE CENTER IN
SPRINGFIELD, OHIO
*www.pinterest.com/
pin/400820435560079209*

One account, surfacing in the late 1920s, has gained wide popularity. Randolph Hock, the manager of the General Lewis Hotel obtained the story from one of his guests, identified only as Werner, from Springfield, Ohio, and a veteran of the 44th Ohio Infantry "… which captured the Confederate battery stationed on this spot. He took Mr. Hock into the rear yard and showed where a mortar had been attached to the log cabin doorway and supported by rails fastened to a chain to the near-by oak tree. Werner explained that because the gun was not more than half supported, it became displaced when fired, and whirled, its shot knocking off the southwest corner of the old Methodist brick church… . This mortar, according to Mr. Werner, was later secured for the courthouse yard at Springfield, Ohio."[548]

A mortar is a short barreled artillery piece, designed to lob projectiles into enemy works at some distance off. By looking at a picture of the relic gun, you can see right away that it has a much longer barrel or tube. As to the gun being fired without a carriage, consider this: General Heth's Confederate force moved rather rapidly from the New River to Lewisburg, and to move a artillery tube that weighs nearly 900 pounds, is no easy task. It would have required a strong wagon, a large number of horses and men to bring it to the battlefield. Once on the battlefield, it would have required a considerable amount of effort and time to move the tube into position and prepare it for action. The Confederates did not have the time, men or equipment to move it in such a way.

There is no doubt about the John Wesley Methodist Church being struck during the battle, as the repaired damage is yet visible, and marked by a sign. The damage, however, is not on the southwest corner of the building, but on the northeast. John Wesley Methodist Church faces (fronts) Foster Street, and the damage is on the upper left side of the wall, as you face the building. Based on the location of the damaged area and the physical location of it, the shot may very well have come from the area of the General Lewis Inn, near the center of the Confederate line. The shot that caused the damage could equally have been fired from a gun located along Foster Street after the artillery advanced.

If the shot in question was indeed fired from the backyard of the General Lewis Inn, it would have came from one of Captain Otey's guns. If it came from the Foster Street area, then it would have been from Captain Lowry's or Captain Bryan's batteries.

According to another tale, when the old cannon was unloaded after the battle, it was found to contain "among other things, about a peck of printers type."[549] An old soldier (Titus), declared that the type was used by the soldiers to print an issue of a soldier newspaper called *The Yankee.*

West Virginia historian and author, Boyd B. Stutler, referred to these two stories as "apocryphal" in 1947. His correspondence with the Clark County Historical

---

548 Ruth Woods Dayton. Greenbrier Pioneers and Their Homes. West Virginia Publishing Company, Charleston, W. Va., 1942, p. 123-4.

549 A peck is equal to about two gallons.

Society president Orton G. Rust, go back and forth about the veracity of the stories. Rust, in one of this letters concerning the type, states that Titus "told me with his own lips the story ...", and that he believed him to be "truthful and intelligent."[550]

According to a small news item on page two of the May 29, 1862 issue of *The Yankee*, several pieces of "large type" was picked up in the camp of the 44th Ohio, and were "originally the filling of [Confederate] shells." This is probably a true statement, and likely gave rise to the story of a large amount of type being found and used to print *The Yankee*. Had they made such a discovery, they would have undoubtedly boasted about it in the columns of their paper.

After years of research on the battle at Lewisburg, I believe these stories are just that – stories. The old soldiers who related them were at an advanced age, and we all know that memory sometimes gets clouded.

At the beginning of the war, nearly 1,200 cannon were taken when the Virginia forces took possession of the Gosport (Norfolk) Navy Yard. There were no six-pounders listed in the inventory, so the piece must have been stored elsewhere in the Norfolk area. It can be safely assumed that the artillery piece was issued to the Wise Legion Artillery at Norfolk, in January 1862, and made its way to western Virginia with Captain Lowry's Battery.

The artillery piece was declared a relic right away by the men of Crook's command. No mention of a "relic" cannon has been discovered in any of the Confederate accounts of the battle. The earliest mention of the gun as a relic of Revolutionary War days appeared in the columns of *The Yankee*. After reporting the capture of four artillery pieces at Lewisburg: two 12-pounders and two 6-pounder rifled cannon, the newspaper added:

---

550 Boyd Blynn Stutler Collection, Ms78-1, West Virginia Department of Archives and History, Charleston, W. Va.

"A Relic of Antiquity – One of the pieces captured by the 44th, at the battle of Lewisburg, is an old revolutionary smooth bore ten pounder. Application will be made to send it to Springfield, Ohio, where the regiment was recruited. ... The improvement in such arms has been so great since it was cast that it is almost worthless except as a relic."[551]

By June 10, 1862, *The Troy Times* referred to the piece as an "old smoothbore revolutionary 6-pounder." The Ohio newspaper undoubtedly used *The Yankee* article as its source.

Sometime after the Lewisburg battle, someone applied to the government – perhaps the Secretary of War, or the Ordnance Department – to have the piece retired to Springfield, Ohio. The application was apparently approved as the artillery piece is now displayed there.

The cannon was first put on display opposite the courthouse in Springfield. Up to about 1925, it stood at the base of the soldier's monument on the memorial plot, near the courthouse. The gun was then moved to the soldier's mound in Ferncliff Cemetery, the resting place of many Northern soldiers.

The artillery piece was presented to the Clark County Historical Society on August 8, 1929, by Captain Harlan E. Titus, commander of the Mitchell Camp, Grand Army of the Republic, and one of the men who helped capture it at Lewisburg. The piece received a fresh coat of paint and was placed on display in front of the Memorial Hall.

By December 1941, the old relic was removed from its rotting carriage and placed on two cement abutments; still displayed in front of Memorial Hall. Here it remained until September 1983, when it was removed from public view, having fell into a deplorable condition.

In 1999, with a new carriage and the tube restored, the piece went on display inside the Clark County Heritage Center. A team of experts examined the old cannon, and determined that it was indeed a smoothbore, iron 6-pounder, cast between 1815 and 1820, well after the Revolutionary War. No visible markings were discovered on the tube to aid in making a positive identification.[552]

---

551 *The Yankee*, Lewisburg, Va., May 29, 1862

552 This was determined through the aid of Tim McKinney and the staff at the Clark County Heritage Center in Springfield, Ohio.

Appendix F

Visiting Lewisburg

Lewisburg, West Virginia, is the county seat of Greenbrier County, and is named for Revolutionary War period General Andrew Lewis. Winner of the 2011 "Coolest Small Towns in America" award, the town offers many quaint shops, restaurants, galleries, and other attractions. Walking tour brochures, including one focused on the Battle of Lewisburg, are available at the Greenbrier Valley Visitors Center, located downtown on the corner of Washington and Court Streets.

For more information on visiting Lewisburg, visit these web sites:

www.visitlewisburgwv.com

www.greenbrierwv.com

Or call 304-645-1000.

DOWNTOWN LEWISBURG
Greenbrier County CVB

CONFEDERATE MEMORIAL STATUE, COURTNEY DRIVE AND
WASHINGTON STREET. THE STANDING SOLDIER IN BRONZE WAS
DESIGNED BY WILLIAM LUDLOW SHEPPARD AND DEDICATED ON
JUNE 14, 1906, "IN MEMORY OF OUR CONFEDERATE DEAD."
Steve Cunningham

BIBLIOGRAPHY

I. Books

Brown, Joseph Alleine. The Memoirs of a Confederate Soldier. Sam Austin Publishing, Forum Press, Abingdon, Va., 1940.

Cavanaugh, Michael A. The Otey, Ringgold and Davidson Virginia Artillery. H. E. Howard, Inc., Lynchburg, Va., 1993.

Chaffin, Tom. Pathfinder: John Charles Fremont and the Course of American Empire. Hill and Wang, New York, New York, 2002.

Chapla, John D. 50th Virginia Infantry. H. E. Howard, Inc., Lynchburg, Va. 1997.

Coggins, Jack. Arms and Equipment of the Civil War. Broadfoot Publishing Company, Wilmington, N. C., 1990

Cole, J. R. History of Greenbrier County. J. R. Cole, Lewisburg, W. Va., 1917.

Committee, Greenbrier Heritage Book. Greenbrier County, West Virginia family heritage, 1997. Summersville, W. Va.: Shirley Grose & Associates, 1996

Cox, Jacob Dolson. Military Reminiscences of the Civil War. Charles Scribner's Sons, New York. 1900. 2 volumes.

Cunningham, D. and W. W. Miller. Antietam. Report of the Ohio Antietam Battlefield Commission. Springfield Publishing Co., Springfield, O., 1904.

Davis, James A. 51st Virginia Infantry. Lynchburg, Va.: H. E. Howard, Inc., 1984.

Dayton, Ruth Woods. Greenbrier Pioneers and Their Homes. West Virginia Publishing Company, Charleston, W. Va., 1942.

Devol, Bvt. Brig.-Gen. H. F. Biographical Sketch. Hudson-Kimberly Publishing Co., Kansas City, Mo., 1903.

Dickinson, Jack L. 8th Virginia Cavalry. H. E. Howard, Inc., Lynchburg, Va. 1986.

Edgar, Alfred Mallory. My Reminiscences of the Civil War. 35th Star Publishing, Charleston, W. Va., 2011

Evans, Clement A., Ed. Confederate Military History. Confederate Publishing Company, Atlanta, Ga., 1899. 12 Volumes.

Fry, Rose W. Recollections of the Rev. John McElhenney, D. D. Richmond, Va.: Whittet & Shepperson, Printers, 1893.

Hechler, Ken. Soldier of the Union: Private George Hechler's Civil War Service. Pictorial Histories Publishing Company, 2011, Charleston, W. Va.

Hewett, Janet B., Ed. Supplement to the Official Records of the Union and Confederate Armies. Broadfoot Publishing Company, Wilmington, N. C., 1994, Part I – Reports, Vol. 2 (Serial No. 2) of 100 volumes.

Humphreys, Milton W. Military Operations, 1861 – 1864, Fayetteville, West Virginia and the Lynchburg campaign. Cotton Hill Publications, Gauley Bridge, W. Va., 1991.

Humphreys, Milton W. Capt. Thomas A. Bryan, Bryan's Battery, 13th Battalion Virginia Artillery, C. S. A., 1862 – 1865. Richmond: Whittet & Shepperson, n.d.

James, James R. To See the Elephant: The Civil War Letters of John A. McKee. Leathers Publishing, Leawood, Ks. 1998.

Johnston, A. S. Captain Beirne Chapman and Chapman's Battery: An Historical Sketch. Union, W. Va., 1903.

Johnston, Jane Echols & Brenda Lynn Williams, Comp. & Ed. Hard Times: 1861 – 1865: A Collection of Confederate Letters, Court Minutes, Soldiers' Records, and Local Lore from Craig County, Virginia. np, 1986.

Kempfer, Lester L. The Salem Light Guard. Company G, 36th Regiment Ohio Volunteer Infantry, Marietta, Ohio 1861-5. Adams Press, Chicago, Ill. 1973.

Lang, Theodore F. Loyal West Virginia From 1861 – 1865. Baltimore, Md.: The Deutsch Publishing Co., 1895

Lewis, Virgil A. History of West Virginia (In two parts). Philadelphia: Hubbard Brothers, Publishers, 1889.

Lowry, Terry D. 22nd Virginia Infantry. H. E. Howard, Inc., Lynchburg, Va. 1988.

Lowry, Terry D. 26th Battalion Virginia Infantry. H. E. Howard, Inc., Lynchburg, Va. 1991.

McAllister, J. Gray. Family Records: Compiled for the Descendents of Abraham Addams McAllister and his wife Julia Ellen (Stratton) McAllister, of Covington, Virginia. Easton, Pa.: Press of the Chemical Pub. Co., 1912.

McKinney, Tim. The Civil War in Greenbrier County, West Virginia. Quarrier Press, Charleston, W. Va., 2004.

McNeer, Harry L. The Letters of John and Susan Morgan: A Story of Everyday Life, Love and Loss in the Civil War Years. Wolf Creek Publishing, 2006, Copyright by Harry L. McNeer.

Mays, James H. Four Years For Old Virginia. The Swordsman Publishing Company, Los Angeles, California. Copyright Lee Mays, 1970.

Miller, James H. History of Summers County: From the Earliest Settlement To The Present Time. np, 1908. Copyright James H. Miller.

Mollohan, Marie. Another Day in Lincoln's Army: The Civil War Journals of Sgt. John T. Booth. iUniverse, Inc., Lincoln, NE, 2007

Monroe County Historical Society. The Notebook of A. N. (Nannie) Campbell. Monroe County Historical Society, Union, W. Va., 2002.

Moore, Frank. The Rebellion Record: A Diary of American Events. New York: G. P. Putnam, 1863, Volume 5, p. 141 – 144

Moore, George Ellis. A Banner in the Hills: West Virginia's Statehood. New York: Appleton-Century-Crofts, 1963 (map)

Morton, Oren F. A History of Monroe County, West Virginia. Staunton, Va.: The McClure Co., Inc., 1916.

Ohio Roster Commission. Official Roster of the Soldiers of the State of Ohio in the War of the Rebellion, 1861 – 1865. 12 volumes. Cincinnati: The Ohio Valley Publishing & Manufacturing Company, 1886 – 1895.

Pendleton, Wm. C. History of Tazewell County and Southwest Virginia 1748-1920. W. C. Hill Printing Company, Richmond, Va. 1920.

Reid, Whitlaw. Ohio in the War: Her Statesmen, her generals, and Soldiers. Cincinnati: Moore, Wilstache & Baldwin. 1868, 2 volumes.

Rice, Otis K. A History of Greenbrier County. Greenbrier County Historical Society, Lewisburg, W. Va., 1986. McClain Printing Co., Parsons, W. Va., 1986.

Robertson, James I. Jr. Soldier of Southwestern Virginia: The Civil War Letters of Capt. John Preston Sheffey. Louisiana State University Press, Baton Rouge, La. 2004

Saunier, Joseph A., Ed. A History of the Forty-Seventh Regiment Ohio Veteran Volunteer Infantry, Second Brigade, Second Division, Fifteenth Army Corps,

Army of the Tennessee. The Lyle Printing Company, Hillsboro, Ohio, n. d. (c. 1903).

Schmitt, Martin F., Ed. General George Crook: His Autobiography. University of Oklahoma Press, Norman, Ok. 1946.

Scott, J. L. 45th Virginia Infantry. H. E. Howard, Inc., Lynchburg, Va. 1989

Scott, J. L. Lowry's, Bryan's, and Chapman's Batteries of Virginia Artillery. H. E. Howard, Inc., Lynchburg, Va. 1988.

Sherwood, G. L. and Weaver, Jeffery C. 59th Virginia Infantry. H. E. Howard, Inc., Lynchburg, Va., 1994.

Stutler, Boyd B. West Virginia in the Civil War. Charleston, W. Va., Education Foundation, 1963.

Sutton, J. J. History of the Second Regiment West Virginia Cavalry Volunteers, During the War of the Rebellion. Portsmouth, Ohio. 1892.

Taylor, George Braxton. Life and Letters of Rev. George Boardman Taylor, D.D. Lynchburg, Virginia: J. P. Bell Company, Printers, 1908.

U. S. War Department. The War of the Rebellion: A Compilation of the Official Records of the Union and Confederate Armies. Government Publishing Office, Washington, D. C., 1880 – 1900. 128 Volumes.

Werrell, Kenneth P. Crook's Regulars: The 36th Ohio in the War of Rebellion. Christiansburg, Va., KPW, 2012.

West, Michael. The Gauley, Mercer and Western Artillery. H. E. Howard, Inc., Lynchburg, Va., 1991.

Willard, Eugene B., Ed. A Standard History of The Hanging Rock Iron Region of Ohio, Volume I. The Lewis Publishing Company, n.p., 1916.

Williams, H. C. & Bro. History of Washington County, Ohio, with Illustrations and Biographical Sketches. H. Z. Williams & Bro., publishers, Cleveland, O., 1881.

II. Manuscripts

G. Dudley Acker, Jr., Flagstaff, Az.

Records of the 36th Ohio Infantry

Albert and Shirley Small Special Collections Library, University of Virginia, Charlottesville, Va.

Diary kept during the Civil War by Milton Wylie Humphreys – Mss 1578

Lynchburg Republican, 1862

Miscellaneous Virginia Papers, 1829 – 1905 – Acc. # 8979-j

Fielding R. Cornett Letter

Alleghany County Court House, Circuit Court Office, Covington, Va.

Sketch of Jackson River Depot Grounds (1859)

Alleghany County Historical Society, Covington, Va.

Photograph of Jackson River Depot

Eleanor S. Brockenbrough Library, The Museum of the Confederacy, Richmond, Va.

Charles C. Baughman Letters & Papers

Carol M. Newman Library, Special Collections, Virginia Polytechnic Institute & State University, Blacksburg, Va.

Smith Family Letters – Ms1996-018

Edwin Houston Harmon Papers, 1856 – 1984 – Ms1990-019

John Preston Sheffey Papers – Ms2001-060

Henrie H. Alexander Letter – Ms1960-002

Donald C. Davidson Library, University of California, Santa Barbara, Ca.

William Wyles Collection – Oscar F. Hale Papers

Emory & Henry College Archives, Emory, Va.

Isaac F. Thomas Letters

Stuart A. Rose Manuscript, Archives, and Rare Book Library, Emory University, Atlanta, Ga.

John E. Harrison Diaries

Thomas Thomson Taylor Papers

Greenbrier Historical Society, Lewisburg, W. Va.

Civil War Files: Battle of Lewisburg

Deaths of Confederate Soldiers in Lewisburg, Greenbrier Co., W. Va. compiled by Raymond Watkins

Personal Recollections told of Battle (undated clipping)

Mr. Kittinger Writes, Greenbrier Independent, April 23, 1926

Letter of Captain Israel Stough to G. W. Tuttle, June 16, 1862

Howard R. Hammond, Covington, Va.

Photograph of Robert James Thrasher

Huntington Library, San Marino, Ca.

Life and Adventures of William G. Felton

Kent State University Libraries, Special Collections and Archives, Kent, O.

Lysander W. Tulleys Collection

Library of Virginia, Richmond, Va.

Executive Papers, Governor John Letcher

Confederate Pension Applications

Confederate Disability Applications

Terry Lowry Collection, South Charleston, W. Va.

Copies of Oliver Parker Letters & Photograph, in his possession

Robert E. & Jean R. Mahn Center for Archives and Special Collections, Vernon R. Alden Library, Ohio University, Athens, O.

Brown Family Collection, letters of Edwin A. Brown

Monroe County Public Library, Union, W. Va.

Life in Irish Corner District During the Civil War, by Mark Crayon.

(published in West Virginia News, February 13 – May 29, 1926)

National Archives, Washington, D. C.

    Records of the Adjutant General's Office, 1780s - 1917 - RG-94

        Battle Report of Lewisburg, 36th Ohio Infantry

    Regimental Casualty Lists, 1861 – 1865

        Reports for Lewisburg, Va., May 23, 1862

    Compiled Service Records

        2nd West Virginia Cavalry

        36th Ohio Infantry

        44th Ohio Infantry

    Regimental Records

        Order Book, 36th Ohio Infantry

        Muster Rolls, 36th Ohio Infantry

    Letters Received by the Commissions Branch – Samuel A. Gilbert file

    War Department Collection of Confederate Records – RG-109

    Confederate Manuscripts – No. 3082

    Union Provost Marshal Records, 1861 – 1867 (M-0345)

    Station Rolls (E-199)

    Compiled Service Records

        22nd Virginia Infantry

        26th Battalion Virginia Infantry

        30th Battalion Virginia Sharpshooters

        45th Virginia Infantry

        50th Virginia Infantry

        51st Virginia Infantry

        59th Virginia Infantry

        Lowry's Battery

Bryan's Battery

Otey's Battery

Chapman's Battery

Confederate General and Staff Officers & Non regimental Enlisted Men (M-331)

John A. King

Henry A. Wise

Unfiled Papers and Slips belonging in Confederate Compiled Service Records (M-347)

Prisoner of War Records (Confederate)

Wheeling, (W.) Va.

Camp Chase, O.

Records of the Commissary General of Prisoners – RG-249

Union Prisoner of War Records (those received at Richmond, May 31, 1862)

Records of the United States Army Continental Command, 1821 – 1920 – RG-393

Volume II, E-961 – Letters Received

Records of the Office of the Quartermaster General, 1774 – 1985, RG-92

Burial Registers of Military Posts and National Cemeteries, 1862 – 1960.

Ohio History Connection, Columbus, O.

Hiram F. Devol – OHS-AV200-b03-f13-05-02.tif

Mss 734 – Samuel J. Harrison Records

Mss 180 – John T. booth Papers

State Archives Series 147 - Correspondence to the Governor and Adjutant General of Ohio, 1861 – 1898, letter of E. B. Andrews, June 9, 1862

VFM 1727 – Sidney C. Baker Correspondence, R. Byrd letter

David M. Rubenstein Rare Book & Manuscript Library, Duke University, Durham, N. C.

Sarah A. Saylor Cibler Papers, 1861 – 1865

Letter Book, 1862, William E. Duncan (L:969)

Preston Library, Archives, Virginia Military Institute, Lexington, Va.

Cadet files of William W. Finney, George M. Edgar

Portrait of Captain George G. Otey

Joyce Applefeller Rarick

Diary of Johann Christian Appelfeller

Special Collections and University Archives, Library and Information Access, San Diego State University, San Diego, Ca.

Asa Sackman Diaries, 1861 – 1862 – MS-0404

State Historical Society of Wisconsin, Madison, Wi.

Ernst Joseph Lindner Autobiography

U. S. Army Heritage and Education Center, Carlisle, Pa.

Civil War Times Illustrated Collection

Letters & Memoirs of James Abraham, 1st & 2nd W. Va. Cavalry

William A. Tall Letters, 2nd W. Va. Cavalry

William H. Dunham Letters, 36th Ohio Infantry

Virginia Historical Society, Richmond, Va.

Shannon Butts Papers

West Virginia Department of Archives and History, Charleston, W. Va.

Boyd Blynn Stutler Collection – Ms78-1, Series 8, Box 9, folder 2, Lewisburg Battle

Civil War Collection – Ms79-18, Series 1, folder 41, Rand, Noyes. Papers, 1862 – 1904

Letters and Diaries of Junius Marion Jones (Ms90-48)

West Virginia Vital Records

Greenbrier County Death Records, 1862

West Virginia Collection, West Virginia University, Morgantown, W. Va.

Roy B. Cook Papers – A&M 1528

Zimmerman Correspondence

Sally Patton Letter

Joseph Pearson Diaries – A&M 3477

David Todd Gilliam Autobiography – A&M 3231

Scott-Palmer Family Papers – A&M 1423

Civil War Correspondence – A&M 1508

Letter from E. H. Harman, May 25, 1862

III. Newspapers

Albany, New York

"From the Kanawha Division" *Albany Evening Journal*, July 8, 1862 (copied from *Cincinnati Gazette*)

Athens, Ohio

"The Battle of Lewisburg, and the 36th Ohio Regiment." *The Athens Messenger,* June 5, 1862.

Beckley, West Virginia

Beckley Post-Herald

"Yesterday and Today: Lewisburg Civil War Cemetery In Need.", July 3, 1959

"Yesterday and Today: Greenbrier Man of Noted Hanger Family.", August 21, 1963

"Yesterday and Today: Hefner Family Has Many Connections", September 7, 1971

"Yesterday and Today: One Of Jones Boys Had Quite A Career", January 23, 1973

Raleigh Register & Post Herald

"Common Grave Contains Bodies of Unknown Confederate Dead", December 8, 1956

Charleston, West Virginia

Charleston Daily Mail

"Old Resident Recalls General Lee Reception", August 26, 1932

"Exciting Civil War Days Recalled by Eye-Witness.", June 4, 1939

The Charleston Gazette

"Lee Week At White Sulphur Springs Comes To Brilliant Close", August 28, 1932

Chillicothe, Ohio

The Ohio Soldier

"The Battle of Lewisburg", April 14, 1888

Cleveland, Ohio

Morning Leader

"From Gen. Cox's Army", May 27, 1862

"The fight at Lewisburg – Our Victory", June 2, 1862

"The Victory of Lewisburg", June 4, 1862

"More Rebel Treachery", June 25, 1862

Covington, Virginia

Covington Virginian

"Civil War Experienced By Covington Resident", October 3, 1968

Dayton, Ohio

"Gallant Conduct of the 44th Regiment O. V.", *Dayton Weekly Journal*, June 10, 1862

Gallipolis, Ohio

Gallipolis Journal

"Army Correspondence", June 5, 1862

"The Fight at Lewisburg, Va.", June 5, 1862

"The Fight at Lewisburg", [Poem], June 5, 1862

"Army Correspondence", June 12, 1862

List of Secesh Prisoners, July 3, 1862

Gallipolis Dispatch

"Army Correspondence", June 5, 1862

Greenville, Ohio

Darke County Democrat

"Army Correspondence", June 11, 1862

"Army Correspondence", June 18, 1862

Jackson, Ohio

The Jackson Standard

"Army Correspondence", June 5, 1862

"Army Correspondence", June 12, 1862

"Battle of Lewisburg" [Poem], September 9, 1886

Lewisburg, Virginia

The Yankee, May 29, 1862 (1993 Reprint)

Lewisburg, West Virginia

Greenbrier Independent

"Our Dead", March 21, 1867

"Removal of the Confederate Dead", June 6, 1867

"Removal of the Confederate Dead", June 13, 1867

"The Battle of Lewisburg.", November 24, 1887

"Reunion: 36th Ohio Infantry at Lewisburg…", May 12, 1904.

"The Reunion Monday", May 19, 1904

"War Reminiscences.", June 9, 1904

"Mr. Kittinger Writes", April 23, 1926

"If Only Those Old Walls Could Talk…" by J. W. Benjamin, March 18, 1976

"May 23, 1862: The Battle of Lewisburg", May 20, 1976

Lynchburg, Virginia

Lynchburg Daily Republican

"Letter From Buchanan", May 26, 1862

"The Fight at Lewisburg", May 27, 1862

"The Traitor Dr. Rucker", May 30, 1862

"The 45th Virginia Regiment", June 10, 1862

Lynchburg Daily Virginian

[Lewisburg], May 27, 1862

Marietta, Ohio

Home News

"Battle in Western Virginia", May 30, 1862

"Later from the 36th Regiment", June 6, 1862

"Battle of Lewisburg, Va.", June 6, 1862

"Another Account – Incidents, &c.", June 6, 1862

"Gen. Crook's Congratulatory Order", June 6, 1862

"From Summersville to Lewisburg and Beyond", June 6, 1862

"More of the Lewisburg Fight", June 13, 1862

The Intelligencer

"Order of Col. Crook", June 5, 1862

"Letter from the 36th Regiment", June 5, 1862

"36th Regiment at Lewisburg", June 5, 1862

New York, New York

New York Herald-Tribune

"From The Mountain Department: A Guerrilla Band Broken Up – Their Arms Captured – Col. Crook's Victory at Lewisburg – A Brilliant Affair", May27, 1862

"From The Mountain Department: The Defeat of the Rebel Gen. Heth.", June 6, 1862

Philadelphia, Pennsylvania

Public Ledger

"From Fremont's Army: The Battle of Lewisburg." June 5, 1862.

Point Pleasant, Virginia

Point Pleasant Register

"Lewisburg Prisoners", June 5, 1862

"Mrs. Welch's dwelling …" ,June 19, 1862

"After the battle of Lewisburg…", June 26, 1862

Pomeroy, Ohio

Pomeroy Weekly Telegraph

"From the Kanawha Valley", May 30, 1862

Raleigh, North Carolina

The Semi-Weekly State Journal

"Engagement at Lewisburg, Va.", June 4, 1862

Richmond, Virginia

Richmond Whig

"Confederate Defeat At Lewisburg …", May 28, 1862

"The Loss at Lewisburg", May 30, 1862

"From Gen. Loring's Command – Lewisburg Evacuated by the Enemy", June 11, 1862

Richmond Daily Dispatch

"The Enemy Reported Advancing Towards the Castle", May 15, 1862

"From the Valley and Northwest", May 19, 1862

"Narrow Escape", May 19, 1862

"Late War News: The Fight at Lewisburg", May 28, 1862

"Otey Battery", May 29, 1862

"The Battle at Lewisburg", May 30, 1862

"The Battle of Lewisburg", May 31, 1862

"The Battle At Lewisburg", June 3, 1862

Richmond Examiner

"Movements and Spirit of the War: Fight at Lewisburg, Va.", May 28, 1862

"The Affair At Lewisburg", May 29, 1862

Richmond Enquirer

"From Greenbrier County", May 30, 1861

Ronceverte, West Virginia

The West Virginia News

"The Reunion", May 28, 1904

Springfield, Ohio

Springfield Republic

"From the 44th Ohio", May 21, 1862

"Col. Crook …", May 23, 1862

"From the Forty-Fourth Regiment", May 26, 1862

"From the Forty-Fourth Regiment", May 30, 1862

"Splendid Conduct of the 44th", June 2, 1862

"From the 44th", June 4, 1862

"The '"Yankee"' of Lewisburg, Virginia", June 4, 1862

"War Correspondence: From the Forty-Fourth Regiment", June 6, 1862

"About the Lewisburgh Fight", June 11, 1862

"From the Forty-Fourth", June 16, 1862

"War Correspondence: From the Forty-Fourth Ohio Regiment", June 20, 1862

Staunton, Virginia

Newsleader

"Staunton Cemetery an Outgrowth of the Civil War", March 14, 2014

Staunton Spectator

"Fight at Lewisburg", May 12, 1862

"Federal Cemetery", November 20, 1866

Troy, Ohio

Troy Times

"From the 44th Ohio", May 29, 1862

"From the 44th Ohio", June 5, 1862

"From the 44th Ohio", June 10, 1862

"From the 44th", June 19, 1862

Union, West Virginia

The Watchman

"The Reunion at Lewisburg", May 26, 1904

"Re=Union of Blue and Gray", May 28, 1904

Washington, D. C.

National Tribune

"Fighting Them Over: Battle of Lewisburg.", June 24, 1886

"The 2d W. Va. Cav. at Lewisburg", August 12, 1886

"The 2d W. Va. Cav. at Lewisburg.", September 9, 1886

"Fighting Them Over: Battle of Lewisburg", November 4, 1886

"The Fight at Lewisburg.", December 9, 1886

"Lewisburg, W. Va.", June 28, 1888

"Gen. Heth's Cannon.", August 2, 1888

"Helped Win Crook's Star", December 26, 1895

"A Fighting Regiment", January 9, 1902

"Gen. H. F. Devol", September 30, 1909

"The Battle of Lewisburg.", December 9, 1909

"Battle of Lewisburg", September 12, 1912

Wilmington, North Carolina

Wilmington Journal

"The Fight at Lewisburg, Va.", June 5, 1862

Wilmington, Ohio

The Watchman

"Headquarters, 47th, Reg., O. V. I", June 26, 1862

Wheeling, Virginia

Daily Intelligencer

"Heading Off Jackson.", May 26, 1862

"The Lewisburg Prisoners.", May 30, 1862

"More Prisoners", July 5, 1862

"More Prisoners", July 16, 1862

"Taking out the Ball", July 16, 1862

Woodsfield, Ohio

The Spirit of Democracy

"Army Correspondence", June 11, 1862

Zanesville, Ohio

Daily Courier

"The Battle at Lewisburg", June 5, 1862

IV. Periodicals

"Gray Forces Defeated in Battle of Lewisburg", by J. W. Benjamin. *West Virginia History: A Quarterly Magazine.* Volume XX, Number 1, (October 1958), page 24-35.

"War in the Streets of Lewisburg", by James T. Siburt. *America's Civil War*, Volume 11, No. 5 (November 1998), p. 54-60.

"A Note on the Confederate Cemetery", by Dr. John F. Montgomery. *Journal of the Greenbrier Historical Society*, Volume. 6, No. 6 (1998), p. 46 - 47

"Sergeant Haddow Writes Home", *Journal of the Greenbrier Historical Society*, Volume 6, No. 6 (1998), p. 48-52

"Notes on Confederate Artillery Service." by Milton W. Humphries. *Journal of the United States Artillery*, Vol. V, (1896), Artillery School Press, Fort Monroe, Va.

"The Burial Site of the Union Soldiers is Marked", by John McIlhenny. *Journal of the Greenbrier Historical Society*, Volume 5, No. 5 (1991), p. 23 -24.

"A Civil War Event", by S. W. W. Feamster. *Journal of the Greenbrier Historical Society*, Volume 6, No. 3 (1995), p. 19 – 37

"May 1862: Why Lewisburg? Heth versus Crook." *Journal of the Greenbrier Historical Society*, Volume 8, No. 1 (2008), p. 10 – 32

"The Battle of Lewisburg", by Col. J. W. Benjamin. *Journal of the Greenbrier Historical Society*, Volume 1, No. 6, (October 1968), p. 24 – 36.

"Eye Witness Accounts of Lewisburg Battle", by Col. J. W. Benjamin. *Journal of the Greenbrier Historical Society*, Volume 1, No. 6 (October 1968), p. 37 – 42.

"Heth's Star Did Not Decline", by Col. J. W. Benjamin. *Journal of the Greenbrier Historical Society*, Volume 1, No. 6 (October 1968), p. 43 – 47

"The Story of a Cannon", by Col. J. W. Benjamin. *Journal of the Greenbrier Historical Society*, Volume 1, No. 6 (October 1968), p. 53 – 54

"War Correspondent Covers Battle of Lewisburg", by Col. J. W. Benjamin. *Journal of the Greenbrier Historical Society*, Volume 1, No. 6 (October 1968), p. 55 – 58

"A History of the White Sulphur Rifles (Company G) and the Scouts and Guides (Company E) of Edgar's 26th Virginia Battalion of Patton's Brigade" by R. Hal Walls. *Journal of the Greenbrier Historical Society*, Volume V, No. 3 (1989), p. 17 – 38

"Had They Stood Their Ground, We Would Have Cleaned Them Out: Ohioans in the Battle of Lewisburg in Western Virginia on 23 May 1862" by Jan Rader. *Ohio Civil War Genealogy Journal*, Volume XIII (2009), Number 1, p. 3 – 10

"Down In The Ranks: Recollections of Captain William F. Bahlmann, Confederate Officer" *Journal of the Greenbrier County Historical Society*, Volume II, No. 2 (October 1970), p. 41-93

The Gallia County Glade, Volume 34, No. 2 (Summer 2009)

The Gallia County Glade, Volume 33, No. 4 (Winter 2008)

"Gooch [Family]", *Virginia Genealogical Society Quarterly Bulletin*, Volume 2, No. 4 (October 1964), p. 67

V. Miscellaneous

"The Battle of Lewisburg" Lewisburg Visitors Center Brochure

Letters of Captain Levi Barber, Jr. Ancestors of Eugene Ashton Andrew http://www.genal.net/138.htm (last visited April 2016)

Overall Family Civil War Letters, June 2, 1862. http://goverall.wordpress.com/overall-family-civil-war-letters/the-letters/5/ (Last visited April 2016

The 22nd Virginia Infantry Regiment History Society. the Official New Website of the 22nd Virginia Infantry Regiment. www.Emmitsburg.net/john/contents/22ndvainfantry/22ndva_index.htm

Chesapeake and Ohio Historical Society. "History of the C&O" www.cohsorg/history/histoy/htm accessed June 12, 2002.

Letters of Charles Ramsey, 44th Ohio Volunteer Infantry Band, copies in author's possession (Lewisburg letter is online)

Gleaves Family Letters, 45th Virginia Infantry, www.gleavesfamily.com/home/letters/html (last visited January 2016)

Staunton National Cemetery, Staunton, Virginia. www.nps.gov/nr/travel/national_cemeteries/virginia/staunton_national_cemetery.html (January 2016)

NOAA History, A Nation At War: Civil War: War Record of Samuel A. Gilbert http://www.history.noaa.gov/stories_tales/samgilbert.html (last visited April 2016)

Jeffrey C. Weaver – New River Notes www.newrivernotes/va/vasecesh.htm (last visited November 2012)

INDEX

W

Walden, William A. 80, 98
Wallace, Fred S. 187
Wallace, John 9, 13
Ward, A.T. 135
Ward, Isaac 187
Warren, Burruss 176
Warren, Larkin 176
Watson, Joseph 176
Welch, Mrs. 110
Welch, Phoebe 108
Werner 216
Wethered, Pere B. 17, 176
Wetzel, George W. 176
Wharton, Charles 187
White, John T. 176
Wickle, George C. 177
Wickline, M.R. 177
Wickline, William F. 177
Wikle, James 190
Williams, David F. 177
Williams, E.C. 177
Williams, James H. 177
Williams, John S. 4
Williams, J.W. 17, 177
Wilson, H. Blair 20, 104
Wilson, James 188
Wilson, Samuel J. 177
Wilson, Sanford 188
Winans, J.C. 15, 23
Wise, Henry A. 210
Withrow, A.W. 178
Withrow, John 68, 113, 152
Withrow, Nathaniel W. 178
Wolf, George W. 147
Woodward, William W. 44, 56, 57, 85, 87
Workman, Claiborne 178
Workman, John A. 178
Workman, Slaven 178
Workman, William C. 178
Wright, James N. 178
Wright, John 188
Wyatt, William H. 178

Y

Yeager, James H. 188
Youart, Robert 86
Young, Peter 188

Z

Zeering, James 190
Zeering, John 190

Made in the USA
Columbia, SC
28 July 2024